PAY

— TO —

PROSPER

USING
VALUE RULES
TO REINVENT
EXECUTIVE
INCENTIVES

RICHARD N. ERICSON
TOWERS PERRIN

WorldatWork.

The Professional Association for
Compensation, Benefits and Total Rewards

WorldatWork
14040 N. Northsight Blvd., Scottsdale, AZ 85260
480/951-9191   Fax 480/483-8352
www.worldatwork.org

Editor: Dan Cafaro
Cover Design: Kris Sotelo
Production Manager: Rebecca Williams Ficker
Technical Review Coordinator: Betty Laurie

To Cynthia, Sarah,
Andrew and John

About WorldatWork®

WorldatWork is the world's leading not-for-profit professional association dedicated to knowledge leadership in compensation, benefits and total rewards. Founded in 1955, WorldatWork focuses on human resources disciplines associated with attracting, retaining and motivating employees. Besides serving as the membership association of the professions, the WorldatWork family of organizations provides education, certification (Certified Compensation Professional — CCP®, Certified Benefits Professional — CBP™ and Global Remuneration Professional — GRP®), publications, knowledge resources, surveys, conferences, research and networking. WorldatWork Society of Certified Professionals and Alliance for Work-Life Progress (AWLP) are part of the WorldatWork family.

For more information, visit www.worldatwork.org

About the Author

Richard N. Ericson specializes in management and reward systems emphasizing principles of shareholder value creation. A principal in consulting firm Towers Perrin, he has more than 20 years' experience in business valuation and incentive design. Ericson holds a B.S. in finance and a B.A. in French literature, each granted summa cum laude from Northern Illinois University. He holds an M.B.A. in finance and accounting from the University of Chicago.

He can be contacted at richard.ericson@towers.com.

About Towers Perrin

Towers Perrin is a global professional services firm that helps organizations around the world optimize performance through effective people, risk and financial management. The firm provides innovative solutions to client issues in the areas of human resource consulting and administration services; management and actuarial consulting to the financial services industry; and reinsurance intermediary services.

For more information, visit www.towers.com

Acknowledgments

I would like to thank my editors, Steve Davies of Towers Perrin and Dan Cafaro of WorldatWork, for their substantial and helpful efforts with this book. I would also like to thank my reviewers, whose insights improved it greatly: Richard D. Landsberg, JD, LLM, RFC, APM, Senior Attorney, Advanced Markets, Nationwide Financial Services; Randolph W. Keuch, Director, Strategic Rewards, Pfizer Inc.; Michael H. Irons, CCP, Senior Vice President, Human Resources, Fleet Capital Corp.; Roy W. Cureton, Jr., CCP, CEBS, SPHR, Senior Director of Compensation and Benefits, Corporate HR Services, Galey & Lord Inc., Swift Denim; Steven Sahara, Director of Corporate Development, Empower Interactive Group; Michael J. Welsh, Manager, Oakmark Global Fund; and Paula Todd and Doug Friske, Principals, Towers Perrin. I thank Gary Locke, Global Practice Leader, Executive Compensation Consulting, Towers Perrin, for his consistent support and temerity in bringing the challenging subject matter of executive pay re-design to market in a number of ways, including this book.

Numerous business executives contributed insights, either directly or through consulting project work. I'd like to thank, in particular, Martyn Redgrave, CFO of Carlson Companies, Larry Edwards, CEO of Global Power, Gary Christensen, retired CEO of Pella Windows, Jeff Fick, CAO of HON INDUSTRIES, Bruce Paradis, CEO of GMAC Residential Funding Corporation, Jeff Warne, CFO of Carlson Restaurants Worldwide, John Cronin of Pillsbury, Charles Velure of Carlson Companies, and Robert Grams of Compensation Strategies. Many current and former Towers Perrin colleagues and associates, including Mike Grund, Scott Olsen, Rob Greenberg, Ben Stradley, Mark Yango, Jeff Kridler, Henry Erlich and Steve Faigen, assisted with aspects of this book or with development of Towers Perrin training programs, publications and consulting tools upon which portions of it are based.

Table of Contents

Chapter 6: Pay for the Right Stuff — Do's and Don'ts
of Performance Measurement at the Senior Management Level 119

Chapter 7: Motive, Means and Method —
Evaluating Financial Performance Metrics 133

Chapter 8: Value-Based Performance Measures 165

Chapter 9: Ownership, Not Gamesmanship:
Setting Targets and Ranges for Performance-Based Plans 197

Chapter 10: Business Units and Private Companies, Phantom Stock and Performance Plans 229

Foreword

A tiny portion of the world's population largely directs the affairs of commerce. A typical Fortune 500 U.S. company has a few hundred of these people. Little companies have from one to a few. They are senior-level members of company management. And they, either alone or working within a team, have material impact upon the value of a private or public business enterprise, or a business unit of either.

Their roles endow them with great impact. But, in the case of most of the bigger companies, they don't own the businesses they run. Instead they manage these enterprises at the pleasure and behest of shareholders and their board representatives. They draw their remuneration in various ways and are responsive to the incentives present in their system of rewards.

This book is about how to design their incentive plans. It asserts that companies should use senior management's incentive pay as a proactive instrument of business governance, one specifically designed to increase business performance. That is, it asserts that companies should *pay to prosper*.

Most companies will significantly revamp their incentive structures for senior management over the next few years. Until now, companies' heavy use of stock options was driven by the "no cost" portrayal of such grants in financial statements and by the 1990s bull market, to the point where stock option grants comprised the bulk of the value of long-term incentives in the marketplace. The balance of incentive pay is based upon companies' troublesome budget processes and flawed financial metrics. Business and stock market conditions have brought problems with the traditional incentive structure to the forefront. Imminent changes in option accounting are creating the "burning platform" for change. Accounting rulemaking bodies are on course to require companies to expense their options and many companies have elected to go ahead and do it voluntarily.

This is a perfect time for many companies to step back and think fundamentally about what role senior management's incentives should play and about how, precisely, they should be designed. It may be the best opportunity in a generation to get things right in this pivotal area. This book is meant to assist in that process and to do so in decisive and specific terms.

Chapter 1 is an overview of the book. The typical incentive structure does not consistently encourage good, value-creating business performance. In fact, it often can reward senior management for bad business decisions. Incentives at most companies should be restructured based upon a set of principles of business governance and value creation called "value rules." Chapter 1 is written to the CEO, since it is in the CEO's interest to adopt better-working incentives as a way to pursue better business results for shareholders. Further, most companies really can't enact this sort of change without CEO support. Chapter 2 conducts a detailed analysis of the typical, stock option-centered incentive structure. We find that it connects actions of key decision-makers only vaguely with the results they drive and that it rewards advancement up the ranks much more clearly than anything else.

You can't set up incentive plans properly unless you have a set of objectives against which to make the many important choices involved in design. Chapter 3 critiques the set of premises that drives current practice and sets out a much more proactive, effective blueprint. Proper incentive plans should address clearly the linkages between business decisions, business results and value creation. To design incentive plans, an organization does not have to specify these linkages from scratch. Rather, as Chapter 4 shows, it can draw upon the techniques of business valuation, where the relevant rules have been set out in a clear and compelling way for many decades. Findings from Chapters 3 and 4 are summarized at the end of Chapter 4 as "Value Rules."

Senior management is in the "decision" business. Their jobs involve not only managing business operations, but making material, long-term and often irrevocable commitments of shareholder resources. And they do so under conditions of uncertainty, or risk. Chapter 5 addresses the many ways in which incentive structures can bias management against reasonable risk-taking or encourage them to gamble too freely with shareholder money, detailing a range of design solutions to the problem.

Hundreds of approaches to incentive plan design exist. What distinguishes them most is their basis for rewards — the methods and media used to capture management's performance. Chapter 6 separates the wheat from the chaff, honing in on the most effective approach for senior management teams — linking pay decisively to sustained business results that create value. Most bonus pay is delivered based upon a few common financial yardsticks like earnings per share, net income, return on equity and revenue. Deficiencies in these metrics are among the main problems with bonus plans, since they allow many poor business decisions to be rewarded. Chapter 7 uses value rules to examine the full range of financial metrics and to show how to use them properly within incentive plans.

Value-based metrics like economic value added, cash flow return on investment and total business return have been in the spotlight for a decade, promising to help improve business results and create more value. But most companies have not adopted these metrics and many complain they are unworkably complex. Chapter 8 demystifies the subject matter. It proves that value-based metrics all have the same roots in value rules. They can be put in place simply and effectively, without the clutter of metric "adjustments" and odd incentive plan designs, and without turning the whole company upside down.

Most goal-based incentive plans use performance targets and ranges that stem from an internal process often involving negotiation. Most bonus goals are based upon budgets, for example. This can lead to internal battles, mediocre performance expectations, and managed business results. Companies don't have to do things this way, and Chapter 9 lays out a set of solutions. Most companies base incentive pay heavily upon corporate results: stock price movements that drive gains on stock options, for example, and corporate-level metrics like earnings per share. In contrast, most of the value of a typical company — as well as most of its executives and most of the business decisions that it might hope to improve through better incentives — are found in business units like groups, sectors, divisions, profit centers and joint ventures. Chapter 10 shows how to tie incentives to business unit results in effective, fair and prudent ways.

With new accounting rules on the horizon, many companies are considering making fewer option grants and instead using other forms of stock-based pay. This is a fundamental shift in how incentive pay is used and also a very big-ticket move since so much of senior management pay comes in the form of stock option grants. Chapter 11 establishes a framework for stock-based incentive design, reviewing the most pertinent choices at issue. It encourages companies to examine in a clear-eyed way what stock-based pay can accomplish for a company and what it cannot.

One of the platitudes of incentive design is that proper communication of incentive plans is pivotal to their success within a business. What's said less often, though, is that the plans themselves are important communication media. When we talk about communication of incentive plans for senior management, the most important thing to recognize is that the medium is the message. Formal communication initiatives will not work if the plan design itself is ineffective. Chapter 12 addresses plan communication, part and parcel with the incentive plan design process, plan terms and prospective business impact.

1

To the Typical CEO

By restructuring senior management's incentives based upon a few principles I call *value rules*, you can improve the quality of many business decisions made at your company and their results for shareholders. You can encourage your senior management team to take better account of the risks, capital requirements and time horizons of actions they take on behalf of the company. And you can get a better yield for your shareholders from the collection of business traits and market opportunities that underlie the value of your enterprise.

Why are these gains possible? Right now, your company's system of incentives does not consistently unify the interests of your senior management team with those of shareholders, nor, for that matter, with yours. As a general matter, your current incentives link performance and pay only weakly. And, in many important ways, they leave open the possibility of getting paid to make poor business decisions.

These are serious problems for businesses. Poor incentives may contribute to common failures in mergers and acquisitions by biasing the selection and evaluation processes and by systemically weakening accountabilities. They may consistently favor short-term results over the long-term ones that weigh much more heavily in value creation. They may encourage executives to manage expectations for their performance more than to deliver the best possible results. They may encourage talented people in the organization to do whatever is involved in moving up the career ladder, and that is not always the same thing as making their best contributions in roles they fill along the way.

You may be getting great business performance right now. It may well have a lot to do with your own business smarts, leadership ability, motivating power and maybe even some charisma. It also may be that you've got all the right people working for you, and they're always doing the right things. Perhaps all the cylinders of your enterprise are firing and you feel you are moving apace. My message to you is that whatever speed you've attained may have been in the face of a stiff headwind from your incentive plans, one that is probably slowing you down and one that risks, at some point, putting you in the ditch.

Incentives, of course, aren't the only driver of management performance at companies. Companies certainly help their performance simply by hiring and hanging onto good people who do the right thing consistently. Nonetheless, problems with incentives and decision-making arise frequently, have significant effects and definitely merit attention.

For many reasons, both business and personal, managers tend to avoid risk. They also tend to focus on short-term results. Also, in many settings, they don't pay much attention to how much of other people's money is being used in their business. These three issues become serious problems when you assess how much value a company creates for shareholders. Balancing risk and return, focusing upon long-run results and being mindful of capital usage are each critical to shareholder value creation. Unfortunately, all three criteria tend to be distorted by the systems that companies use to track business performance and reward key employees.

Incentives lie at the heart of the business, connecting senior management's actions with rewards. Like Adam Smith's "invisible hand," your system of executive rewards affects many important actions by people throughout your company. Incentive plans may imbue the full range of senior management decision-making with biases, and bias is the boll weevil of value creation. The bigger such problems are at your company, the more you'll prosper by fixing them.

Your Company Could Be More Successful

You and your senior management team are in the decision business, committing investor resources to business activities and seeing them through to success, often over a period of many years.[1] Like any company, if you somehow could have avoided some past mistaken decisions and pursued more successful ones, your business performance would have been better. The future will be no different in this regard. Value creation in your business — and the role of your senior management group — is very much about choosing. It is about coming up with a range of real choices, accentuating the positive ones and eliminating the negative. If you could improve business decision-making in a broad and systemic way, you could get a materially better yield from the opportunities surrounding your businesses.

Consider the biggest mistakes your business has made over the past 10 years. Or, if you prefer, consider the biggest ones made by other companies around town. When companies recount such errors, they do not always describe good business decisions that simply did not work out. Rather, they often point out some problems with decision-making — things like short-term bias, organizational inertia, indifference, either insensitivity to risk or disproportionate fear of it, or an unconditional growth mandate driving everything the company does. They describe problems that contributed to their business mistakes and that risk creating more in the future. Consider whether each mistake would have occurred if everyone in senior management had incentives that:

- Directly encourage every person in senior management to take a long view

- Create a clear and direct stake for them in the results of their business decisions

- Attach a fair, unbiased cost to the use of new investor capital as well as fair credit when it gets sent back to investors

- Balance business prospects and risks as would an investor

- Attach first-dollar[2] stake and accountability to the money the company budgets, spends and earns each year

- Put the bulk of incentive pay — rather than some fraction of it — directly within executives' line of sight

- Rebalance the system to favor team performance decisively over narrower individual interests

- Set the platform afire, creating peer pressure, overcoming bureaucratic inertia and starting up a real contest for performance.

Would all of the mistakes you envisioned have been made, under these circumstances? And would your business success stories have been impeded by such a system?

You and your senior management team make decisions that affect results of the entire company. But that does not determine how you, personally, will be judged or rewarded. As CEO, you are in the "total shareholder return" game. For your tenure to be judged as successful, you need to outperform most other companies by generating above-market returns for your company's owners, the shareholders.

Statistically speaking, your game is a hard one to win. In your annual proxy statement, within a few pages of the table showing how much you're paid, there's one comparing your stock price performance to that of peer companies or a common stock index. Your chance of generating a line of returns for your shareholders that isn't below the peer line or roughly on it, but appreciably above it, is maybe 40 percent (based upon typical variability in stock returns). The other 60 percent? That is your chance of being middle of the pack or below.

You may offer really superb products and services, sell them at good prices and margins and beat tough rivals for market share. You may run the most efficient operations in your industries or grow to the point where you're the dominant player in each of them. You may beat all the CEOs you know in the race for earnings growth. None of these things assures high stock market performance. Why? These business scenarios may not create value for shareholders. The longer-term income outlook, capital requirements, or the risks of any of these scenarios may be unprofitable in an economic sense. Also, your shareholders may have expected more. Your stock price is based upon the hopes investors hold about future performance of your company. To them, current disappointments may portend bad news that plays out over the longer term.

You may already be a winner. You may have won this game every year for years, putting your company in the top deciles of stock performance rankings. Unfortunately, your future performance is subject to the same caveat as an investment manager's — past returns are not a guarantee of future results. If you have had outsized expansion in your stock price, it surely implies outsized expectations for future business results. You have to beat those to retain the pole position. The stock market ratchets up performance expectations a bit like a golf handicap, but it adjusts more quickly and can't be fudged for long. Overall, stock markets are efficient, updating expectations and prices so thoroughly that the pattern of future stock price movements is predicted best as a statistical "random walk" rather than any function of past business results.[3] The constant demand of such markets is not merely "what have you done for me lately" but "what will you do for me next?" At the same time, it is quite possible to generate above-market returns with little or no growth in enterprise size or income, depending upon the shape of investor expectations and the charges they assess for the risks and capital involved.

One thing is certain, though. All of the strategies, prospects and results of your business will be distilled by the cruel, reductive math of business valuation into your stock price. Since you have very large holdings of stock-based incentive grants and stock, share price movement determines not only whether you are seen as a success, but also how much you get paid.

These inferences about your performance and rewards stem from basic rules of business valuation and from the basic characteristics of your incentive pay plans. I've spent over 20 years advising companies in those two areas — business valuation and executive incentive design. Executive incentives are concerned with the linkages between executive decisions, business results and value creation. The techniques and financial models used in business valuation are concerned largely with the same things. You should be concerned with these things, too. They're called value rules.

Value Rules

Value rules are basic facts of business governance, performance measurement and valuation that should shape incentive pay at the senior management level. They are derived and explained in Chapters 3 and 4, but here are the most salient points:

- Management's job is to run the enterprise in such a way as to maximize the wealth of shareholders.[4] Incentive plans must support this goal by creating a high degree of line of sight from actions to results to rewards. They must be specific and proactive, encouraging business decisions that create value and discouraging those that don't.

- Incentives, like investor interests, should be unlimited, long-term, concrete and continuous. They must take account of the capital market criteria and performance expectations that actually determine value creation.

- Three basic financial variables describe the value of a business enterprise: long-run operating income, capital usage and the cost of capital. These drivers must be represented in proper proportion in incentive pay.

- Companies must make sure executives, whether found at the corporate level or in business units, have a decisive stake in the businesses they run. They also must immunize incentive pay from the effects of financing decisions, like whether to repurchase shares, and pay little or no attention to the way accounting treats the various forms of compensation.

- Incentive plans should be kept clear and simple to create a direct, enduring stake in value creation that needs limited adjustment or revision over time.

Value rules are at once straightforward, obvious, and revolutionary. They invalidate the bulk of presumptions and practices used by companies when designing incentives, specifically discrediting the standard architecture that now delivers almost all of management incentive pay:

- Heavily stock-based long-term incentives (mainly stock options), favored largely for their accounting treatment and having little connection with the efforts of most recipients

- Bonus plans whose targets are based upon internal negotiation

- Traditional metrics and performance schedules that do not reward good business results consistently and are strongly affected by financing decisions

- An overall structure based almost entirely on corporate-level performance, oriented strongly toward the short term, and constantly being re-negotiated, adjusted or redesigned.

You Don't Run Your Company

This is the primary reason, from the CEO's perspective, to abandon the traditional incentive structure and adopt a much more proactive one. The people in your senior management team — a few dozen to a few hundred executives in a medium to large company — make the bulk of business decisions on the part of shareholders. Cumulatively, they hold much more information than you about the truest, best sources of business advantage and gain within your company. They are in a position to decide which ideas get advanced to you and which do not. Their scope of authority means they take many actions without needing to consult you at all. In many other matters, you properly defer to them based upon their expertise and credibility. They also decide, in a largely voluntary way and using the many tools and tactics at their disposal, which business initiatives are executed faithfully and which are not.

You do not always know what they are thinking. They do not always do what you say. As a group, they have greater effective decision rights than you and perhaps far greater power overall. Your position vis-à-vis them is replicated in their own relation to successive tiers of subordinates, in a process cascading throughout the enterprise.

Incentives are present at every level in that cascading process. To an extent that may or may not surprise you, your company is run by its system of incentives. This system has important effects upon who gets into your senior management team, how long they stay and what they do while they are there. It mirrors good and bad aspects of your management culture. It affects whether your senior executives are competent decision-makers, team players, committed contributors and effective leaders. It affects whether they hold a long view, a balanced sense of business risk and return and a proper concern for use of investor resources. Its effects upon selection and promotion strongly influence whether you have a winning team or not. Its effects upon business decision-making may determine whether they will win or not.

Incentive pay is the centerpiece of your system of executive rewards. Management's task, ultimately, is to run the enterprise in such a way as to generate strong returns for its owners over time. Annual and long-term incentives are the parts of the system that address that duty directly. The other parts — salary, benefits and perquisites — are there to fulfill other objectives, like offering a competitive pay package overall. Companies should regard the incentive parts of executive pay as proactive instruments of business governance.

Senior Management Performance
Has Become More Decisive Than Ever

The world is getting more and more competitive and executive performance is ever more decisive in determining business success or failure. The secular trend toward free trade is producing greater international competition. Better information and communication technology has made most companies more efficient while increasing the pace of innovation and change. The Internet enables most companies to communicate all around the world right now at zero marginal cost and allows many to run large parts of their business at greatly lowered cost. Free, frictionless global capital markets facilitate expansion and funding of new competitors everywhere in the world. Efficient transportation and logistics extend market reach for many enterprises, further reducing geography as a competitive barrier. Privatization and deregulation are trends in many markets around the world.

Companies have to work harder to create a competitive edge and maintain it for any length of time. Many things that used to confer an enduring competitive advantage are now diminishing. Enterprise scale is no longer a clear avenue to market power. The heightened pace of change means that being ahead in technology is less enduring as an advantage. Protection and subsidies of all types are less common than they once were.

In a world like this, human capital is decisive since it is one of the few remaining sources of competitive edge. To an increasing extent, it is the whole game. More and more companies are saying things like "our assets all walk out the door at the end of the day." This once was a platitude of the human resources department. It now is a genuine business reality just about everywhere. And it is never truer than at the senior management level where very disproportionate decision-making power resides. Now more than ever, companies should be using the explicit terms of incentives at this organizational level to encourage high performance.

Your Current Incentives Have Almost
Nothing to Do with Your Own Company

Most companies believe their incentives are tailored to their own circumstances, but actually, they're right off the rack. Companies do have genuinely different circumstances and business strategies, but these apparently aren't driving how they set up incentives. They all use the same option and stock-heavy long-term incentive mix, the same internally-focused target setting in bonus plans, the same flawed metrics drawn from a short list of the usual suspects. They think they have to do this to be competitive. Many don't know of better methods. In the end, the general mechanism of incentive pay at your company appears dictated by what other companies do.

Never mind where your incentive designs came from — you don't even run the plans themselves. You don't make the real decisions with respect to variable pay for senior management. The stock market does. It sets performance expectations, continually judges results and prospects, and decides the payouts on the bulk of incentive pay. It thinks so little of your internal target-setting processes and metrics that it favors its own, when different, 100 percent of the time. Companies effectively have ceded power over this key instrument of governance. You shouldn't be willing to do that any more than the framers of the U.S. Constitution would have allowed Congress to forego the power of the purse.

How can companies with differing cultures, challenges and strategies all end up with the same incentive structure? They're driven by things companies do have in common. Unfortunately, these common beliefs, the ones that actually drive incentive structure, often are nothing but counterproductive illusions:

- The purported efficacy of stock-based incentive pay
- The fictional "zero cost" accounting treatment of stock options
- The assumed expediency and wisdom of linking pay to budget goals
- The putative simplicity of traditional metrics
- The supposed necessity to draw incentive pay into the game of near-term EPS expectations.

These are the pillars of the current incentive system, ones we will demolish in the early parts of this book. Then:

- We'll see effective alternatives to stock options that have been used to advantage by innovative companies for years.
- We'll prove once and for all that the accounting portrayal of incentives does not matter to stockholders; we'll address the past biases toward option usage as well as future ones that may arise under new accounting rules.
- We'll examine tested methods for target setting that improve not only the efficacy of incentives, but also the company's planning processes.
- We'll see a range of ways to align incentives with value creation and overcome the deficiencies of traditional metrics.
- We'll demonstrate how to use incentives to deliver the results that investors do care about.

Using value rules, you'll be able to convert incentive pay into a force that drives higher business results. You also will be able to improve the quality of your working life as CEO. You can improve some of the most important and, at once, nettlesome aspects of your job — budget negotiations, internal equity disputes, allocation of capital resources and other persistent corporate headaches. You can deal fairly with high performing people and businesses miffed by effects of bad performance in other parts of the organization. Some executives and management teams can outperform others year after year, after all. You can keep the bad ones off the property and the good ones on, with decisive effects upon overall results.

With new structures for incentives and target setting, you can encourage high performers to join your business, stay and contribute. You can encourage business unit heads and functional leaders to be utterly forthright about business prospects and resource needs. You can improve the quality of important business processes — budgeting, long-range planning, capital expenditure and acquisition review — and make them less difficult by removing pay-related biases.

Pay Isn't Everything

Companies really shouldn't have systemic biases and flaws in business decision-making, ones they have to remedy using new incentive plans. Rather, they already own many of the solutions. The field of business valuation, and of corporate finance more generally, is focused on how companies create value for shareholders. It is a field replete with sophisticated tools that help companies create the most value from the prospects they have — things like discounted cash flow analysis, risk and cost of capital estimation, and probabilistic inference and simulation. These methods can be used to get a better economic yield from just about any company's set of business opportunities. Most big companies use at least some of these tools.

But financial tools and those who wield them can't overcome by themselves the biases that exist in companies. They aren't powerful enough to realign a broad range of management decisions in favor of shareholder value creation. They tend to be used on a narrow range of episodic decisions like large capital expenditures and acquisitions. They tend to be understood well only by a cadre of staff with specialized training. Lastly, and most importantly, their potential influence tends to be thwarted by the separate, often inconsistent systems that companies use to measure their business success and distribute rewards.

The general ethos of corporate performance and value creation ought to encourage management to set high standards and act consistently in favor of long-run value creation. Instead, many companies find that management focuses too strongly on the short-term. If your management rewards system is focused mainly upon moving up the corporate ladder, it may not consistently ask people to focus upon long-run results, balance risks well, and set high expectations for their segments of the business. The thing it encourages people to manage really well is expectations of their performance and their own image within the organization. Moreover, your company requires growth to provide a plausible supply of the promotions you're using as reward currency. In this regard, the traditional rewards system is a bit like a Ponzi scheme. It's valid only until the pyramid's growth slows down. This may be one of the reasons companies have been so eager to grow through acquisitions, even when particularly risky or expensive.

Creating Value or Taking Stock?

Everyone in senior management has a duty to ensure value creation, not just the finance people, and everyone has a ton of incentive, in theory, to do just that. After all, your company is spending a ton of money on executive incentives. For a typical company with revenues between $5 billion and $10 billion, the annual bill for incentives is $100 million. Of that, $75 million is the annual value of stock option grants and other stock-based long-term incentives. That is an indisputably real cost that is borne in cash or in equivalent shareholder dilution. It also is a cost soon to appear, under new accounting rules that are on the way, as an explicit expense in company income statements. The other $25 million goes out the door in the form of management bonuses and in any long-term incentive (LTI) plans that are settled in cash.

All that money in stock-based incentives in particular ought to rivet senior management's attention to the stock price. It ought to push all their decisions in the direction of value creation. When they make any decisions that destroy value, they're reducing their own stock and option gains, right? And stock and option gains are the main way in which they make money.

Those are valid points. Before we move sharply away from the current incentive system, we need to be sure we are right about the deficiencies of stock-based pay. Stock-based incentives don't come with instructions on how to create value. That leaves executives to make their own inferences about which business actions will increase the stock price and any option gains. Do they do this well? Not consistently. For example, lots of top executives and board members think their share prices move up or down in tandem with earnings per share (EPS). Actually, many poor, value-destroying management decisions can increase EPS in the short run. Further, the general statistical connection between EPS and value is much weaker than what people often assume.[5]

An option-heavy incentive structure is one that relies on executives naturally understanding how to optimize the share price. That is a stretch, since market valuation is a complex and specialized science. Market movements have complex origins that regularly bewilder investors. Also, lots of executives think their stock price moves around for reasons they can't control. That means they regard their stock value and option gains as being largely out of their hands. These folks are right. In the time frame relevant to incentive pay, stock price movement is not driven mainly by business results but by overall stock market movement, industry stock price action and other factors. So, even if an executive at the top level of your organization feels that he or she can have an impact big enough to be felt in consolidated business results, that executive cannot expect stock-based incentives to reward him or her reliably for it. Farther down the ladder, consider your business unit executives. Their team may be running a business worth billions of dollars, yet their actions might have only a trivial impact on where the stock price goes. Strictly speaking, for most executives, options offer no real performance incentive — no plausible cause-and-effect linkage from actions to results to pay.

The Real Incentive System

The main driver of rewards for your senior management group over the years has been their progress up the corporate ladder. That is the real incentive mechanism within corporate executive ranks. Pay rises hugely as a result of promotions. Doing what's necessary to get promotions is well within the executive's line of sight and control. Compare that to the vague, distant effects an individual might have on any option gains. *The only clear incentive created by the typical, option-dominated rewards structure is to do whatever it takes to get more stock options.*

But what if I'm wrong about all this? What if options do work well, if not as a directive performance tool, then as the general currency of hiring, retention and rewards? If stock options were effective as a general medium of rewards, you'd expect to see stock option usage connected with company success. You do not. The preponderant finding from the many academic studies in this area is that stock option usage does not contribute materially to company performance.

Stock options, as well as most of the balance of the costly incentive structure, do not in any direct way encourage individuals to contribute their best. When it really gets down to it, company systems for performance-based pay rely extremely heavily upon the company's ability to judge individual merit and contribution and match them with promotions, salary increases and the higher incentive and benefits opportunities that attend each. But individual merit and contribution can be hard things to judge. And a group of people with high individual performance ratings may not generate high levels of business results. The whole system would work better if it directly encouraged individuals to take those actions most productive to value creation, utterly irrespective of whether they count toward individual performance, bring individual accolades or secure the next job or the current one. There already is plenty of money in the pay system to be earned with attainment of rank. Individualism, apart from team results, does not need to govern senior management's incentives, too.

With more effective incentive plans, the people in your organization have a clearly defined stake. In response, you can expect them to make personal commitments to the success of your particular business, rather than keeping their skills liquid and their resumes polished. By contrast, when the path to reward is unclear and un-entrepreneurial, executives are discouraged from devoting their human capital to the enterprise.[6]

Most of these issues with incentive plans have been around for a while.[7] For guidance, we can look at some of the past attempts to correct them. In the early and mid-1990s, a value-based management (VBM) movement sprang up to address a few of the relevant issues. Unfortunately, most of its interventions were about *doing* one or another of a few metrics like *economic value added* and *cash flow return on investment*. Many advocates in the 1990's VBM movement insisted all the company's processes needed to be turned upside down to accommodate the new metrics. In most cases, they did not. Companies already possessed building blocks like well-specified analytical and valuation tools, adequate tracking of capital and business results by business unit and sensible people in charge of it all. Where they needed to focus — where they found real business problems with financial measurement warranting broad intervention — was mostly in the incentive plans. This is where the rubber hits the road, where financial results are tied to incentive pay and therefore to executive behavior.

The VBM advocates had some ideas about incentives, but they relied too much on metrics alone in their efforts to remedy the issues. They attempted to use them to police every business action and accounting decision made in the company. When applied within pay plans, metrics like economic value ended up being over-adjusted and unworkably complex. They also were used mainly within annual incentive plans rather than in the long-term plans where most of senior management incentive pay is found. And they tended to accompany their unfamiliar, over-engineered metrics with incentive plan structures that were equally complex and foreign. Most companies passed on these approaches and many who tried them have since abandoned them.

This Picture is Coming Soon to a Boardroom Near You

Many companies are on course to make some of the changes indicated by value rules. If you haven't yet started talking about option expensing, you will. I've got a lot to say about that later. For now, let me just note that, now that everyone understands that stock options are on track for less favorable accounting treatment, boards are questioning how much value people really place on them and how much effect most option holders really have on stock price gains.

You may confront the fact that, in typical circumstances, unlike those that prevailed in the 1990s, options often will be marginally in the money at best during the key few years following grant. Stock options will be seen as high-maintenance, a real mixed bag in terms of business benefits and of no differential accounting advantage. You'll be inclined to cut back on who gets them and how many you grant, and you may ditch them entirely. Stock options were way, way overdone. Now they're on their way out, both as a common device for broad-based rewards and as the centerpiece of senior management pay.

Next, you'll probably start thinking about the obvious first alternative: using stock grants rather than option grants as the central feature of senior management's long-term incentives. This approach has the advantages of creating immediate stock ownership, being more effective as a retention device, and paying management in a medium they value more highly — in relation to economic cost — than option grants. But you'll run into this problem: restricted stock grants can allow senior management to make a ton of money even when their performance stinks. The fact is that competitive long-term incentive pay involves large grants of something and that something should be performance-based or it should be a non-starter. Restricted stock as the new long-term incentive currency? That dog won't hunt.

In the next obvious step, you'll turn your attention to performance shares. These are grants of stock that are earned or vested over time based upon company performance against pre-set goals. You'll consider replacing all or part of your stock options for senior management with performance shares, ones based upon traditional metrics set at the corporate level. Surveys in mid-2003 indicated that, in reaction to accounting changes, performance shares were favored as the main alternative to stock options.

Everyone is going to get that far. What I recommend is that you go much farther to have a more complete and effective outcome. To do the job right, do these things:

- Rather than basing performance share grants entirely upon corporate goals, you should consider using goals struck at the business unit level. You don't have much in the way of business unit incentives now. The bonus plan is said to be a business unit incentive, at least in part, but really it just encourages everyone to manage expectations and results into a modest range in the near term. You don't have much in the way of *long-term* incentives at the business unit level, either, and for bad reasons. The accounting advantages of corporate-level stock options won most battles over business unit pay before they started, causing most companies to issue corporate stock options to business unit executives rather than using potentially more effective forms of LTI struck at the business unit level. In other cases, concerns about counter-productive effects on corporate-wide teamwork won out, overlooking the fact that the business units at issue are almost always largely separate, with their own financial statements, substantive degrees of autonomy and at least some bonus pay that is already based upon unit results.

- You may want to consider using cash-based long-term incentive plans at the business unit level rather than continuing your heavy use of corporate stock. The folks receiving these awards typically aren't executive officers of a public registrant, after all. You may have been paying them with a lot of stock-based incentives simply because of market practice and accounting considerations rather than any real governance argument. You'd probably find it feasible to use performance unit plans (basically long-term bonus plans) or phantom stock plans, especially in the more separable, autonomous business units. Once the accounting advantages of stock options are gone, the bulk of the other common arguments against this approach will dissolve.

- Traditional financial measures have many dangerous flaws, and nowhere more than at the business unit level. Here, we see operating income and revenue delivering bonus pay most often. But the fact of the matter is that executives can deliver lots of income and revenue without creating any value at all. Companies need to improve the measurement methods they use at the business unit level before they can base more incentive pay upon them. Existing methods are an unstable vehicle. If you increase the load on them by allowing them not only to deliver bonuses, but long-term incentive pay, you may end up in the ditch. To link the system to long-run value creation, you need to feature long-run income of the business unit, its use of capital and the opportunity cost of that capital. This book describes a range of good ways to do this. You don't need to use any one particular metric or plan design.

- At the corporate level as well, you need to be sure the incentive system encourages long-run value creation. As one element of this task, you need to address deficiencies of metrics like EPS, return on equity (ROE) and net income. Solutions simply need to reflect the value drivers that senior management affects most closely: income levels and capital usage, with the balance between them driven by the cost of capital.

- We're talking about making far heavier use of performance-based pay, so we need to focus on where performance targets come from. At this point, your entire cash incentive structure rides on internally set goals. This can cause at least moderate sandbagging and possibly great concerns about unfairness. It can result in payouts that connect poorly with outcomes for shareholders. The company should base its goals not upon budgets, but upon external, shareholder-oriented benchmarks like investor expectations and valuation criteria. These can be applied at the corporate and business unit levels.

- Finally, take a close look at the performance and award ranges, weightings and leverage that comprise the rest of the incentive apparatus. These things can have surprisingly strong effects upon decision-making behavior. Our recommendations: set them in a deliberate way, rather than based upon habit or competitive practice. That is, formally measure the inputs and outputs of the whole system — the amount of possible variation in business results, the influence people have on them and pay outcomes — through simulation and testing. Then, you'll know what you're paying for, across the full range of scenarios that may prevail.

Commit to these directional changes at the board level and hand the details of design and implementation over to your senior staff.

Everything I Need to Know
I Learned in Financial Kindergarten

Sounds simple? It is. Value rules cover every business decision, every configuration of business results, just about every situation in which business success warrants reward. Value rules provide a simple way to reward executives for producing value-creating business results. They stem from the most basic linkages between business results and business value, ones that should form the core of incentive plans.

Once you have a pretty good picture of a company's future prospects and risks, it is easy to rough out its valuation or, equivalently, to have a good starting point for the design of incentive pay. To do so is just a matter of applying valuation models in a roughly sensible way. From this starting point, it really is pretty hard to make a big mistake; for example, to take an enterprise truly worth, say, eight times current operating cash flow and somehow end up valuing it at a multiple of six or 10.

Valuation isn't easy, actually. But what makes valuation hard is two things that we don't really have to do when setting up value-based incentive plans: assessing future risks and prospects and coming up with precise results. Neither of these tough standards applies when applying valuation techniques to incentive design. When we are setting up incentives, we don't have to know that much about what the future holds. Rather, we just need an adaptable mechanism for sharing results in a proper way *once they have occurred*. And a rough rather than precise standard is a proper one in this context. We are trying to create a general alignment between value-creating decisions and results, one that holds up under a range of circumstances over time.

We need to get a handle on the future to set reasonable targets, yes. And we also need incentives that are consistently and properly directive. That requires a certain level of precision. These needs are met by the long-term nature of incentive structures that comply with value rules and by their many fallbacks and governing devices. The only parts of the science of business valuation we need to apply are the easy parts — the basic models translating a given set of results into an estimate of value.

We're talking about appraisal, but we're not valuing an 18th century maritime clock or a vintage roadster. When valuing a business interest, we are looking at something that has prospective financial results. Whether your company is public, private, or a business unit of either, it can be valued based upon reasonable criteria for pricing risk and return, ones applied by capital markets that do this kind of thing all day. By translating these fundamental valuation principles into well-designed incentives, we:

- Encourage creating the greatest stream of long-run income instead of managing income into a narrow range in the near term

- Provide complete accountability for the use of capital and for its opportunity cost from an investor's perspective.

The plans we create in this way are called "incentives," so they involve reasonable line of sight from a participant's viewpoint. And, as we said, they're well designed, so they are competitive and prudent.

Incentive Dynamics

Here is a question that many companies should consider when looking at new incentive plans. Why is it that senior managers act like bystanders so often when business disasters are unfolding in front of them? Companies often make overpriced acquisitions based upon synergies they're not likely to achieve, for example, and fritter away overhead on ill-advised initiatives, all in full view of powerful people who know better.

Perhaps they're taking direction from their incentive system. We've noted the traditional system of rewards pays mainly based upon one's place in the organization. This invites decision-makers to be a bit concerned about financial consequences of bad moves, to be sure, but it also gives a nod to politics, to not rocking the boat and to protecting one's own turf. It can allow insularity, inertia or hubris to run their destructive course. It can enable a management team to euphemize failure as a source of valuable "learnings."

Value rules are a bit different in their emphasis. They deliver pay not based upon an individual's place, but upon forward progress of a team. They advance these three catchy messages in response to any big, bad business decision: "Kill it. Kill it now. Kill it dead." Value rules create outrage over bad decisions because such actions dip into the pockets of everyone in senior management. They also create a certain urgency about successful initiatives.

I just used the term "urgency" in the context of something positive. Does that happen often enough in your business? Proper incentives broaden and energize the stakeholder group for any materially sized business initiative. This may affect how the whole business is run. It could change how you approach your job. You'll be using incentives to ask your key decision-makers to put their money where their mouth is. You'll be using incentives — and their effects on the many aspects of the decision-making process that you can't read or direct — as a supplement to your own business judgment, persuasive powers and authority. Lastly, let's remember that the big business decisions all bear your *imprimateur*. If you put in place an incentive system meant to engage the senior management workforce more strongly, that means the matters they'll be minding more actively are, to a certain extent, yours. You'll be inviting a broad group of senior managers to get involved in some productive way and to express what they know when the big decisions are being made, rather than waiting to second-guess the results in private. This may well change your dialogue with the senior management group. You'll be dealing with co-investors rather than functionaries. This will encourage a lot of good information to come to the forefront as big choices are being made by the company, potentially improving the process of business decision-making and many of its outcomes. And, once a decision is made, it encourages everyone to get on board and get it executed.

Bottom Lines

Money helps all this to happen, and it should be used in this way. Companies should use senior management incentives purposefully; to help them prosper. They should *pay to prosper*. Instead, they leave this tool in the shed unused. This book is about how to employ the company's structure of incentives in an active way to get better business decisions and better results from senior management. This is the best way to use incentives — to encourage high business performance in a proactive way rather than acknowledging it in a distanced and vague manner after the fact.

It is not easy to get better performance out of a business. The virtue of this performance initiative is that it does not involve turning the whole business upside down. Rather, it concerns a limited group of people over whom you hold much sway. It does not depend upon actions of your competitors or upon market conditions you cannot affect. Rather, it is about getting better economic yield from business opportunities under all market conditions. It is comparatively easy money. Getting it done is completely within your control. And it can't really happen without you.

Your required reading ends here. Read on if you wish, of course. The balance of the book concerns matters whose scope clearly warrants your attention. But, most importantly, be sure your human resources and finance folks take a look. With your visible concurrence and consistent support, they can take it from there, and your company can get the gains promised. Thanks for your time.

Endnotes

1. Consulting firm Strategic Decisions Group coined the saying, "Management is in the decision business."

2. Or euros, yen, pounds or other currency. U.S. dollars will be used in this book as the reference currency.

3. For descriptions of the statistical behavior of equity prices, see Nobel Prize winner Eugene Fama's book, *Foundations of Finance*, as well as Burton G. Malkiel's *A Random Walk Down Wall Street*.

4. This is a general tenet of the area of economics called "agency theory."

5. For a representative example of statistical evidence, the report, *Company Performance and Measures of Value Added*, by the Research Foundation of the Institute of Chartered Financial Analysts, examines a wide range of metrics and value creation. Findings make clear that the bulk of variation in stock prices is not driven by differences in measured performance.

6. These effects are detailed by Tom Davenport in his book, *Human Capital*.

7. For example, John England cited several of the problems with stock option grants in the article, "Don't Be Afraid of Phantom Stock" (September/October 1992 issue of *Compensation and Benefits Review*).

2

The Typical
Incentive Structure

Meet Homer. He is the top manufacturing executive for a group of businesses within a *Fortune 500* company headquartered in the United States, and his incentives are quite typical for someone in a senior management job. Here's how they work:

- Homer receives an annual bonus based one-half on corporate results and one-half on his business unit's results. He does not have much impact upon corporate goals, but he and his management teammates have strong influence upon results of their business unit.

- Business unit results — that is, results of his group — are measured by operating income. This metric basically encourages Homer and his teammates to increase operating income through the range eligible for reward under the bonus plan. This method does not take account of capital usage (through a measure like return on invested capital, for example) or business risk, so Homer and his teammates seek to get capital for growth and invest it irrespective of yield, as long as it contributes something to operating income.

- Targeted performance levels are set each year within a budget process, one involving some negotiation between business unit teams like Homer's and corporate management. By managing expectations, Homer's team can make good bonuses over time without delivering their best results. They might want to manage the timing of income, too, deferring revenue and accelerating expenses when above the plan's maximum payout level and vice versa.

- Homer receives a large stock option grant each year, and the size of the grant is based upon his rank in the organization. He has no impact on the overall stock price, so to him, this grant is an overall results-sharing arrangement rather than an incentive in any active sense.

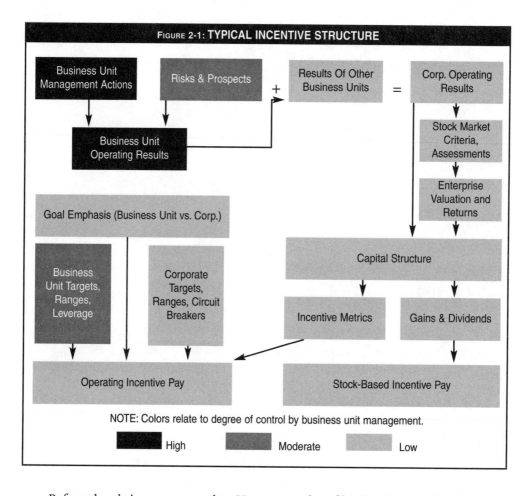

FIGURE 2-1: TYPICAL INCENTIVE STRUCTURE

NOTE: Colors relate to degree of control by business unit management.

Before they bring any reward to Homer, results of his business unit are diluted by results of other business units, interpreted by the stock market in an opaque process, affected by the overall company's capital structure and filtered by the specific terms of incentive plans. The process is a roundabout one, and Figure 2-1 depicts it aptly in this regard. The black boxes show things over which Homer and his team have reasonably strong control — business decision-making and business unit results. They also have some control (denoted in dark grey) over the risks and prospects of their business activities. They have some influence over target setting in their own business unit and perhaps over other aspects of plan design at that level. The balance of the structure of incentive rewards — the bulk of it — is out of their hands.

What Are We Paying for Management Incentives?

To understand how companies can do a better job inspiring their executives to build shareholder value, let's take a look at what's usually on the table in the way of incentive plans. Corporations use a variety of management incentives that include cash-based plans like bonuses, multi-year performance plans, phantom stock, as well as stock-based incentives like stock options, restricted stock and performance shares.

As we noted in Chapter 1, Homer's company uses up about $100 million per year in investor resources to provide management incentives. How does a typical company this size end up with so much incentive cost? First, let's look at the size of the company. Homer's parent company has consolidated revenue of $7.5 billion. Using typical margins and valuation multiples, let's say it has income of $500 million and a market equity valuation of $7.5 billion.

Next, let's add up the cash plans. Management bonus plans cost a typical company of this size 5 percent to 6 percent of net income. Other cash operating incentives cost another 1 percent or 2 percent. Let's be conservative and say 5 percent of net income is the total cost of cash-based incentives for management. Our example company has net income of $500 million, so the cash cost of operating incentives is about $25 million.

Lastly, let's add in the economic cost of stock-based grants. This company is typical, so it grants about 2 percent of its shares annually in the form of stock-based incentives (survey averages from the 1998-2003 period are in the 2 percent to 2.5 percent range for annual share usage). A grant of 2 percent would be a grant of stock-based incentives against shares worth $150 million, or 2 percent of $7.5 billion:

- That consists mostly of options, 80 percent or more based upon typical market data. So we have option grants totaling $120 million. Options for an average company — with typical terms — are worth 40 percent or more of face value at the time of grant. Present value at grant is a reasonable, common basis of measuring the economic cost of option-based pay and expressing it in a way that is consistent with other elements of pay. So we have $48 million in option cost.[1]

- The other $30 million is issued in a typical mix of restricted stock and performance shares. We value these grants at 90 percent of face value after taking into account the mix and some relevant risks faced by participants.[2] So we have $27 million in the form of these grants.

The total cost of stock-based incentives is $75 million ($48 million + $27 million). Cash costs for the bonus awards are another $25 million, for a total of $100 million. There is no question that the company is spending a lot on management; their incentives alone amount to 20 percent of consolidated net income. Disagree with these figures? Use different ones like $50 million or $150 million. Any way you slice it, this is a big cost to company's owners, and the cost goes up when you add in salaries, benefits and perquisites. And this expense is largely a corporate construct; upward of $90 million of it is based upon collective rather than business unit results.[3]

What Are We Trying to Buy with Incentives?

To assess costs and benefits of incentives, we need to address what they are meant to do for the company. The system of management rewards is intended to help the company meet important objectives:

- Attract and retain top-caliber management by providing an overall pay package valuable enough to meet market demands

- Encourage desired behaviors and values like teamwork, information sharing and support for many business initiatives

- Enable the company to reward advancement and encourage candidates to compete through high performance

- Provide flexibility and tax benefits.

These are laudable goals. For the price of incentives plus the costs of other aspects of the total rewards package, the company ought to be able to buy a lot of all of them. Salary is not a formal incentive arrangement, for example, but it can be used to encourage good performance. The fact that a person has a senior management job at all reflects performance, and merit pay and promotions are meant to encourage high individual contribution. But companies apparently believe these and many other organizational dynamics aren't enough to assure good performance, because they devote an enormous quantity of resources to something they call incentive pay.

Calculating the direct cost of executive pay and relating it to a few goals is only the beginning. The key cost/benefit indicator, where incentives are concerned, is their efficacy in encouraging better business performance.

To judge that, let's talk in detail about the typical company and about Homer, the typical participant. He is the head of manufacturing for a group that accounts for one-fourth of the value and results of the consolidated enterprise. He's paid competitively, with total direct compensation worth $450,000, which consists of:

- A salary of $200,000

- Annual bonus potential of $90,000. This year, he'll get his target bonus if operating income in his group and corporate EPS each grow by 8 percent.

- A long-term incentive grant worth $160,000 annually, all in the form of stock options from the parent company. The annual size of his grant is $400,000. It is valued using typical methods at 40 percent of face, so it is worth $160,000.

The total cost of his pay package is $550,000 once you add in another $100,000 in perquisites and benefits. The formal incentive plans within his total compensation add up to $250,000, or $90,000 in potential bonus and $160,000 in long-term incentives.[4]

Homer's Performance and Homer's Pay

Now let's take a look at how Homer's performance might affect his pay. He has a pretty strong connection to results of his group, so pay based upon group results should be reasonably compelling to him. There are gaps between Homer's actions and the financial performance of his group over time, to be sure, but they are not a big hindrance to incentive efficacy for someone like Homer for two reasons:

- Homer doesn't drive his group's results by himself, but his overall team has a very strong ability to drive them over time. Homer and others might argue that their duties are very specialized — not matters always judged fairly by team results. A reasonable response to someone at Homer's level is that, if the activity isn't something that is going to help overall results over time, he probably shouldn't be spending much time on it. Within the context of an incentive, everything important that Homer does ought to be in the vein of making financial results at his group better than they otherwise would be. That standard works most of the time for Homer's participation in corporate-wide efforts as well.

- Homer and his team members face business risks, but these do not invalidate his incentives. Their actions are not guaranteed to deliver results, but they are accustomed to this kind of uncertainty. We're paying them to make the best decisions in the face of those risks, to devise bets that win. The risks in Homer's pay package are inescapable as a practical matter; he'd face similar risks if he went to work somewhere else.

Now let's look at the precise workings of Homer's incentives, focusing on the stock options that make up the biggest part of his incentive package. Do Homer's options provide him with an incentive to produce better performance? Lots of people complain that the stock market moves around for reasons outside of management's control and so they question whether stock-based incentives work as an incentive, strictly speaking, for most plan participants. On the other hand, some argue that the results of management's actions do end up represented in the stock price over time.

Then there are people who say both are right. I'm in that third camp. The stock market does a good job of reflecting economic performance over a long period of time. Companies face a timing issue, though, when they rely too much on stock market outcomes to deliver incentive pay. In the nearer term, the period of one to three years that is most relevant to incentive design, the price of the stock moves around mainly for reasons unrelated to company results.[5] Although executives typically feel that business results are the thing they deliver during this critical period, their stock gains are driven mostly by other factors. If they wait 10 or 15 years, they can be quite confident that the stock price over that time will have synched up, by and large, with the company's performance. But that's just too long for purposes of anything we'd call an incentive.

It's also true that stock prices consistently reflect the present value of the future cash flows that shareholders hope to see a business produce. The stock market is a grand discounting mechanism, one that takes into account:

- Results management can deliver over the next few years given the opportunities they have

- Longer-run prospects and risks for business generally and for the company's particular industry or industries

- Valuation criteria like security yields and the price of risk.

The fact that stock prices are based upon expected future results provides a partial solution to the timing issue noted earlier. Management is rewarded now — through stock and option gains — for taking actions that are expected to play out in future business results. If investors in the market start thinking management isn't going to deliver, they penalize the stock price (and option gains) sooner rather than later.

So accountabilities aren't lacking in the system in a general sense. It is responsive to actual and expected business performance. But clarity is lacking and so is line of sight. Most management types don't have a very clear view of the market's valuation mechanism. If they did, we'd see them behave differently in areas like option exercise behavior and acquisition policy. Instead, they demonstrate little timing "edge" in their own share sales and routinely make acquisitions that destroy value.[6] Also, most don't have much influence upon the overall company's valuation.

Running the Numbers

Remember that the stock-based part of Homer's pay is the biggest part at $160,000, and that bit costs his company $75 million per year. The company understands that there are some problems with stock-based pay, but believes nonetheless that these grants work toward a general goal of encouraging key people like Homer to create more value for owners. How much do option gains really have to do with the performance of Homer, his fellow group management members and his group? Let's put some numbers on it.

Homer's group has an operating income target for this year of $200 million. His group represents one-fourth of the overall company's consolidated income of $800 million. Applying a 37.5 percent tax rate reduces overall operating profit to $500 million. Since the company has no debt and no other income and expense, the $500 million in after-tax operating profit is the same as net income after tax.

Let's say that Homer and his team come up with some cost reductions that can increase his business unit's operating income to $220 million, or 10 percent above target. These performance improvements, if enacted, are seen by all as permanent. And they don't cost anything to produce. This is hard to do, but Homer's group can pull together and do it. He'd make some money under his bonus plan for doing this, but we'll get to that later.

For now, let's see whether he gets paid through the company's most expensive incentive plan — his grant of options under the stock-based incentive plan. Let's assume his group undertakes the cost reduction effort and gets the hoped-for results this year. The stock market agrees that this year's income gain is permanent, an enduring increase of $12.5 million in after-tax cash flow every year from now on. In fact, let's assume the stock market is providing more or less perfect performance feedback, adjusting the stock price by exactly the present value of the performance improvement. That would be the absolute best case in terms of the efficacy of the stock market as a pay delivery system, so it is a place to start.

Let's say the company's cost of capital is 9 percent. Measured at the end of the year, this performance improvement is worth about $150 million, consisting of $12.5 million in extra cash flows accumulated this year plus the present value of cash flows for many future years ($12.5 million plus $12.5 million divided by 9 percent: beginning-of-year convention regarding timing of cash receipt). This is a perpetuity valuation method, one we will cover further in Chapter 4 and use a lot in later applications.

Homer's overall company is worth $7.5 billion, or 15 times earnings. It has 150 million shares outstanding and the price per share is $50. At the end of the year — with performance at target — let's say it would have earned a cost-of-capital level of return for its owners and be worth 9 percent more. That's an ending equity valuation of $54.50 per share or $8.2 billion. This estimate is before paying out any cash flows to owners in the form of dividends or share repurchases, with capital market criteria and expectations unchanged, and with the stock market valuing enterprises using traditional discounted cash flow analysis.

Homer's performance improvement increases valuation at year-end by a bit less than 2 percent, or $150 million divided by $8.2 billion in year-end market capitalization. Homer's option grant, whose overall value was $400,000, delivers an incremental gain to him of about $8,000, or $1 per share.

Homer also might make some money on other options that he's been granted in the past. But we're not looking at those right now. We're just assessing the impact of the $160,000 in long-term incentives we granted to him this year.[7] So, in a static world with perfect markets and foresight, Homer gets paid $8,000 on this year's grant for actions that created $150 million in value. This is a pittance in relation to his overall pay, so let's just dismiss it, assume the stock option grant has no incentive value in this case, and move on to a bigger example.

Let's suppose Homer and his pals increase income permanently by $60 million this year, or 30 percent, again with no investment required. That's great performance in most businesses. The operating income jump by itself is in the 84th percentile in the S&P 500 over the past 10 years.[8] The percentile probably is even higher for an established, profitable company beating its budgeted operating income by 30 percent. Accompany that with no capital increase — no investment required — and Homer's group's performance is at the top of the market in relation to any normal standard.

Does he get paid under the stock-based incentive plan? Well, the gain is now three times as high at $3 per share or $24,000 of his option grant. It still is a small part of his pay, but it's enough to get his attention. For our incentive scheme to work, however, Homer has to believe that the corporate stock price will trend roughly $3 higher than it otherwise would have at some point in the future when he's exercising his grant. In effect, he needs to believe that the stock market is holding his incremental gains in a kind of "lock box." Lacking that, he certainly won't see his options as an incentive. In terms of good performance this year, he and his group went about as far as they can go. If his options don't pay him for this, they'll never pay him for his performance.

A Drop in the Bucket

So, is he getting paid, and should he believe there's a lock box? At this point, we don't know. Let's look at how stock prices move around. The $3 gain equals a 6 percent movement in price. The range of likely movement in a typical year — statistically the range the stock price has a 70 percent chance of ending up within — is about $40 to $70 per share.[9] As it works out, Homer is likely to see price changes of $3 or more — owing to all kinds of valuation factors — within a typical month. Here are some things that could offset his $3 per share gain:

- An increase of 40 basis points (0.40 percent) in the cost of capital used by the stock market to price company shares. If expected yields on corporate equity move around in a way similar to corporate bonds (standard deviation of one percentage point or so per year), you'd expect at least this level of movement almost every year.

- Similar movement in either the price of risk — that's the premium in yield that investors demand in order to bear the risks of equity investments — or in very long-run expectations for expected growth.

- A 10-percent decline in income — one seen as enduring — in the other businesses. If their targeted income is $600 million in total and they came in 10 percent below that, it would offset all of the huge $60 million in gains earned by Homer's group.

Smaller movements in each of these factors could combine in such a way as to wipe out Homer's gain. Larger movements could boost the price, making Homer's incremental contribution hard to distinguish as incentive pay.

Overall, his change in incentive pay for helping boost the company's income is a drop in the bucket. Most people in the senior management organization are like Homer, whether they are found at corporate or in business units. They have big jobs. They have a strong impact on some important part of the company. But they have modest to negligible effects upon the stock price. The $75 million spent on stock-based incentives went mainly to people like Homer. If it was meant as "performance incentive" pay in any strict sense, it was largely wasted.

What Did the Money Go For?

Participants do make gains on option grants, though. If it isn't related to their performance, it is reasonable to ask, what did it go for? I developed a valuation/pay simulation model to answer this question, one that attaches reasonable levels of movement and predictability to three factors that influence the movement of a company's stock price.

- Performance of the executive's own business unit and its contribution to shareholder value. This is measured based upon a valuation formula applied to business unit results, a particular variant of the metric total business return (TBR), which we will examine in detail in later chapters. It is designed to capture the valuation implications of current business results.

- Performance of other business units based upon their measured TBR. We could add effects of corporate actions as a separate item, but instead we'll assume that source of uncertainty is reflected in combined results of the other units.

- Stock market factors that affect valuation, such as interest rates, equity risk premia and long-run growth expectations for the economy and its various sectors.[10]

Using the model, I ran a few thousand random scenarios of Homer's stock price gains. I took care of the "anticipatory pricing" issue by ascribing perfect foresight to the stock market and allowing near-term performance variation to compound into stock prices for a typical option holding period of five years.[11] So the stock market was assumed to be able to perfectly predict Homer's future company performance, an approach that accorded higher efficacy to his stock-based incentive pay.

Here's what I found:

- Over the five-year holding period, only about 10 percent of the variation in Homer's option gains is related to performance of his group, meaning decisions made by Homer or his team, or to risk and prospects of the industries in which they work.

- About 30 percent of Homer's range of gains is driven by the performance of the other businesses or by corporate actions.

- The balance, 60 percent of the variation in pay, is not related to company financial results. It is due to market factors utterly outside the control of Homer or most anyone else involved with the company.[12]

Of the $160,000 devoted to long-term incentive pay for Homer, only $16,000, or 10 percent is an incentive plan, and $144,000 is a random, uncontrollable pay source like lottery tickets. *As far as incentive value is concerned, Homer may as well be getting option grants from some other company.*

Now, perhaps Homer has influence beyond that of his business unit. In that case, the linkages are a bit stronger than 10 percent since he has some impact upon organization-wide results. And perhaps a head of another, larger business unit has even more. Corporate executives, with their organization-wide span of influence, ought to be in an even stronger position to drive stock prices and their own pay under option plans.

But our analyses as well as general statistics on movement in stock prices show that the normal variability in the stock market tends to swamp the effects of individual company performance during the period when executives normally hold grants. Executives hold options for about five years on average. Over that time frame, less than half of the gain on a typical option normally can be linked statistically to consolidated company performance; 40 percent in the case just examined.

These observations don't mean there is anything wrong with the stock market. The stock market is doing its job perfectly in all our examples. It is reacting properly to company performance as well as other important factors affecting security prices. The market is more than efficient in this simulation. It is omniscient. But the stock market's job does not include paying Homer in a sensible and productive way. Look at it this way; the stock market does not even know Homer. It should not be put in charge of administering the bulk of Homer's pay to reflect his performance contribution.

The fact is that Homer's piece of the $75 million in stock-based incentive cost doesn't really work as an incentive for him. Whether it works for executives in other, larger business units is called into question as well by the analysis. Ditto for most folks at corporate. And partly true for even the top few officers of the company.

Financial researchers have run a few numbers on stock-based incentive pay as well. Generally, they find no statistical linkage between corporate use of stock options at the senior management level and company performance.[13] Indeed, stock options by themselves, as opposed to ownership of full shares of company stock, appear to have some adverse effects upon company decision-making. Options protect executives from downside in the stock price, and this is particularly true in the option-heavy pay structures of top corporate officers. When these folks have a ton of stock options, they are more inclined to roll the dice on acquisitions. And most acquisitions fail. Companies influenced by holders of large blocks of shares, on the other hand, particularly when the block-holder is the CEO, are significantly less inclined to go down that path.[14]

There is a legitimate performance play involving stock options. Some companies use unusually large amounts of stock, options and other corporate resources as a means of attracting the best talent and to get the best results. Some of them succeed with this remuneration strategy. But that does not speak to the efficacy of stock-based pay as a performance incentive device by itself. Those companies might have succeeded just as well by offering boatloads of cash rather than options in their attempts to attract and retain the best.

Accounting "Advantages" of Stock Options

Companies run numbers on options, too, but they tend to focus too much upon EPS effects. Use of options is driven in large measure by their accounting treatment. Unlike most kinds of incentives, stock options have not (yet) required a charge against earnings. Companies fear that if they use other kinds of incentives and are obliged to account for them as expenses, their financial results will tumble and the stock market will penalize them.

In a January, 2002 publication, I contributed to the debate by writing, "Overall, belief in the book advantages of options — in the idea that options accounting keeps stock prices higher than they otherwise would be — appears to be a broadly held financial illusion. This is unfortunate since the focus on bookkeeping skews incentive design greatly and renders it ineffective for most participants."[15] A few months later, some surprising developments provided a perfect opportunity to test this prediction. In mid-2002, more than 100 companies announced they would voluntarily record option expenses in their income statements. My colleague, Michael Grund, and I studied stock market reactions to these announcements. Figure 2-2 is a chart with our results. It shows announcing companies' stock price performance in typical "event study" format. In this case, it sets forth announcers' stock prices, normalized to a common value of $10 per share at the time of announcement and adjusted for market movements. (See Figure 2-2.)

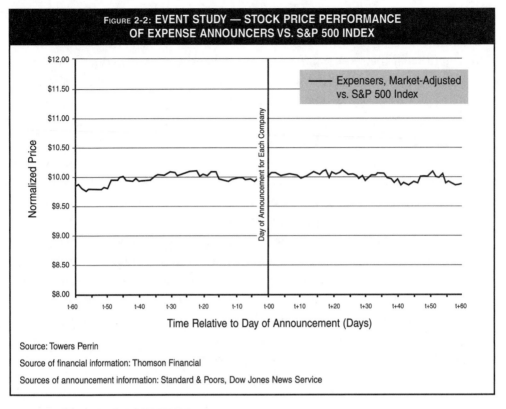

Source: Towers Perrin

Source of financial information: Thomson Financial

Sources of announcement information: Standard & Poors, Dow Jones News Service

If there ever was going to be a test of whether stock option accounting matters to shareholders — and whether the favorable book treatment of one incentive or another should be pursued in the hope of improving one's stock price — this was it. After all, in the summer of 2002, corporate America sorted itself into an experimental group of option expense announcers and a control group consisting of everyone else. If the market saw option expensing as a bad thing, this line would blip or trend downward as this remarkably bad earnings surprise was received and assimilated into prices. It did not.

These companies announced that they would record option costs, resulting in a material and persistent reduction of earnings. This is the scenario that many companies worry about — a voluntary choice regarding pay and its accounting effects that reduces earnings and, they fear, the stock price. When companies are faced with such a choice, they almost always choose to use options heavily to keep the accounting charges down.

These 103 companies simply chose to go ahead and take the hit to earnings. The stock market shrugged it off as a non-event. Stock prices of those that expensed did not dip at the time of announcement nor during the surrounding time periods when the market might have been anticipating or digesting this information. Overall, stock price movements of the expense announcers were indistinguishable from those of the average S&P 500 company.

Why? Because expensing isn't news. The stock market already was well aware of stock options and their economic cost, so the prospect of a change in accounting to recognize these facts provided no new information, certainly, at least, for widely followed stocks. Those that expensed weren't all pikers, either. The pro forma effect of option expensing in this group averaged 10 percent of earnings, and companies with larger prospective earnings reductions did not experience any larger share price reductions. Companies may have believed that the fictitious accounting portrayal of stock options was allowing them to escape the economic consequences of making these grants, but as predicted, this was a broadly held financial illusion.

These findings do not suggest that companies should expense their options voluntarily. Nor do they suggest that companies should not expense them. Rather, they indicate that for a typical company, it doesn't matter. Overall, accounting treatment of stock options is a non-issue to the stock market, just as it was in the case of past studies of inventory, depreciation and merger accounting rules.[16] This should be a relief to many companies, because, as of early 2004, new rules requiring option expensing appear imminent.

Companies should stop worrying about the accounting treatment of incentive plans. After all, the biggest accounting advantage imaginable — outright "no expense" treatment of a really enormous pay cost — turned out to be literally worthless. Jay Pritzker, billionaire philanthropist and founder of the Hyatt Hotels chain, used to call accounting "the language of business." He was right to assert that you need to know about accounting to really understand business dealings. But owners of private companies like the Pritzkers do not follow every order issued in that language; they work for their own accounts. All together now — *accounting does not matter*.

Money Talks. What Do Stock Options Say?

Communication is another area of concern with grants of stock and stock options. For these grants to act as an incentive in the classic cause-and-effect sense, management needs to know how to make those business decisions that cause stock-based incentives to pay off best.

Do they? Not clearly. Stock and options say, "Go forth and create value," but they don't come with instructions on how. Rather, they are complex financial claims whose returns are driven by many things completely outside of management's control during the time frame most critical to incentive pay. To function as incentives, option grants would have to convey something about what executives should do to receive an incentive payment. Options, and the underlying stock prices upon which they are based, are silent on the critical matter of expected performance or desired actions. There's no plan, no schedule of goals, nothing but the published results of trades among third parties.

Options might work well as incentives if most executives had a good understanding of how various business decisions are likely to translate into financial results and stock value. But outside of the finance function at a company, not many executives have that kind of specialized training. One of the duties of company financial management is to step into this gap of financial knowledge, helping the organization make business decisions that create stock market value for shareholders. They do this by applying analytical tools like discounted cash flow (DCF) analysis to matters like acquisitions or major capital expenditures. But that process — its timing, scope and time frame — is not consistent with the structure of incentive pay. So the expected results upon which many big-ticket business decisions are made (e.g., acquisition synergies) may not figure directly into the usual budget-based incentive plan goals. If accountabilities are weak, then the finance department's valuation skills won't have much effect.

Companies have the financial tools to direct business decisions consistently toward value creation: valuation models, risk assessment methods and the like. But they don't apply them to the full range of business decisions that have implications for value creation. And when they do, their influence can be subverted by a separate budget process or by other problems with incentive design and administration. When the company really wants to do a deal whose economics are questionable, the executives supporting it either come up with the numbers or just bypass that charade and call the deal strategic or a business imperative. Is this really happening, and is it widespread? Well, something is. Most deals are expected to fail, and most do.

Certainly, there are legitimate, important reasons for using stock and options to compensate executives. Options work pretty well, for the most part, as a kind of embarrassment insurance, making it less likely that executives will have earned huge sums when shareholders got little return (although there is hardly a guarantee, given customary granting practices and the occasional repricing). Options also offer some flexibility and control in the timing of income recognition for tax purposes, but this advantage can be accomplished just as well with maturity, exercise and deferral features of cash plans. For some startup companies, technology businesses and other dynamic, high-growth situations, options can work better than other kinds of incentive devices. But most companies don't fit that profile, and their use of stock options has gone far past the point of diminishing returns.

The Currency of the Realm

For the past decade or more, the long-term incentive game always has been won with the trump card — the accounting advantages of stock options. This has had the unfortunate effect of biasing corporate practice toward heavy use of options rather than other, potentially more effective incentives. It also has created the illusion that options are low cost or even free in an economic sense.

If public company managers and boards think options are cheap or free, they're going to spend them like monopoly money. This no doubt has contributed to the excessive dilution levels that prevail at many companies. It also may have led them to hand out options to everyone in sight. With today's higher focus on option costs, award sizes and eligibility are beginning to contract.

The demand curve may have some issues as well. In many instances, the issuance of an option is a rather poor trade from the company's perspective, because participants don't think they are worth much. When a typical company like Homer's issues option grants at its $50 share price, it is doing the same thing as handing out $20 bills, based on the assumption that a grant's value equals 40 percent of face value. Participants, on the other hand, may think they are being handed a $5 or $10 bill. Why?

- The grant, in a sense, is worthless at the time it is made. That is, no gain has yet been earned.

- The concept behind options and the underlying dynamics of stock valuation are complex.

- Most of the likely gain in an option grant occurs during the five- to 10-year term following grant — a time frame heavily discounted by individuals, perhaps properly, because most exercise their options well before expiration.

- Most participants have little impact upon the stock price, lessening their engagement in the exchange and lessening the value they're likely to attach to the grant.

The appeal of stock options increased greatly during the 1990s simply because just about everyone was getting gains. Indeed, when stock prices are rising, many option holders regard the stock market as a highly prescient arbiter of their own business prowess. As stock market returns have become predictably more modest, many of these views have changed. The problems with options now are appearing in stark relief. The option currency was hyped for years, but now it is about as strong as the ruble.

So what are we left with? Companies are continuing to pay senior management mainly with stock options, because they're the coin of the realm. Options may work well enough for that purpose — simply assembling a pay package to meet competitive market in terms of both size and structure. If you want to hire or keep someone, you give him or her coins. You don't think these coins are worth much, companies say? Here, have some more coins.

It isn't a very efficient approach. The problem with stock options as currency is they lack what monetary economists call "money-ness." That's the extent to which your coins serve as a unit of denomination, a medium of exchange, or a store of value. Options don't work well as any of these things, and in fact must be converted into cash before they can. Not only are options a step or two removed from being an incentive for most people, but they're a big step removed from even being useful as remunerative specie. In a race for money-ness, guess who wins? Cash does. Incentives involving whole shares of company stock come in second and may be admirable performers if used properly. Stock options come in at the back of the pack.

Some companies see some money-like advantages to stock options because they don't require a cash outlay. In other words, they think it is a good treasury decision to fund this particular commitment by issuing new shares rather than parting with cash. Avoiding the cash outlay is seen as making the grant somehow zero-cost, ignoring the obvious dilution cost to owners and the fungible nature of cash.

What to Do About It

Due to imminent accounting changes, some companies are questioning the efficacy of options and concluding that they would be better off if they had stronger connections between pay and performance within their long-term incentives. This book discusses ways to achieve these connections. We've looked at stock options mainly, so far. That's a sensible place to start, because, as the infamous bank robber Willie Sutton said, "That's where they keep the money." In coming chapters, we'll look closely at many other issues needing remedy within the senior management pay structure.

When we do, we'll use the simulation model that we employed in this chapter. The model performs a kind of overall test of plan design — a simultaneous test of targets, ranges, measures, weightings, leverage, and other aspects of calibration. It is designed to test precise terms of incentive plans.

Results often are striking. Bonus plans, for example, even purportedly simple ones, tend to be rather complex systems. It actually is difficult much of the time to figure out whether a particular business decision or scenario will increase pay. And many common plan designs allow for situations that reward poor business actions, sometimes even more so than they reward the accomplishment of improving performance and value.

There often are instances, some more familiar than others, in which operating incentives like bonus plans might encourage:

- Short-term price gouging or unprofitable sales growth

- Income and expense shifting at year-end due to plan thresholds or range maximums

- Very little performance improvement, since performance ranges are so wide they nullify award leverage

- Applying very biased and inconsistent costs of capital to investment decisions

- Low-yielding, value-destroying investments

- Sandbagging tactics instead of sticking to high standards that bring better results.

Capitalist Tool?

The executive incentive structure at most companies has developed into something very distant from the model of entrepreneurial capitalism. Consider this. Homer works for a public company owned by private sector shareholders. It operates around the world in free, competitive markets in an era reflecting hundreds of years of evolution of the capitalist system. But, in important ways, the company's incentives appear to have been designed in the old U.S.S.R.

The incentive system that pays Homer is based upon central planning and the needs of the collective. We've seen that what Homer and his team contribute in terms of performance goes into its collective, corporate results. Rewards are meted out from there based upon centrally determined success metrics like earnings per share (EPS), stock price gains and business unit targets set in a central planning process. What is Homer's system "about," in the most elemental sense? It is about central control.

What Homer's team and the rest of senior managers contribute to the system is performance. How they get paid, in contrast, is based mainly on their rank. The pay system is based upon pay levels needed to meet competitive pay norms at various echelons in the company. The general philosophy is "from each according to ability, to each according to competitive need."

Figure 2-3 shows competitive pay levels for Homer, his boss, the group CEO and the corporate CEO.

Homer knows he can earn tens of thousands of

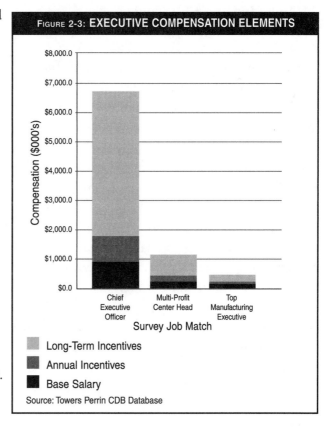

FIGURE 2-3: **EXECUTIVE COMPENSATION ELEMENTS**

Long-Term Incentives

Annual Incentives

Base Salary

Source: Towers Perrin CDB Database

dollars more this year in incentive pay if his business can bring operating income to the target level or beyond. But the main way he gets paid is simply by hanging onto his job. And if Homer can do what's needed to move up into his boss' job, he can increase his pay *hundreds of thousands every year*. His boss is looking at even higher bounties if he can somehow move up the ladder.

How might Homer move up? Well, the typical arrangement of *realpolitik* pays some attention to performance, but, as in the socialist system, politics are pivotal as well. Overall, it pays Homer to manage expectations, deliver moderate performance and not question that of others.

To keep up the supply of promotions it uses as its principle rewards, Homer's organization needs to be in a constant state of expansion. *The Communist Manifesto* provided a growth plan for the communists. Homer's company has a similar manifesto called a "strategic plan" with basically similar instructions — grow for growth's sake. Unfortunately, the preferred avenue for high growth is to annex neighboring enterprises irrespective of the costs involved.

For most executives, the rewards system prevents genuine ownership just as communism abhors private property. Executives actually have lots of legal claims connoting ownership or a derivative of it in the form of stock and stock options. They can flex their ownership muscles by, for example, returning the proxy they receive each year around May Day. But, in their areas of responsibility, they have relatively little direct ownership in results; little in the way of a money claim on the success of actions they take in their business. In an Orwellian turn of phrase, the philosophy behind this approach sometimes is called the "ownership" movement.

Like a planned economy, Homer's company does not benefit from having a free market of business initiatives vying for resources, and rewards systems that charge properly for their use. Homer's rewards system does have some concept of capital, but, as in a collectivist system, it is hard to figure out who owns it. Some parts of the business can't get the capital they need for growth. The system is depriving them of access to the means of production. Others get unlimited use of their business capital with little consequence, like a rent-controlled dacha.

Homer's company's approach to rewards may cause results to drop off like Andropov. Its generally weak framework of stakes and accountability may lead to a bloated, mediocre organization that drains talent and initiative. After all, the energetic ones do eventually make their way over the wall. The company may correct for these problems from time to time with workforce purges. But in doing so, it may leave the survivors with a cynical view, unable to see the *Izvestia* in *Pravda* or the *Pravda* in *Izvestia*.[17]

Kidding aside, the news and the truth are that capitalistic companies are making some of the mistakes that caused so much failure and misery in the collectivist system. They've erected a wall between actions of their decision-makers and incentive rewards. What they should do now is quit Stalin. They should restructure their incentives for greater business impact. They should *tear down this wall*.

Endnotes

1   This is the cost of the grants themselves. Administrative costs can be substantial for stock-based incentive programs, particularly for those companies making grants in many countries around the world.

2   A restricted stock grant with three-year ratable vesting is worth about 95 percent of face value. Performance share values often fall in the 75 percent to 90 percent range depending upon risk. Restricted stock weighs more heavily in the typical mix, so 90 percent is a reasonable, rounded approximation.

3   Almost all of the $75 million in stock-based incentives is driven by overall corporate stock price performance since it consists overwhelmingly of stock options and restricted stock grants. Performance share plans are denominated in shares and also are based heavily upon consolidated financial results (or upon total shareholder return). More than half of the $25 million in cash incentives typically is driven by overall corporate results. Executives at the corporate level typically have all their cash incentives based upon corporate results. Business unit executives have substantial amounts at risk based upon corporate results, both through the explicit weightings placed on corporate performance within plans and through "circuit-breakers" based upon corporate results. Cash long-term performance plans are heavily corporate in terms of both measurement and participation.

4   The incentive part of pay actually is a bit higher than that, since his bonus affects his measured pay for purposes of the retirement plans, and his defined contribution plan reflects company performance.

5   Example of statistical results from CFA Institute cited in Chapter 1.

6   For example, see *The Synergy Trap: How Companies Lose the Acquisition Game*, by Mark Sirower, 1997, The Free Press.

7   That is, we're looking at the $75 million we granted in total in this area. If we said he made a gain of $24,000 because he had three grants, we'd have to compare that gain to $480,000 in option grants (or $225 million for the overall company), so we'd just end up with the same proportional conclusions. If we throw in even more past grants — vested but unexercised options and shares retained after exercise — we're simply looking at accumulated wealth rather than any active, current incentive policy.

8   Based upon operating income variance around a 10-year trend line, measured across a large sample of companies.

9   Based upon a normal distribution of continuously compounded total shareholder returns with a mean of 9 percent and a standard deviation of 30 percent, and a stock with a 2 percent dividend.

10 This variable was simulated by attaching a 1.4 percent standard deviation to the cost of capital; an approximation of the combined effects of independent, random movement in the cost of capital and in long-run growth expectations, each being normally distributed with a standard deviation of one percentage point.

11 Simulation model specifications: Market-based parameters were assigned to incentive plan terms and financial performance. Typical variation was applied to operating income in the near term (15 percent root mean square error around 10-year regression trend line) and this variation drove the 10,000 scenarios examined. Default assumptions about capital usage and capital structure were used to convert each scenario's operating income into the measures used in the annual incentive plan (constant capital structure in market value terms, excess equity cash flows used for share repurchases at ending share price each year). The most common measures were used at the corporate and business unit levels (EPS and operating income). Using this information about financial performance, annual incentive plan payouts were simulated. The annual incentive plan was assumed to comprise modal

award ranges and leverage (80-120 percent performance range, 50-200 percent payout range). A random error of one percentage point from most likely forecast for growth in operating income was used to determine the target used in the annual incentive (this was done in order to simulate uncertainty, but not bias, in the annual incentive target-setting process).

Stock returns (and option gains) were simulated using a 10-year discounted cash flow (DCF) model with separate assumptions applied to near-term, medium-term and longer-term performance. Year 1 financial results in each scenario were the same ones used in simulating the bonus plan. Medium-term results were based upon adaptive revision of the DCF forecast based upon variation in one-year results. Modest random movement was attached to long-run expectations for business growth and also to the cost of capital (levels of variation resembled the variation in long corporate bond yields). The model's outputs were also validated by market norms; overall, the DCF simulation generated a pattern of stock returns resembling the stock market (continuously compounded shareholder return with a mean around 10 percent, a standard deviation of about 30 percent, and variance driven about one-half by consolidated financial performance over a five-year period). The 50 percent explanatory power attributed to financial performance was higher than typical. This was done in order to give some weight to the stock market's antici-patory nature and to its ability to reward for business decisions based upon expected rather than actual results.

The simulation of the incentive structure focused in this case upon a typical participant: a member of top management of a business unit. Movement in business unit financial results was assumed to be largely within the control of business unit management, or at least to represent a tolerable or customary risk. Variation in results of other businesses was assumed to be outside of the control of business unit management, as were market valuation parameters like the cost of capital and very long-run growth expectations. In this example, the overall "line of sight" figure of 20 percent is the amount of variation in cash and stock-based incentive pay that is explained by variation in business unit results. The other 80 percent of the variation in incentive rewards was driven by variation in the cost of capital, in long-run growth expectations, in performance of other business units or in the outcome of the annual budget process.

12 Results are consistent with a range of direct statistical tests of the connection between metrics and value and also with published research such as the CFA Institute study cited in Chapter 1.

13 "There is no relationship whatsoever," said Dan R. Dalton, dean of the business school at the University of Indiana, of his 2002 study examining research on linkages between stock option usage and company performance, quoted by David Leonhardt of the *New York Times* (study: Dalton, D.R., Daily, C.M., Trevis, C.S., & Roengpitya, R. "Meta-Analyses of Financial Performance and Equity: Fusion or Confusion?" *Academy of Management Journal*, April 2002). Separately, Kevin J. Murphy indicates, "Although there is ample evidence that CEOs (and other employees) respond predictably to dysfunctional compensation arrangements, it is more difficult to document that the increase in stock option incentives has led CEOs to work harder, smarter, and more in the interest of shareholders." (Murphy, K.J. "Executive Compensation." In O. Ashenfelter & D. Card [Eds.], *Handbook of Labor Economics*. 1999).

14 Sanders, W.G. "Behavioral Responses of CEOs to Stock Ownership and Stock Option Pay," *Academy of Management Journal* 44: 477-492. (2001).

15 "Addressing Structural Issues in Executive Incentive Design," *WorldatWork Journal*, First Quarter 2002.

16 Seminal studies of LIFO conversions made this point starkly clear many years ago, as has much empirical research since. Regarding LIFO conversions, see the Sunder article in the 1973 *Empirical Research in Accounting,* and Biddle and Lindahl in the *Journal of Accounting Research*, Autumn 1982. The more general point about the stock market's preference for the economic portrayal of events (cash flow) over their accounting characterization is one upheld broadly for decades and a finding made clear in any review of relevant financial research. Examples include Hong, Mandelker and Kaplan on purchases versus poolings in *Accounting Review* in 1978, an SEC study on R&D announcements published by the Office of the Chief Economist in 1985, Copeland and Lee on exchange offers, stock swaps and their EPS effects, published in *Financial Management* in 1991, and Kaplan and Ruback on the importance of cash flow in driving business value, "The Valuation of Cash Flow Forecasts: An Empirical Analysis," NBER working paper 4274.

17 *Izvestia and Pravda* are the two major news dailies in Moscow, the former meaning The News and the latter meaning The Truth. The old saying from the days of communist-controlled propaganda in the press was, "There's no News in the Truth and no Truth in the News." Other quotes attributed variously to Marx, Lenin and Ronald Reagan.

3

Incentives and the
Role of Management

O nce during a trip to Paris, a client asked to meet at Café de Flore, a place still
frequented by the literati set that gave it its post-war fame. During our
conversation I was going on in French, feeling fluent enough to use some
big words like *philosophie de rémunération*, or compensation philosophy. A gentleman
sitting in a group at the table next to us seemed to wince each time I used the phrase.
My client later remarked that the man was a noted philosopher. I was embarrassed. By
applying the term *philosophie* to the pedestrian matter of pay, I had seemed to vulgarize
his life's work.

I've since become more comfortable with the phrase "compensation philosophy."
Philosophy connotes high-minded matters and ones of some societal import. I believe
we approach those standards when examining executive incentives. Executives control
trillions of dollars in business capital, opportunities and ideas. Their incentive plans
affect how they put all of that to use on behalf of many millions of stakeholders.

Companies that use their resources effectively are companies that succeed and
enrich their owners. When they do, they enrich society more broadly. Wal-Mart, for
example, creates more value for consumers than it does for its owners. It does this
through the value it delivers to its customers and through its effects on retail industry
competition and pricing.

Ideas Have Consequences

In such an exercise, stated goals matter. Wal-Mart chases business success, and
along the way creates value for consumers. The thing that makes the capitalist
system work best — to society's greatest overall advantage — is business
competition for profits and value creation.

Milton Friedman put it succinctly when he said, "The social responsibility of
business is to increase its profits."[1] I might quibble with the metric "profits,"
preferring the phrase "long-run shareholder returns," but that's what economists
mean by profit anyway. Society's highest and best use of its business resources is

to maximize the financial success of competitive enterprises. This approach creates the most wealth for a society overall and for the bulk of its citizens. It is then the task of the public sector to regulate, tax and redistribute results in the manner desired by a democratic society.

Even if the term "philosophy" were an overreach, you'd have to have some term to refer to the ideas upon which compensation design choices rest. In a contest of terms for this foundational concept, the main alternative to "compensation philosophy" is "compensation strategy." That phrase carries the unfortunate implication that incentive pay investments don't have concrete results and therefore need rationalizing as "strategic."

There are lots of anecdotes that make the point about how goals matter. We don't have to travel far from the Café de Flore to find one. One evening when I was a student in Paris many years ago, I was out in a restaurant with friends. I mistook the French term "ordures" for the verb "to order" and ended up asking our waiter to serve us kitchen garbage. You have to be careful about what you ask for. Incentives may be read as instructions to management, even as orders, regarding what to do with the business. Incentive plan terms give mistaken orders all the time. Management sometimes serves up garbage instead of performance and gets paid anyway. Perhaps as often, a *pièce de résistance* goes unrewarded.

Another French story — this one fictional — serves to show how ideas about performance and reward have consequences at a tactical level. In the Zola novel *Au Bonheur des Dames*, the local shopkeeper Baudu faces a new kind of competitor emerging in Paris in the second half of the 19th century, a department store modeled fictionally on Galeries LaFayette. Mr. Baudu scoffs at the big store's big-volume approach, divulging to his apprentice that "L'art n'est pas de vendre beaucoup, mais de vendre cher" — The secret is not to sell a lot, but to sell at a high price. Mr. Baudu was a margin guy, and that is not a good thing to be when the big store opens up down the street. These new department stores were category killers in all categories, and Mr. Baudu was economic road kill a few chapters later.

Principles and goals matter. You can call them a pay strategy, a remuneration philosophy or something else, but these ideas have consequences.

Accentuate the Positive, Eliminate the Negative

The anecdote about Mr. Baudu is not only fictional, but set in the distant past. What if a business could turn back the recent past, reversing the biggest mistakes it made over the last few years? However it may have performed over that time, wouldn't it look a lot better with the biggest bad things expunged from the economic record? Sure it would. Every company makes at least some mistakes, and they often are big.

Edmund Burke, describing the standing environment for people at the tops of important organizations, said they must be "formed to the greatest degree of vigilance, foresight, and circumspection in a state of things in which no fault is committed with impunity and the slightest mistakes draw on the most ruinous consequences ..."[2] That's the way it is in business. Senior management often makes big bets. At their level, doing something often is a big bet, and so is doing nothing. When they win or lose on behalf of owners, they often win or lose big.

Could the company somehow have avoided at least one or two of the mistakes? For many companies, the answer is an easy yes. They had a bad acquisition, an ill-conceived new product, or a failed reorganization. In other instances, complacency can leave even a very successful business franchise vulnerable. As a former CEO of 3M once put it, "Success inoculates against change." When describing bad turns in a business, executives do not always tell of solid business decisions that just went bad. Rather, they often recount the writing that was on the wall for all to read, the trail of management decisions that ignored it, and the persistent decision-making issues that make it a risk the next time around, too.

So, should the enterprise work to avoid mistakes? Sure, but it should not make it job one. Mistake avoidance can be taken to the point where it outlaws the proper risk-taking involved in business success and value creation. Just like scrap reduction, customer satisfaction and so many other nodes on the causal chain to value creation, an ethic of mistake avoidance has its point of diminishing returns. In the context of executive decision-making, the real enemy is bias. For example:

- Risk-related biases can paralyze the company or, on the other hand, encourage it to gamble too freely with other people's money.

- Short-term bias may exclude much of the landscape of business opportunity.

- The system of rewards may bias managers to pursue individual accolades, empires, and advancement over greater team results.

- Growth biases may lead to over-investment in mediocre businesses, overspending on product and promotion, overpriced acquisitions and other wastes of corporate assets.

- Biases against investment may starve the business of capital needed for perfectly good growth opportunities.

Bias is the boll weevil of value creation. If you have biased decision-making processes at the senior management level, your company is a mistake-making machine. Do you think your system of executive rewards has a role in creating biases or cementing them in place? What if your key decision-makers all had financial interests that:

- Directly encourage every person in senior management to take a long view

- Create a clear and direct stake for them in the results of their business decisions

- Attach a fair, unbiased cost to the use of new investor capital as well as fair credit when it gets sent back to investors

- Balance business prospects and risks as would an investor

- Attach first-dollar stake and accountability to the money the company budgets, spends and earns each year

- Put the bulk of incentive pay — rather than some fraction of it — directly within executives' line of sight

- Rebalance the system to favor team performance decisively over more narrow individual interests

- Set the platform afire, creating peer pressure, overcoming bureaucratic inertia and starting up a real contest for performance.

In this system, successes clearly and directly expand the overall pool of wealth available to investors and management while mistakes — lost opportunities and wasted money — reduce it with equal clarity. Anyone proposing a money-wasting initiative or an overpriced acquisition is grabbing for the checkbooks of fellow senior managers. Anyone with a good idea has lots of support.

Now, what are the best things your company did over the past five or 10 years? If this new incentive structure had been in place, would it have discouraged those good decisions? Isn't it just really hard to imagine how it could have? After all, what good business decision involves a combination of high risk, high investment needs and persistently low income?

The main principles of value creation are simple. At the same time, they are broad, flexible and powerful. Arcane hedging strategies, long-term strategic plays and risky business ventures all can create value so long as their eventual results are likely to exceed a fair rate of return on the capital involved. A high-tech venture stock portfolio with a 75 percent failure rate could easily create value, for example. So could equally risky forays into oil exploration or development of new consumer products. A policy of swinging for the fences can be sensible, after all, if you're Sammy Sosa.

Incentive plans that comply with value rules aren't going to discourage anything management should be doing. That is the easy part. All incentive systems accentuate the positive, containing some incentive for high-quality decision-making. They have lots of biases, to be sure, and they tend to obscure the incentive linkages. But directionally at least, they certainly allow good things to happen to good people.

The issues have to do with the bad stuff. Badly designed incentives allow bad decisions to pay off. That does not prevent management from making good decisions on its own. An altruistic premise may hold. Management may do only those things that create value for shareholders, get rewarded for those and simply abstain from the many bad decisions eligible for reward within their incentive scheme.

People usually do the right thing, after all, in business and society more broadly. But, just in case, society has laws. Laws don't need to accentuate the positive. Civil life offers everyone the opportunity to pursue happiness in all those areas where it doesn't harm others. Where laws get specific is in eliminating the negative.

That's where they should focus. In crime and in many other matters, when something goes wrong, it goes really wrong. Even a petty criminal commits crimes over and over until caught, all the while causing direct material loss, anguish and fear, and higher costs on everything for everyone. A little vigilance and justice are a relative bargain. Well-designed incentives are a great enforcement bargain for shareholders — a freebie, in fact. They enforce against economic lawlessness, costing nothing more than traditional incentives. Actually, when value rules are broken, the well-designed incentive structure *reduces* pay costs relative to the traditional structure.

The point of value rules, however, is not to reduce the general value of incentive opportunity. My standing presumption is that incentives are set in a marketplace, and there is some rationale for their cost. The market changes, of course. Changes in the supply and demand curves for stock options probably have shifted since 2000 as companies increased the perceived opportunity costs of these grants and executives reduced their perceived value. Greater pressure on compensation committees and their advisors could make for a more parsimonious supply of incentive resources. The elasticity of demand for specific executives may rise or fall over time, and changes in enterprise values may shift the whole demand curve for management's services.

It is the job of the executive labor market to sort out all of that, and results of that market action will come through clearly enough in pay surveys over time. This discussion, in contrast, simply concerns value-based incentive design; it is neutral on matters of pay level and, for that matter, everything else. Our task starts by measuring the levels of competitive opportunity in the marketplace. *When we transform that opportunity from a traditional structure to a value-based one, we are changing the circumstances of pay, not the level. The new plans pay well for value creation and not at all for its reverse.*

It's Time to Thin the Herd

A company's value is the sum of its business opportunities, the ones likely to play out in actual business results over time. If a company sorts its opportunities based upon their likely contributions to value, channeling resources to the winners and starving the losers, it will increase returns to investors. This may seem like a simple concept, but traditional incentives don't even try to address it. Instead, they base rewards upon a largely undifferentiated mix of outcomes from all of these business opportunities: good and bad ones, ones found in one business unit or another, ones a particular individual can affect and ones he or she can't. They allow incentive pay to flow in an insufficiently discriminating way. To comply with value rules, incentives need to get a lot more specific.

Incentive programs should sort the herd of business opportunities into those that create value and those that don't. They should work a bit like the grid in Figure 3-1, used in Otto von Bismark's Prussian army to draw distinctions among army personnel.

FIGURE 3-1: DRAWING DISTINCTIONS		
	Smart	Stupid
Industrious	1	2
Lazy	3	4

Quadrant 1 is full of smart and industrious people suited to the highly responsible top staff jobs in an army. The smart and lazy ones in Quadrant 3 are suited to the highest command. They're smart, so they know what ought to be done, and they're lazy, so they're going to be comfortable ordering others to do it. Both are fine attributes for a general. Even the stupid and lazy ones in Quadrant 4 can be forced into productive military use, at gunpoint if needed, so there's nothing unworkable about their traits. They could perform brilliantly, in fact, as long as they consistently follow orders coming from the smart quadrants.

The big problem concerns those in Quadrant 2. They are stupid, so they're inclined to poor judgments and bad decisions. And they're energetic, so they're running around making a lot of them. Your incentive plans pay out for many decisions that destroy value, so they can create this kind of problem. They can take a bad decision, one clearly in the stupid column, and promote it into the high-energy row by attaching a cash bounty to it.

This grid discriminates where your incentive plans may not. If your overall system of promotion and rewards is not rigorous, for example, it can allow some stupid, lazy folks from Quadrant 4 to get into senior management and then ride for free in a system of low stakes and vague accountability. The smart energetic ones from Quadrant 1, on the other hand, may not be a problem. Some people argue that incentives don't matter to the types of people found in Quadrant 1. Perhaps they're right, but there are those instances when these talented people leave for other jobs to be better rewarded for their contributions.

Personally, I'm not always able to judge exactly who is in which quadrant. It seems to me like the lazy and stupid ones sometimes try to act like they're really from Quadrant 1. Also, people can move from one quadrant to another; the ambitious folks in Quadrant 1 may move to Quadrant 4 over their careers, the cumulative result of having always done things the army way rather than the right way. Then there are the lost weekends over in stupid/energetic Quadrant 2 when, for example, normally sensible executives go shopping for acquisitions in the dot.com sector.

Company executives are pretty good at figuring out who is in what quadrant. They often have very good systems for selection, promotion, development and reward. Senior managers often are very good judges of character and ability. It is one of the traits that got them where they are. And they basically assume that if you have the right people in the jobs, you'll get the right decisions and the best performance. They believe they know the individuals in their large, diverse senior management group well enough to be sure they're getting people into the right roles and on the right tracks. They seem to want to operate as Lyndon B. Johnson did as Senate majority leader, knowing all his colleagues' personal traits very well, finessing and cajoling them with remarkable success.[3]

But as good as executives may be at making character judgments about the people who work for them, companies should not assume they possess these skills at the institutional level. Since the organization does not always provide a perfect screen for the people it hires and promotes and the decisions they make, the incentive system, at a minimum, should not allow the stupid quadrants to annex the others. Incentives can do a more thorough and constant job of enforcing value rules, outperforming everyone in all the quadrants in this particular task. Ordering the incentive system to enforce value rules is a smart play on the whole grid.

Origins and Effects of Current Incentive Practice

Problems in current incentive practices may take their toll on business results — and therefore upon overall corporate performance — in a multitude of ways:

- Talented, confident people want to have a stake in their own success, so they leave to find jobs where their contributions receive more recognition and are rewarded accordingly. Those most comfortable being insulated from the results of their own decisions are those most likely to stay.

- Business unit management teams may set stretch goals, take proper risks and pursue excellence. But sandbagging and income management can be reliable paths to the same pay result, creating an environment of mediocre expectations, internal inequity and general dissonance.

- Management may discount the longer term. Short-term thinking and risk aversion — encouraged by the system of annual bonus rewards — work directly against long-run value creation in many businesses.

- The pay system typically allows free riding on corporate results. This is the main way one gets paid. Executive incentives are said to encourage partic-ipants to drive business performance, but where most pay dollars are concerned, they create a passenger's perspective.

Left to run its course, the incentive system may retain mediocre people, drive down ambitions and create disappointing results.

Why do we have that system, and how did it get that way? To begin, it is based upon rather subjective foundations. Some presumptions, like the following, are held commonly and apparently hold sway, since most incentives are designed to conform:

- "Our shareholders are looking for near-term EPS results."

- "Our stock option grants encourage a broad segment of our workforce to focus on shareholder value creation."

- "Our bonus plan applies a strong emphasis on consolidated results. This encourages organization-wide teamwork."

- "Using our budgets as incentive targets helps build accountability to the budgeting and business planning processes."

- "Our pay packages reflect market norms, helping us attract and retain talented people for key jobs."

- "We have had to rely on stock options. Everyone else uses them so executives demand them. Also, we could not take the EPS hit involved when using other kinds of long-term incentives."

- "Incentives can't contribute to company performance unless they're understood clearly, so we use a simple and familiar approach."

Shareholders want short-term EPS? One of the central findings of financial economics is that shareholders disregard EPS results whenever they conflict with underlying economic performance. Another clear finding is that shareholder criteria are overwhelmingly long-term. Lastly, EPS and many other familiar yardsticks can be improved by business actions that do not create shareholder value, and shareholders surely do not want that. A system of rewards that pays for bad management decisions is a triumph of hope over reason.

Encouraging value creation? Stock-based incentives offer such poor line of sight for most managers that they have no plausible impact upon performance. Stock options in particular — though huge in amount and heavily concentrated on corporate officers — have no consistently discernable linkage with performance. The main thing that an option-heavy rewards system encourages is to do whatever is involved in getting more options.

Corporate bonuses encourage organization-wide teamwork? Teamwork is critical and should be encouraged with incentive pay. But the teamwork that is relevant for most at the senior management level has to do with one's immediate team: the group of managers running a group, division, profit center or other business unit. Corporate performance measures offer plausible incentive effects only for the corporate-level executive cadre. Basing pay of others on corporate performance distances their incentive pay from their own work, discrediting the very idea of an incentive. Conversely, matching rewards more closely with one's scope of responsibility reinforces important notions of accountability and ownership. This kind of "matching" is hard to accomplish as a rule, but is relatively easy at the senior management level; there, generally speaking, you can identify where the buck stops.

Linking pay to budget-based goals reinforces the budget process? Incentives subvert the company's planning processes at least as much as they reinforce them. As one author in the Harvard Business Review put it a couple of years ago, "The corporate budgeting process is a joke and everyone knows it."[4]

We need to mimic the market in every regard? The amount of pay opportunity needs to be close to market to be competitive, but the structure does not. Companies can restructure pay to do a much better job of appealing to the high performers they are targeting.

Your incentives have to be option-heavy like everyone else's? The bloom is off the rose, at this point, where the stock market's appeal as a rewards system is concerned. The accounting advantages of stock options always were an illusion. Their imminent expiration is contributing to disillusionment with stock options.

The traditional approach is simple? Hardly. We saw in Chapter 2 that the typical incentive structure is very complex. The budget process is lengthened and complicated by its linkage to pay. And the familiar, "simple" metrics that deliver most bonus pay are not only complex, but also prone to manipulation.

Pundits often describe executive pay levels as scandalously high, an embarrassment of riches. But the levels of pay are not the primary issue. They are, for the most part, a competitive outcome of the market for executive labor and for commerce and capital, more generally. The executive labor market has problems, but they are being worked out of the system in large part, with changes in option accounting being an important part of that process. There is wealth-related embarrassment in the system, but the issue is more an embarrassing poverty of reason than an embarrassment of riches.

Off The Rack

Another common assertion about company incentive structures is that they are distinctly tailored to fit the company's particular circumstances and challenges. Actually, they're right off the rack.

Of all the characteristics of company incentive structures, the most striking is their *sameness*. Long-term incentives consist 80 percent or more of grants of vanilla stock options.[5] Bonus targets are based upon budgets almost all of the time, while their metrics almost always are drawn from a short list of traditional yardsticks. They're even more alike when you look under the hood. When tested and simulated, they have largely equivalent degrees of line of sight and correlation with the operating drivers of value creation.

Companies do have genuinely different circumstances and business strategies, but these apparently aren't driving how they set up incentives. The outcomes are all the same, so it must be that they are based upon things the companies do have in common:

- They all endorse the axiom that equity interests align the motives of management with the well-being of shareholders, and they usually have stock available for use in long-term incentives. So their long-term incentives are nearly 100 percent stock-based.

- They all have shareholders who seem to talk mainly in terms of EPS, so they use this most often as a corporate measure. Net income and return on equity are other popular corporate measures. At the business unit level, performance discussions are most often about revenue growth and operating profit, so that is what is used. The answer to the question, "how do people talk about our business results?" often is used to answer a different question, "how should we pay our key decision-makers?"

- They comply with the same accounting rules, ones that historically accorded "zero cost" treatment to stock options. As a result, as of 2003, companies tapped stock options to deliver more than four times as much pay as the other alternatives combined.

- They all run a budget process each year. This information is readily available for use as the basis for bonus targets, and companies don't have valid, tested alternatives, so bonuses are based upon performance against budgets.

There is a lot more expediency than efficacy visible here. And yet, everyone acknowledges that executive pay is a big, big deal. Assembling and motivating a high-quality executive team is seen as one of the top priorities of the CEO.

Companies cite a hyper-competitive, fast moving and risky business environment. They believe that incentives are critical to success in this entrepreneurial world, and then they use incentives that are centralized, leveled and essentially bureaucratic. Regardless of industry or business circumstance, the incentive structure tells executives how to make money by moving performance expectations down the scale and their career up the ladder.

The design process is another part of the issue. Competitive practices are followed without due skepticism. Programs are adopted in a one-off fashion without a rigorous look as their overall effects. Incentive policy involves huge cost commitments, yet the financial behavior of these obligations rarely is studied when creating them.

When rolling out a new plan, a common success metric is whether the management group is pleased with the result. But unanimous contentment should not be a measure of success in these matters. A well-designed plan framework — one that is likely to improve business results — is going to *add new information* to the process and encourage people to do things differently. In a typical company moving from the traditional system to a more effective one, it will increase the line of sight, leverage and effective upside of incentive opportunities. At the same time, it may reduce the range of circumstances eligible for reward simply by eliminating those that destroy value for owners.

This is going to make the confident, contributing and successful people happy. On the other hand, if you have value destroyers, free riders, and chiselers around, they're not going to be happy. And here is the toughest thing — you don't always know who they are. There is a bit of an asymmetric information problem here; senior managers running various parts of the business know their true prospects for business performance and contribution better than anyone. Facing this, the best tactics unify the interests of the parties and encourage them to share all they know.

The typical design process deals with each of the high- and low-performing constituencies in the worst way. A putatively consensus-based process allows the biggest whiners to get their way. And the typical end result — one with lots and lots of loopholes — is the one that appeals least to the high performers. The process is set up to serve the wrong people.

In the inescapable comparisons that executives will make, some will see themselves as worse off under the new plan than the old one. Someone is not going to be pleased. The typical approach based on consensus really amounts to a unanimous approval requirement. No wonder the outcomes are so undiscriminating. Nor is it any wonder that HR hesitates to act in a decisive way in this area without a mandate from the CEO. Otherwise, they're alone against a big pack of wolves, including a couple that were left hungry.

Outside advisors can be subject to the same pressures. These range from the general "don't rock the boat" admonitions familiar to anyone who is trying to improve business performance, all the way up to verbal assaults. In my own project work, the most aggressive objections were from executives in the process of running their businesses into the ground when no one on the outside knew it yet. The conversation about new incentives was very threatening to them, since it involved marginally viable performance demands or at least a vague notion of accountability for capital usage. Here is what happened in three memorable cases:

- The head of a large manufacturing business within a public company vigorously disputed his incentive targets one year, questioning the basic idea of whether business unit management should be required to get any return on the capital used for acquisitions and other initiatives. A year later, news accounts of subsequent business results and his firing made it clear that the executive's costly, failed actions had erased a third of the company's market capitalization.

- In one meeting, a divisional management team carped on for hours about the unreasonableness of their performance goals. They swatted down any comparisons of their abysmal results with industry standards, other divisions within the same company, and the very notion of a standard for return or growth. They just insisted, in effect, that they weren't viable in the market, but that their low budgets nonetheless warranted market-level bonuses within a going-concern premise. Economic gaps this size reconcile themselves quickly, this one within the year. After many attempts to sell the business unit at any premium over fixed asset values, the parent company shut it down, fired everyone and liquidated.

- A public company CEO insisted that he should be given a large ownership interest in a newly formed ventures unit as encouragement to make it a success for parent company shareholders. I counter-argued that the success of this business unit would be reflected fairly within his corporate-level incentive gains. I also noted that to insulate subsidiary-level gains the way he was suggesting is not proper for pay of a corporate-level executive. Shareholders have no such protections, after all, and corporate-level executives should have enterprise-wide accountability to match their authority.

This message was not well received. He filled in a client feedback form with odd but unambiguously negative statements about our intervention. Then, he got himself another advisory team and all the shady pay deals he asked for. In this case, it took the board years to fire him. By that time, he had racked up millions in unwarranted gains under the ventures incentive deal, unaffected by the fact that he had imploded the corporate stock price.

Pleasing everyone should not be a goal of executive incentive design. Sometimes, if you experience some pushback, it means you are doing the right thing. One of my first experiences working in a former employer's executive compensation consulting practice gave me a sense of the landscape. A colleague chided me for my suggestion to explore the subject of performance measurement within the scope of a client project. It seemed to me like a very reasonable thing to talk about, but the consultant was certain that it was presumptuous. Whether due to gaps in skills or inclination, the fact is that many advisors will not help companies move forward in pursuing more effective incentives, notwithstanding their reputation as experts in the field.

The issues are systemic. Overall, in this area, companies have a poorly informed design setting, excessive concern over bookkeeping effects, abysmally flawed premises and naked conflicts of interest. Companies should discard the prevailing views and adopt new principles based upon supportable facts, paying attention to how people actually behave and how businesses actually run. Instead, for now, companies continue rolling the stone of business performance up a steep hill, with only half-hearted assistance from their incentive plans. If companies are going to do a better job with these programs, they will have to take a hard look at what they are doing. They're going to have to commit to some standards. They will have to break some eggs. And the CEO, based upon his or her own self-interest and on behalf of the company's board and shareholders, will have to champion the redesign process and its products.

Form Follows Function

Our sample executive, Homer, is in senior management. He is a typical executive in an executive incentive plan. He reports to the head of a business unit like a group or division. Group head of manufacturing, let's say, though he just as easily could be the head of finance, marketing or human resources for purposes of this discussion. His own decisions, and his influence upon his peers, subordinates or superiors, have a tangible effect upon business results over time.

Designing incentives for Homer should be easy. His role and his characteristics pose no serious problems with measurement or accountability:

- His actions affect results so we can judge his performance or that of his team based upon results. It may take a few years for some of the things the team does to show up in measured results, but they will, one way or another.

- He knows his business. He and his fellow group executives understand the cause-and-effect and timing dimensions of most business decisions they make. So we can tie his pay to simple measures of business success and not have to write him a script for how he is going to get there. We're on the wrong side of the asymmetric information divide, so if we try to micro-manage his actions through complex schemes of incentive goals, we will have many, many ways to lose.

- He is a fairly good judge of risk. You don't see people like Homer losing money at Three Card Monte while on their way to the OTB parlor. They're not a very good market for extended warranties on toasters, either. On the contrary, they're pretty good intuitive statisticians. That's good. It means they will make better business decisions. So we need to set up pay structures that pose a reasonable chance of paying off. Otherwise, people like Homer will discount what we give him.

- Homer, for his part, is relatively entrepreneurial in terms of his risk tolerances. He is comfortable being held accountable for his actions and for business results, and he doesn't find the normal uncertainties inherent in his own business to be unnerving. In fact, he sees himself as being subject to those risks under just about any career scenario: staying in his current job, changing companies, taking on a start-up gig or becoming CEO of a smaller company in the industry. So, as a general matter, the company can make his pay variable. They can even make him put his money where his mouth is. If we're talking about 1,000 Homers, we might hear squawking from the 200 whose bonuses are coming in well below target this year. But just about all of them will sign up for a program involving a lot of results-based pay as long as they have reasonable influence and commensurate upside.

- He is not comfortable with risks that are way out of his control or that don't have anything to do with his business. Those are bad risks. These would include risks related to performance of other groups or divisions within his company or to fluctuations in the stock market's valuation of his company that are unrelated to its business results. Many people are like this. If they feel they have some control over an outcome, they are more comfortable bearing its risks. Casinos and lottery commissions know this, and they exploit it in more or less pure form. For Homer, these risks are not only more irksome than entrepreneurial risks, but also more avoidable. He can make these risks go away by changing jobs and getting a deal that is based more upon his own performance. If his pay program subjects him to big money consequences of risks that are out of his control, that is going to be a problem if our company is trying to retain Homer or people like him. If we subject Homer to a lot of risks that are far beyond his control, one way or another he will make us pay for it.

- He's got a reasonably long-term perspective. If we put him in incentive plans that allow him to accumulate wealth over time as the results of his performance pile up, he's likely to find that acceptable. We don't have to try to bridge any time span with nonfinancial "value drivers" or "leading indicators" of success to incentivize Homer on a reasonably timely basis. Most of the things Homer does are things that, if effective, show up in measured results within a reasonable period of time (one to five years). Even if Homer's group makes a big acquisition, for example, it probably will be expected to generate results meeting some reasonable standard for returns within three to five years. And he'll be here to get paid when it does. If he puts up much of a fuss about this, it might signal that he doesn't think he'll be around to see through the success of the deal he is proposing, or perhaps that he isn't confident about it. If he thinks that, we'd like to know it, and the incentive scheme helps us flush that information out into the open. Again, this is a basic tactic in the face of informational asymmetries, one left unused in the traditional systems. It uses the incentive structure to directly encourage information-sharing and mutually beneficial decisions. There is no big timing difficulty here. On the contrary, time is on our side.

- Homer likes money. He uses it in the traditional way — as scorecard points in an ongoing competition with his college buddies. He'll also spend some on cars, houses and stuff at the pro shop. Our Homer, well, let's just say that he is interested in knowing what he can do to get more money. We often see him searching, devilishly, for linkages between his actions and money. If his rewards system provides this linkage, it probably will affect what he does at work. If his pay is mostly unrelated to his performance, or if it actively discourages him from taking the kinds of difficult and uncertain actions that are often involved in improving business performance, his performance probably won't be as good. Actually, if Homer really wants to spend his career doing his best and getting paid for it, and he isn't getting that kind of deal, he'll probably just leave and get it somewhere else.

- Homer is not a perpetrator. We don't have to use the precise terms of incentive plans to police all of his actions. Most of what he does, he'd do the same way if he owned the business himself. If we simply put him in incentive plans that draw a reasonably clear line from good business results to high personal wealth, then we won't have to worry too much about him spending all his time trying to manipulate them. The Hippocratic oath applies here — first, do no harm. At a minimum, don't set up systems that stand in the way of good performance.

- Lastly, for someone at Homer's level, incentive plans are the biggest part of how he gets paid. So, when we design incentive arrangements, we probably have his attention.

This is the ideal situation in which to be designing incentive plans and hoping they'll work. All we need to do is set up something that tracks good business results in a reasonably clear and complete way, then tie pay to that over a period of years. Homer knows his business, and he likes money, so he can take it from there.

How do these traits affect pay design? Well, the more line of sight, the better. Incentives have an important agency role in the enterprise. Without line of sight, they cannot work. It is counterproductive to put the bulk of pay at risk based on things that senior leaders cannot affect. Based upon their roles, senior management is fairly paid based upon actual business results measured over time. They are properly held accountable for performance expectations and for getting returns on investor capital they use. If not them, then who?

Another of Milton Friedman's arguments is useful here. Consider a situation in which you are shopping for something for yourself. Clothes, a DVD player, a dozen spider monkeys, it doesn't matter. If you are shopping for yourself, you are diligent in getting the best value for your money and in getting exactly what you want. In a second case, you are shopping for someone you don't know. You might still be careful with your money, but you are not likely to zero in on getting the perfect item for them to the same extent as you would for yourself. In a third case, you are spending a third party's money to buy something for a stranger. At this point, you are not as careful either with the money spent or the choice that is made. The first case is what we mean by ownership when talking about management incentives. It means you have a direct stake both in the resources used and the benefits they create. The third and worst example is the incentive system in place at most companies.[6] The source of the capital and its rewards are found only at a great distance.

The role of incentive plans should not be complicated at the top management level. Top management teams have a strong influence upon the overall company or a business unit within it. They apply hard-won experience and business knowledge in pursuit of high performance. Performance is the difficult part of the performance/rewards linkage. At this level in the enterprise, delivery of incentive rewards should be a kind of economic afterthought. Since top executives are expected to make a long-term commitment to company success, and since they have broad and long-term impact and accountability, it is fair to judge their success by examining actual business results over time.

Incentives should be restructured to part course in three ways from the model prevailing at so many companies today. They should:

- *Shift pay opportunities toward explicit goals and measurable results.* This can be done using cash incentives and better functioning stock-based incentives. Focusing more strongly upon measurable business results — upon the controllable parts of the value creation process apart from the random element of stock price movement — greatly increases line of sight by clarifying the linkages among business decisions, results and incentive rewards. As Carlson Companies' CFO Martyn Redgrave puts it, "Incentives should be focused on actual business performance that creates value, not upon the short-term vagaries of the stock market." As part of this shift, I suggest specific improvements in the methods used in setting incentive targets and ranges and in measuring performance.

- *Shift the operating incentive structure toward the longer term.* Short-term bias and risk aversion can be addressed directly by shifting long-term incentives away from pure options and restricted stock into long-term performance vehicles. This moves incentive pay directly into line with long-run results and centers it in the executive's field of vision. Another part of the solution here is to inject more stability into the bonus plan. HON Industries, Inc., the Iowa-based office products manufacturer, did each of these things. Jeff Fick, chief administrative officer at HON, notes that better incentives helped the company significantly outperform competitors during tough conditions that prevailed in the industry in recent years.

- *Shift long-term incentive opportunity toward the business unit level.* This is done by weighting business-unit results more heavily within performance-based plans or by instituting phantom stock or subsidiary equity plans tied to business-unit value. This suggestion is sometimes controversial at companies, but it really should not be. Most companies have distinct groups, divisions and profit centers using bonus plans which disaggregate results along these lines. Even a moderate shift toward business unit-based pay would increase line of sight greatly from the weak level that prevails. Bruce Paradis is the CEO of GMAC Residential Funding Corporation, a business unit that has grown to the point where it accounted for more than 10 percent of GM's operating profit in 2002. He reports that subsidiary-level incentives have been critical to his business's ability to attract high performers and to deliver strong performance for years.

Competitiveness

When proposing a big change in pay structure, one may end up so far from competitive standards that the pay package just won't be effective in recruiting and retaining the best people. It is a good idea to look at the general notion of competitiveness to figure how it should drive design. A lot of what pay does for company performance is simply to allow an organization to provide enough pay — enough salary, bonus, options, whatever — to get the high-performing people it needs to come, stay and play. We're not focusing on the amount of pay here. Rather, all of our examples assume that the overall cost of pay and incentives to the enterprise will not change. We simply slice and dice the typical company's $100 million annual price tag for incentives into different pieces with different designs, examining effects upon the overall efficacy of the system.

So we're talking about being competitive in money terms, but not necessarily in design terms. Being competitive does not mean mimicking every aspect of what other companies do. A well-designed incentive plan should take account of market data and the goal of assembling a competitive overall pay package. Trying to keep top management pay below market is a very poor way of saving money. It leads to mediocrity, turnover, or both. Keeping pay systemically above market, on the other hand, is just a waste of corporate assets.

So a key task is at once to provide competitive pay levels and well-designed incentives. Providing competitive pay levels at most companies need not be a big mystery. One can measure middle-of-market rewards as well as the performance level to which it corresponds. When companies want to pay at the upper end of the market, they almost always cite "cream of the crop" hiring tactics in pursuit of high performance. These high performers should bring about performance levels that fund their higher rewards. Some companies also say they set high goals for performance so they must set their pay objectives above the market's median. In each case, the company's general performance/award scale may be equivalent to market norms; they may simply have affixed the label "target" to a higher point on the scale. If not, then the company may simply be paying out more incentive reward than is appropriate at its performance level, pointlessly overpaying senior management. Overall, once a typical company has its competitive market defined well, there are not a lot of valid reasons to depart greatly from its 50th percentile.

When looking to market norms for useful clues, companies also should pay some attention to the competitive mix in terms of fixed versus variable pay and long-term versus short-term liquidity. Like overall pay levels, those parameters are set in large labor markets characterized by plenty of information, so they probably reflect some kind of efficient solution.

The particulars of design of various plans, on the other hand, appear to be mainly a bureaucratic outcome rather than one reflecting market sense, and so can be discarded. Redesigning plans means departing from the seemingly magical combination of stock options and budget-based bonuses offered by everyone else. Do this without hesitancy. Moving away from stock options means delivering more pay in cash and whole shares, each of which is a more appealing currency. Using bonus target setting methods other than internal budgets is a more transparent approach, one with more overt standards and one at least as appealing to an outside candidate.

If put to better use, incentives can be quite helpful in the dynamics of selection. Well-designed plans will appeal to those who are confident they can make a contribution and will discourage those who are not. An incentive plan's terms can be a highly effective way to ask someone to put their money where their mouth is.

There is a performance edge to be had with better functioning incentives, and companies should chase it. Existing programs at most companies are not doing the hard work of addressing differential contribution. Existing programs are collectivist and altruistic, and in the end, ineffective and naïve. In a company with performance problems, traditionally designed incentive plans do a lot of enabling.

The point of competitiveness is not to have incentive systems that appeal to anyone off the street. If you have that, you are wasting money. Private companies provide some astute guidance here because they, more directly than public companies, spend their own money when they go out to recruit executives. They use signing bonuses and other goodies here and there to get the good candidate in the door when really needed. Public companies, on the other hand, seem willing to hand out big equity grants and other remarkably lenient terms to lots of people. As Friedman might observe, they act as if they are shopping with someone else's money.

Retention, like competitiveness, is a commonly stated goal for incentive design. When companies consider the retention effects of their incentive plans, they should keep in mind that a business is not a family. In business, love is conditional. Well-designed incentive plans create highly conditional attachments. When performance is generally good, they encourage the high contributors to stay and continue to prosper. Also, in these cases, they apply some exit costs like forfeitures of in-the-money grants and of the continuing stream of new grants and bonus opportunities.

The retention problems occur when performance is persistently poor. And, here again, companies are not discerning enough. They often issue stock grants to whole swaths of the senior management workforce, for example, just to be sure these folks are pasted in place no matter what occurs. This tactic can create an utterly performance-free path to wealth.

Fairness

Along with competitiveness and retention effects, fairness is a key concern when considering big changes to pay structure. But departing from the traditional structure does not necessarily endanger fairness. Actually, fairness is an endemic problem in the traditional incentive structure. This is ironic, since companies go to great lengths and expense to be fair. They pay a lot of attention to competitive market standards for pay, and few major companies deliberately hold their pay levels below that standard. They define fairness by paying fairly in relation to market, and that is expensive for them.

They also define fairness as internal equity, using incentive plans that tend to equalize incentive payouts for peers across wide swaths of the organization. Everyone who is in, say, the 20,000-option granting tier gets the same grant and the same gains through the vesting period. Since much of bonus pay is based upon corporate results and the whole bonus may be clipped by the corporate circuit breaker, the bonus plan has more leveling effects. And, of course, base salary isn't greatly variable unless the executive is fired, and that part of pay is pegged by market and internal equity more intensively than anything else.

So these systems seem to define fairness not as equal opportunity, but as equal outcome. What are the chances that an executive like Homer is going to like that? He probably doesn't think that pay outcomes should be homogenized. He's likely to see the pay system as fair as long as it holds people to reasonably consistent performance standards and rewards them accordingly, even if those outcomes are rather divergent. To Homer, you see, income inequality is not prima facie evidence of a bad pay system. Actually, to Homer and many other heartless capitalists, the exact opposite is true. Income inequality is a likely outcome of a system that encourages competition and high performance by linking differential success with higher reward.

But let's forget all that stuff about incentives for a moment. Maybe only the truly best folks get raises, kudos, winks, nods, and bigger and better jobs. Maybe the company is a grand, omniscient meritocracy, a marvel of central planning. Maybe, but Homer probably won't see it that way. Compensation consultants interview people like Homer all the time. High performers are okay with being held to a fair standard and with seeing divergent outcomes. But it really sticks in their craw when people in other parts of the business seem to be getting away with easier targets that they've negotiated or when they just get stuck with unfairly high performance goals themselves. Equal bonus outcomes are not a solution in these cases — they are a symptom of the problem.

The overall effect is unfortunately ironic. Companies spend a lot of money to ensure fairness with respect to the external market. They have a good sense of the external market, but much of the perspective they apply when assessing fairness really has to do with its internal dimensions. They go to lengths to get level outcomes since they're quite concerned about internal equity. Sometimes, they're not sure they have a system that allows them to differentiate performance confidently and therefore to differentiate pay fairly. And even if they did, they can imagine many internal equity problems that would arise if they tried to use such a system in a decisive way. One response is to use incentive plans that greatly level pay outcomes, but this has the unfortunate side effect of short-circuiting most incentive effects. Executives see the outcomes as very homogenized, often feeling they don't get paid fairly for what they contribute. This, to them, is the big issue with internal equity: there's too much of it.[7]

You have to figure that at least some key members of a typical company's management probably are walking around thinking the system is unfair. This may not be the end of the world, this dissonance they feel, but it is another factor that lessens the efficacy of incentive pay within an enterprise. It is not the feeling Homer's company was trying to achieve when it sank $100 million into incentive pay this year. To be fair with that money and best serve everyone involved, companies should channel it into the organization based upon proper, consistent and clear indicators of real economic contribution.

At a typical company, the incentive structures are the cumulative results of years of making decisions meant mainly to track market norms, get good accounting treatment and reflect a few other default preferences. Instead, companies should deliberately set out how, precisely, incentive policy will help the company prosper.

In other words, incentive design should be about how the company will implement value rules.

Endnotes

1   *New York Times Magazine*, September 13, 1970.

2   "Letter From the New to the Old Whigs" (1791), *Selected Prose Of Edmund Burke*, edited and introduced by Sir Philip Magnus (1948).

3   See Robert A. Caro's book, *Master of the Senate: The Years of Lyndon Johnson.*

4   *Harvard Business Review*, November 2001: "Corporate Budgeting is Broken. Let's Fix It" by Jensen, Michael C.

5   Source: Towers Perrin's executive compensation databases.

6   Friedman used the third example to describe government spending.

7   Internal equity is falling in importance in company systems for broad-based (mainly nonmanagement) rewards. Towers Perrin surveyed 1,294 companies in 2003 concerning their rewards and performance management processes. Fully 35 percent cited internal equity as an important current objective, but only 18 percent cited it as one for the next three years. Linking pay to key organizational success factors, on the other hand, rose in importance from 49 percent currently to 60 percent over the next three years.

4

Business Valuation
and Incentive Design

Management incentives need to focus on what management does. Management's job is to make decisions that maximize shareholder value. The role of incentives is to encourage that. To do so, the incentive mechanism must comprehend how incentives influence executive behavior, what actions management can take, and how they affect business results and company value. We've already looked at behavioral effects of the incentive system and the scope of management's charge. We must now explore the last and most important of these linkages; the one between business results and value creation

As it turns out, we're rather fortunate in this endeavor. There's a well-developed field of inquiry within financial economics dedicated to this exact issue. It is called business valuation. Business valuation — in particular, the financial models used in this area — is about how to convert a given set of future business results into an estimate of shareholder value. This chapter looks at a basic, but broadly applicable and powerful valuation model. We'll see what it has to say about the financial underpinnings of executive incentives. Then, we'll take these insights, along with the ones derived earlier concerning business governance and management's role, and compile them into value rules.

Stealing the Playbook of Business Valuation

We use a particular form of business valuation model called the discounted cash flow (DCF) model. It is not the only method that can be used to value a business, but it provides results consistent with other valuation methods so it stands as a proxy for them. This approach involves assembling a specific forecast of a company's capacity to generate income, its capital needs and the rate of return it needs to achieve on any new investments in order to create value. Once assembled, the DCF forecast allows us to make direct inferences about results, value and investor returns that are particularly suited to our purposes. In particular, the model's breadth and specificity support the financially intensive elements of incentive design, like setting performance targets and ranges, devising metrics, and benchmarking incentive-related costs and dilution.

The very simplest prescriptions of business valuation can be used to overcome the problems common in incentive plans at many companies today.[1] To keep the exposition straightforward, we have adopted basic concepts and methods in valuation and finance as more or less unquestioned "givens." Despite many areas of ongoing debate in this field, its basic premises are widely accepted by companies. Our task concerns how well they actually apply them. Problems with incentive plans number among the main reasons companies fail to exploit financial tools more effectively.[2]

Basic DCF Model Example

The DCF model has the three basic moving parts: operating income after taxes, capital usage and the cost of capital (See Figure 4-1).

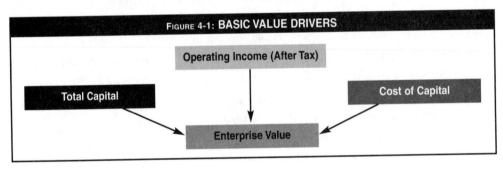

FIGURE 4-1: BASIC VALUE DRIVERS

The DCF method is based upon the idea that the value of a business equals the present value of the cash flows that it can distribute to its owners over time. These cash flows are called "free cash flows" or FCFs. They consist of the funds produced by the company's operations, less the reinvestment requirements of the business (that's the money the business needs to fund growth and replace assets as they wear out).

What remains is the cash available to satisfy the claims of all the investors in the business — the holders of its debt and equity. Free, in the context of FCF, means freely available for distribution to investors. FCF is all that investors as a group get from the business over the long run, and its present value determines the value of all of the capital they have invested in the company.

DCF analysis consists of two general steps: making a forecast of these free cash flows for a very long period of time, then figuring out their present value. To make the exercise practicable, this future free cash flow forecast normally is divided into two parts:

- **A specific forecast of company operating results and FCF for a finite period of time, often 10 years.** Strictly speaking, the company's present collection of competitive advantages — the business attributes it holds now that may enable it to earn above-market returns — are assumed to play out within the course of the forecast term.

- **A residual valuation of the company, representing its predicted value as of the end of the forecast term.** This consists of the value of all the free cash flows expected in the many years beyond the forecast term. Residual valuation typically means translating the company's ongoing earning capacity at the end of the forecast term into an estimate of its value at that date. It typically is computed under an assumption that no additional value is created after the end of the forecast term. If "t" is the number of years in the forecast term, residual value is financial shorthand for the value of FCF expected in years t + 1 through infinity.

The DCF model determines the present value of all the FCFs expected during the forecast term. To this, it adds the present value of the residual value. The sum of these present values is equal to "enterprise value," or the total value of all the debt and equity capital invested in the enterprise.[3]

Figure 4-2 demonstrates the basic mechanics of DCF valuation.

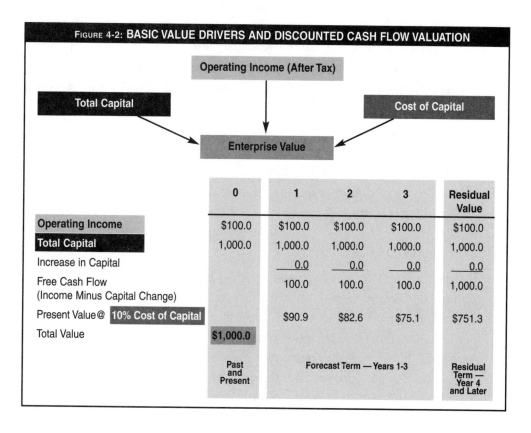

FIGURE 4-2: **BASIC VALUE DRIVERS AND DISCOUNTED CASH FLOW VALUATION**

Operating Income (After Tax)

Total Capital

Cost of Capital

Enterprise Value

	0	1	2	3	Residual Value
Operating Income	$100.0	$100.0	$100.0	$100.0	$100.0
Total Capital	1,000.0	1,000.0	1,000.0	1,000.0	1,000.0
Increase in Capital		0.0	0.0	0.0	0.0
Free Cash Flow (Income Minus Capital Change)		100.0	100.0	100.0	1,000.0
Present Value @ 10% Cost of Capital		$90.9	$82.6	$75.1	$751.3
Total Value	$1,000.0				
	Past and Present	Forecast Term — Years 1-3			Residual Term — Year 4 and Later

Key concepts are summarized briefly:

- **Basic drivers.** This basic, abbreviated version of the DCF model reduces the model to its principal drivers. After-tax operating profit and capital are specified for each period. Capital is the amount of debt and equity capital invested in the business. FCF is equal to after-tax operating profit minus the change in capital. The cost of capital is the discount rate used to convert projected FCFs to present value. These three basic drivers of the DCF model — after-tax operating profit, capital usage and the cost of capital — form the foundation of a range of incentive design methods, *ensuring their fundamental linkage with the principles of value creation.*

- **Free cash flow.** The forecast does not involve any new capital needs; rather, capital used in the business remains fixed at $1,000. So FCF is equal to $100 each year, or $100 in profit minus $0 in new capital requirements.

- **Time segments of forecast: Forecast term and residual term.** This simple example has a three-year forecast term, so FCFs are forecast for each of three years. The residual value in this case represents the value, as of the beginning of Year 4, of all the cash flows expected in Year 4 and in later years. Overall, the DCF model takes into account all expected future cash flows.

- **Cost of capital.** The cost of capital for this company is 10 percent. This means that this company needs to provide overall rates of return to investors equal to 10 percent in order to compensate them fairly for the risks they bear by having their capital tied up in this business, taking into account prevailing returns on similar investments in capital markets. Higher risks would increase the cost of capital and reduce value and, conversely, lower risks would reduce the cost of capital and increase value.

- **FCF forecast term.** FCF for the first year is equal to $100. The basic model assumes that each year's FCF is received on the last day of the year. To determine the "present" value of the first year's FCF — its value as of the beginning of the forecast period — we must discount it for one year. Its present value is computed as $100 / (1 + 10 percent), or $90.91. The $100 FCFs expected at the end of each of Years 2 and 3 are discounted for two and three full years, respectively.[4]

- **Residual value.** This is the value of the FCFs expected in Years 4 through infinity. It is determined in a two-step process. This DCF model assumes that FCFs either remain at $100 per year, basically forever, or that the company's performance scenario is the valuation equivalent of this zero-growth perpetuity. Either way, the company is forecast to create no additional value during the residual term, so valuation at this date is a matter of converting the company's ongoing earning power into an estimate of value. The value of a perpetual stream of free cash flows is equal to their annual amount ($100) divided by the cost of capital (10 percent), or $1,000 in this case. This value, which is stated as of the end of Year 3, is further discounted at 10 percent for three years to convert it to present value terms at $751.31.

The result of these computations is the present value of all the FCF expected to be generated by the business over a very long period of time: $1,000, consisting of $248.69 of forecast term FCF and $751.31 of residual value. Since these FCFs represent all the returns to be received by all debt and equity capital investors over time, their present value represents the value of all the capital invested in the enterprise. If the company had total interest-bearing debt of $400, then the value of equity would be equal to $600, or $10 per share if stockholder's equity consisted of 60 outstanding common shares.

Valuation Perspective: Operating Results and Total Capital Usage

The basic version of the DCF model starts with operating income after taxes. Operating income is stated before subtraction of interest expenses, so it is a measure of income that is earned on behalf of both debt and equity capital investors. In this regard, operating income is constructed from a "total capital" perspective. Net income, in contrast, is stated net of the effects of any interest expense. That means net income is a measure that is constructed from the "residual" perspective of an equity holder; it is the income left over after satisfying debt financing costs. Like operating income, the capital construct used in the basic DCF model is measured from a "total capital" perspective as well; it includes capital advanced by both debt and equity investors.

The same notion of capital can be computed by looking at the asset side of the balance sheet. "Capital," or the sum of debt and equity capital invested in the business is generally equal to "net assets." In Figure 4-3, both capital and net assets equal $40. Net assets consist of the things the investor capital was used to buy: net working capital, fixed assets and other assets. Net working capital consists of the most liquid of the assets used in operations — mainly cash,

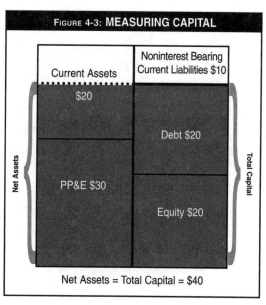

FIGURE 4-3: MEASURING CAPITAL

Current Assets $20

Noninterest Bearing Current Liabilities $10

PP&E $30

Debt $20

Equity $20

Net Assets

Total Capital

Net Assets = Total Capital = $40

receivables, and inventories — net of the most liquid operating liabilities — mainly accrued expenses and payables. Current assets equal $20 while the nondebt current liabilities total $10, so net working capital is $10. Fixed assets consist of the land, building and equipment used in business operations (plant, property and equipment, or P,P&E). Other assets often consist of intangibles like patents, brand names, or goodwill recognized in a merger or acquisition. This company has $30 in fixed assets, no intangibles and net working capital of $10, so net assets total $40. Debt and equity also total $40 at book value.[5]

The model determines market value from a total capital perspective: the present value of FCFs is equal to enterprise value, or the total value of the debt and equity capital invested in the business. This approach isolates equity value by subtracting debt from enterprise value. That means the model tells us everything we need to know about the connection between business results and business value without paying much attention to capital structure.[6] For reasons we will detail in a few pages, the total capital perspective should be applied to the greatest extent practicable in executive incentive plans.[7]

Free Cash Flow (FCF)

FCF is the amount of money a company's operations make available for distribution to capital investors. A general formula to compute FCF is:

> **Operating Income**
> − <u>Taxes on Operating Income</u>
> **= After-Tax Operating Income**
> + <u>Depreciation (a noncash expense)</u>
> **= Operating Cash Flow**
> − Additions to Net Working Capital and Other (Operating) Assets
> − <u>Capital Expenditures (Net of Disposals)</u>
> **= Free Cash Flow (FCF)**

The shorter version of FCF we used earlier is simply operating income after tax minus the change in capital. This is because the terms following income in the computation — depreciation, net capital expenditures, and net working capital additions — add up to the net increase in capital.[8] The more detailed way to get at FCF would be to look at the details of the company's cash flow statement, ignoring changes that have to do with financing (e.g., interest payments or share issuance). In an uncomplicated company, these three definitions of FCF are equivalent. From here on, we'll define FCF in the simplest way based upon its main drivers, income and capital usage:

> Operating Income After Taxes
> − <u>Change in Capital</u>
> **= Free Cash Flow**

This simplified FCF computation allows us to look at this key financial concept in the most basic way. Operating income after taxes is the profit generated by business operations. The change in capital is the amount of that profit that needs to go back into the business. Free cash flow is what remains.

In any given year of a DCF forecast, FCF can be positive or negative. Many high-growth companies experience negative FCFs as they make large investments and even incur current losses in the hope of achieving future profitability. Expectations about FCF have to turn positive eventually, though, for its present value to be positive and, therefore, for the company to be valuable at all.

Over time, positive free cash flow is what the company's operations provide for its investors. It funds all the returns that capital investors as a group get from their investments. Figure 4-4 describes the various possible fates of FCF.

Debt holders get interest payments and return of debt principal. Stockholders get dividends. FCFs also might be used for share repurchases, increasing the company's price per share and enlarging shareholder returns along the way. FCF might be accumulated in liquid assets or other non-operating assets and held on behalf of shareholders.

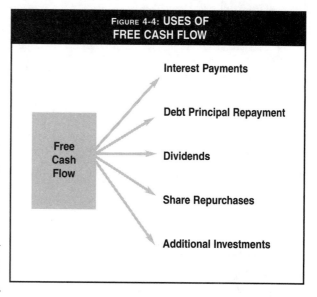

FIGURE 4-4: USES OF FREE CASH FLOW

Free Cash Flow

Interest Payments

Debt Principal Repayment

Dividends

Share Repurchases

Additional Investments

In these cases, the value of the business (and shareholder returns) will reflect not only FCF from operations, but also those expected from these extra assets.

In the general, simplified examples used throughout this book, companies are assumed to distribute any FCF to investors in one way or another, not to let it pile up inside the enterprise. This means the capital levels used in each DCF forecast are levels of capital necessary to support business operations and forecast growth and do not include any "excess" or "non-operating" capital.

Financial Performance vs. Financing Decisions

The "total capital" basis of measuring both income and capital reflects a basic principle of corporate finance: the separation of operating and financing decisions. Changes in capital structure — in the debt/equity composition of enterprise capital — can distort many performance measures. Figure 4-5 demonstrates how financial leverage affects measured performance. A venture

FIGURE 4-5: THE LEVERAGE EFFECTS OF DEBT ON RETURN ON EQUITY (ROE)

	Return on Invested Capital (ROIC)	Leverage Effects	Return on Equity (ROE)
Operating Income After Tax (OI)	$10		$10
− Interest (After Tax)		− $1 in interest	− 1
Net Income (NI)			$9
Capital	$50		$50
− Debt		− $15 in debt	− 15
Equity			$35
ROE (NI/Equity)			26%
ROIC (OI/Capital)	20%		

with return on equity of 20 percent (equal to return on invested capital in the zero-debt scenario) can be converted into one with 26 percent return on equity if financed 30 percent by debt. In that case, after-tax interest costs of $1 reduce income to $9, but equity capital falls to $35, so ROE rises to 26 percent.

Though we saw that FCF has a few possible destinies, the DCF model treats them all alike. One dollar of future FCF, irrespective of whether it is meant for debt repayment, share buy-back or something else, contributes the present value of one dollar to the value of the enterprise. However, all FCF may not be of equal value to owners. Until new tax laws took effect in the United States in 2003, share repurchases often were seen as a much more tax-effective way to distribute FCF than taxable dividends (they still permit shareholders to defer recognition of income). Corporate tax laws in many countries favor at least some debt financing.

Nonetheless, companies should separate incentive policy from financing policy generally. Here is why:

- *Not many people in the organization can affect the company's financing policy.* When incentive plan metrics are affected by capital structure, a broad group of managers are made free riders or victims of such policies.

- *Allowing plans to be affected by capital structure poses some risks of manipulation.* Stock option grants typically do not reward management for making dividend payments, but they do pay for capital gains. In this regard, they encourage share repurchases rather than dividend increases. This practice is encouraged further by bonuses based upon EPS, since repurchases expand EPS as well. At the same time, using debt to fund growth makes measures like ROE and EPS overtly "game-able" in company incentive plans. (See Chapter 7.)

- *The company does not need to pursue financing transactions to mimic their incentive side effects (e.g., IPO, subsidiary IPO, issuance of tracking stock).* Incentive policy itself is an operating decision and not a financing decision. The principle of separating these transactions applies not only when measuring performance, but also when choosing the incentive media (the mechanism to deliver the incentive). Again, the essential thing is to create a financial interest in enterprise value creation, not to paper executives with a particular type of security. That's particularly true in the United States where there is little difference in the overall tax profile of cash and stock-based pay.[9]

- *If a company wants to create LBO-like incentives, it does not need an LBO transaction.* Rather, it simply needs to create a decisive financial interest in business success, one taking reasonable account of the three main drivers of value: operating income, capital usage and the cost of capital. This approach will encourage management to optimize current FCF and long-run earning power (residual value) of the company in particularly strong terms, as would the economics of some LBOs and other private equity transactions. (Demonstrated in Chapter 10.)

- *Financial executives and CEOs ought to be encouraged to use capital structure to create value for shareholders to the extent they can.* Because stock-based incentives in one form or another surely will remain a big part of how these few are paid in the future, they undoubtedly will have a strong incentive to pursue such gains. That alone should be sufficient, so other incentive plans need not be warped by capital structure.

- *Maximizing the overall returns of the enterprise for its owners is the same thing, practically speaking, as maximizing returns for shareholders.* Shareholders are residual claimants on returns, after satisfying largely fixed debt claims. This means that greater enterprise returns accrue directly to shareholders. To encourage executives to maximize shareholder returns, companies need not isolate the shareholder perspective in metrics and plan structure.

Income and Capital: Is This Really All You Need to Know About Results?

Operating income after tax and capital are the only company performance variables included in the basic DCF model. Within the DCF model, operating income after tax and any changes in capital are netted against each other, and the cash that is left is FCF. The other big value driver, the cost of capital, is based upon external variables like business risk and upon market norms for expected return. So, as far as company performance is concerned, FCF is the entire game.[10]

Is FCF really a complete enough concept to capture the company's entire contribution to value creation? After all, stock prices move all over the place, generating big capital gains or losses. Total shareholder return (TSR) — dividends plus capital gains (or losses) — can be very large or small. The FCF part of the valuation story, one of modest dividends, share repurchases, perhaps some debt paydown, does not seem large enough or variable enough to drive all of a company's stock price action. What if a stock price, for example, just goes way up without any movement in the current FCF picture? To explain that scenario of how a business delivers returns to equity investors, and many other such scenarios, do we need to go beyond FCFs? The answer is "No." A basic FCF-driven model fully explains all performance-driven stock price movements. The key concept is that DCF values a business based upon *future* FCF. If a company's stock price rises greatly, generating large capital gains to owners at that time, the price movement normally is reconcilable to enlarged hopes about future cash flows (or perhaps to a lowered cost of capital, but that's a separate matter from business results). Figure 4-6 provides an example in which a company's income is expected to jump by 20 percent.

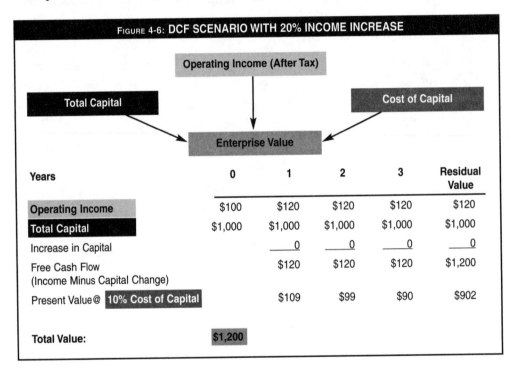

FIGURE 4-6: DCF SCENARIO WITH 20% INCOME INCREASE

Compared to the base case presented in Figure 4-2, expectations for company income jump by 20 percent in the first year and remain at that level. This expands FCF and valuation in scale to $1,200.[11] The DCF model provides proportionally reasonable results in many other cases as well. And, when we run simulations using just this basic model, we get stock price behavior over time that is very close to market norms.[12]

Since the DCF model is based upon a long-term forecast of FCF, it would seem to require that investors stay around for the long run. We know investors don't always do that. They can sell their interests, capturing a particular level of return and immunizing themselves from future movements in FCF or value. Does the DCF framework, with its reliance on long-run cash flows, fail to apply when investors may not be around very long? Actually, it works just fine. If investors sell their interests in the business, the price they get will be governed by the expectations about future FCF that exist at that time. We can rely on the new investors to pay attention to FCF and to discount such expectations based upon risk. In short, current investors can be expected to value their investment consistent with the DCF model and so can all their successors. All that current and future investors as a group will ever get from the enterprise is FCF, so expectations for income and capital performance will drive its value now and at every time in the future. Overall, when we use FCF's moving parts to judge business performance over time, we are capturing every bit of performance that drives value and warrants reward.

FCF and the Irrelevance of Accounting Choices

One of the key findings of financial economics is that accounting choices are not important when determining business value. The "event study" regarding option expensing announcements, covered in Chapter 2, contributes to the evidence in this area. The key driver of value is FCF. Using the DCF model, we can see this clearly. Consider the accounting choice made when capitalizing expenses. If a company capitalizes and amortizes $100 in current expenses over two years, it attaches $50 of that expense to Year 1 and $50 to Year 2. Under this approach, year 1 income falls by only $50 rather than by the full $100 amount of the expense. This might increase measured financial performance and pay in Year 1 in a traditional incentive plan.

However, this accounting choice does not affect FCF or value. The $50 in outlay that did not run through expense must go somewhere in the company's financial statements, and FCF tracks it no matter where it goes. If the outlay does not run through the income statement, it generally is posted (or "capitalized") to the balance sheet. That means the $50 reduction in Year 1 expense is accompanied by a $50 increase in capital. FCF is equal to income minus the increase in capital, so it reflects the full $100 outlay.

The next year, the $50 that was capitalized is taken back into income, reducing it by $50. But, when computing FCF, this income reduction is offset by the $50 capital reduction that occurs when the $50 deferred balance is taken off the balance sheet. So the FCF impact in Year 2 is zero. FCF places the cash impact of the expense into the year in which it was incurred. The capitalization has only temporary effects upon income, so it does not affect the longer-run earning power that drives the residual value. Overall, this accounting maneuver is like most — it has no impact on real value drivers or company value.

The details of the DCF model make clear the more general maxim of financial economics: what matters when valuing an enterprise is not how results are portrayed in the financial statements; what matters are the economic effects of results and their impact upon risk-adjusted free cash flow over time.

- *Accounting doesn't matter.* Incentive plans should reward management only for economically meaningful results over time, not for their accounting portrayal in the short run. Incentive design should be based not upon bookkeeping expediency, but on business efficacy.

- *Well-designed incentive plans feature the drivers of the DCF model consistently — income, capital and the cost of capital — and they do so within a structure focusing upon long-term performance.* Many metric "adjustments," particularly those made in connection with value-based metrics like economic value added or cash flow return on investment, are meant to convert accrual accounting to cash. In an incentive structure focused upon economic performance over the long term, many such adjustments are unnecessary. As demonstrated, the timing differences involved in accruals make little difference when measuring longer-term performance, and they reverse themselves out of an FCF computation anyway.

- Incentive metrics do need adjustment from time to time for issues that arise, including some that concern bookkeeping. Effects of large capital expenditures, for example, often are spread out over time, just to be sure the incentive plan does not discourage good investments. But these adjustments need not cloud or dilute the plan.[13]

When Valuing a Business, the Past Is Relevant only as a Prologue

The value of an enterprise today is based upon expected future cash flows. This has some very specific implications for what does and does not matter when valuing a business, and the DCF model exposes these crisply:

- Past income levels, strictly speaking, do not matter. They literally do not enter into the computation of value. They only are relevant to the extent they provide evidence of what the company's future earning power might be.

- The same is true for historical capital levels. By themselves, they are irrelevant to the value of a business. What matters — and what affects FCF — is the future change in capital. Past capital levels may be useful, but only in estimating future capital needs. They may provide evidence of the level of investment needed to support operations when they grow.[14]

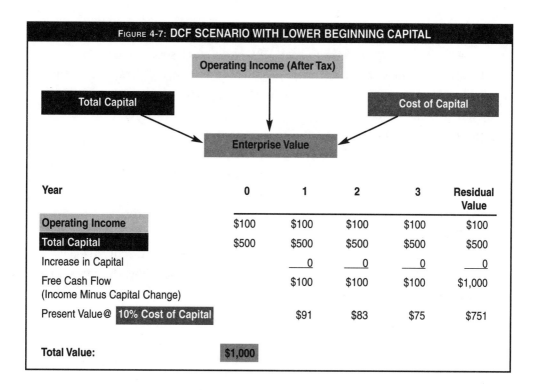

FIGURE 4-7: DCF SCENARIO WITH LOWER BEGINNING CAPITAL

Operating Income (After Tax)

Total Capital

Cost of Capital

Enterprise Value

Year	0	1	2	3	Residual Value
Operating Income	$100	$100	$100	$100	$100
Total Capital	$500	$500	$500	$500	$500
Increase in Capital		0	0	0	0
Free Cash Flow (Income Minus Capital Change)		$100	$100	$100	$1,000
Present Value @ 10% Cost of Capital		$91	$83	$75	$751

Total Value: $1,000

Figure 4-2 showed a valuation of a company with $1000 in beginning capital (Company A). Figure 4-7 shows another company (B) identical to the one in Figure 4-2, except it has an initial level of capital of only $500.

Despite different beginning capital levels, the companies have the same value. That is because income remains at a level of $100 per year and capital, though lower at $500, does not change. FCF remains at $100 per year. Company A might be thought of as a business unit that was just acquired for a price equal to its value of $1,000. Using the purchase method to account for the acquisition, it appears in the acquiring company's financial statements at its cost of $1,000, which consists of fixed assets and net working capital valued at $500 plus non-amortizable intangibles valued at $500. Company B can be thought of as the same company on the day before its acquisition caused $500 in purchased intangibles to be recognized on a balance sheet. It is the same company, with the same future risks and prospects, so its value is the same. If historical income of either company had been $50 rather than $100, the company still would be valued at $1,000. That's because prospective earnings and FCF at $100 are what determines value. If past income had been $50, then forecast results simply would be higher than historical levels. In that case, historical earnings would have under-represented future earning power and would have been less helpful in predicting future results.

Here are the implications for executive incentive design:

- *Long-run FCF expectations drive value.* Yet, companies should emphasize actual, historical business results in their executive incentives. We bridge this gap when we consider management's proactive role within the enterprise. First, managers make decisions now that affect performance for years into the future. Second, they are expected to make a multi-year commitment to their roles within the company. The motivational aspects of proper incentives work the same way; they create a continuously forward-looking interest in several years' worth of business results. This forward-looking perspective is paralleled in the structure of the DCF model. Plans designed to be consistent with the DCF model encourage good decision-making at all times by creating a stake in, and accountability for, consequent long-term results. Absent this key dynamic, shifting the pay structure more heavily toward operating incentives would render it very short-term.

- *Historical capital levels by themselves are irrelevant to valuation, but they can have a huge impact upon incentive plan design and target setting.* The biggest problem with the treatment of capital in incentive plans is the vague, incomplete way in which this key value driver and its opportunity cost affect pay. The second biggest problem arises when companies try to fix the first one by attaching a more prominent role to capital. This can create serious unintended consequences. Differences in the basis of historical capital levels can distort measures like ROIC, ROE and economic value added, as well as the methods used to set targets for these measures. Incentive plans should ignore historical capital levels, or immunize participants from the issues they cause (except in some instances where historical capital can provide a contingent benchmark for setting goals).[15] The role of capital within an incentive plan should be to reward high returns on new capital usage, not to penalize investment or impose other forms of bias.

- *Many techniques used in value-based incentives focus heavily upon a company's long-run earning power.* Often, they look at current income as a source of information about the company's ongoing earning power, valuation and future performance requirements. The economics of traditional incentives also rest on the presumption that a given increase in income will be persistent enough to warrant reward. When administering plans from one year to the next, companies must consider whether actual income levels form a reliable basis for delivering pay in ways that incentive procedures intend. This is prudent regular maintenance for any incentive plan involving metrics and targets.

Forecast Term FCFs and Residual Values

Value creation is about the impact of near-term actions upon long-run performance. Stock prices are based upon very long-run expectations for company performance. That's why a company's stock price tends to be a multiple — often large — of this year's earnings or dividends. Investors are buying shares based upon hopes for a very long-run performance. Our DCF scenario is an example: Investors would be willing to pay 10 times one year's returns to own this particular business, and higher multiples than that are common.

Our initial DCF scenario actually is a special case of the DCF model, one called a zero-growth perpetuity. The company's forecast consists of FCFs of $100 in each of forecast Years 1, 2 and 3, and in residual-term Years 4 through infinity. As we saw when performing the residual value computations earlier, this kind of DCF forecast can be valued by dividing the annual FCF by the cost of capital. That is why the company is worth $1,000. It is the $100 in FCF divided by the 10 percent cost of capital.

The perpetuity method is a "warranted value" concept in the sense that it isolates the value warranted by the current level of operating results under an assumption they will persist unchanged. This sometimes is called "capitalized operations value" for the same reason. It is not only a valuation estimate for a zero-growth situation. Rather, it covers a more general class of scenarios in which, like the zero-growth forecast, the company does not create any more value. (See Figure 4-8.)

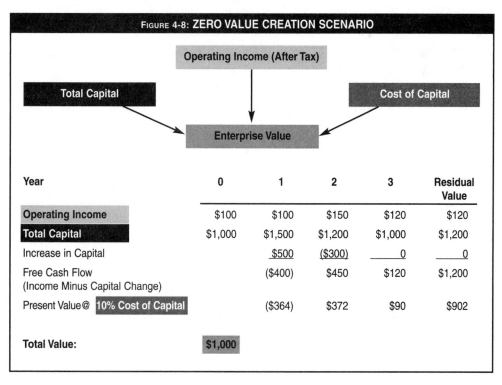

FIGURE 4-8: ZERO VALUE CREATION SCENARIO

Year	0	1	2	3	Residual Value
Operating Income	$100	$100	$150	$120	$120
Total Capital	$1,000	$1,500	$1,200	$1,000	$1,200
Increase in Capital		$500	($300)	0	0
Free Cash Flow (Income Minus Capital Change)		($400)	$450	$120	$1,200
Present Value @ 10% Cost of Capital		($364)	$372	$90	$902

Total Value: $1,000

Value creation means getting new ROIC in excess of the cost of capital. Companies do this by making new investments with high returns, selling off assets whose prospective returns are poor in relation to their potential sale price, or squeezing higher returns out of existing capital. The scenario in Figure 4-8 didn't accomplish these things. In Figure 4-8, the $500 increase in capital occurring at the end of Year 1 increased subsequent income (Year 2 and later) by only $50; this 10 percent ROIC level did not create any excess earnings or value once the company's 10 percent cost of capital is considered. The separate $300 sale of assets in Year 2 didn't create value since its implied ROIC was at the cost of capital as well. And the company didn't increase earnings as a separate matter from capital changes. Capitalized operations value remains at $1,000.

Most companies are worth more than their capitalized operations value. This means that investors expect they will create value in the future. At the same time, DCF forecasts typically assume that the competitive advantages enabling value creation will diminish over time due to competition. A company may well beat such expectations, outdistancing competitors for an unusually long time as Wal-Mart, IBM and McDonald's did for sustained periods in the past. But the typical company's stock price suggests that investors are not willing to pay for such hopes in the current value of company shares. More typically, stock prices and the conventions used to explain them are consistent with this pattern of assumptions:

- *A company's most compelling advantages and strategies are expected to provide their greatest performance gains in the next three to five years.* When stock analysts develop forecasts for companies, this is the time frame in which they tend to assert any specific expectations for income growth and for returns on new investments. Companies do the same thing with acquisition pro formas and long-range business plans.[16] For most companies, performance during this key mid-range period also sets the level for results in the balance of the typical 10-year forecast term and affects their trajectory. Overall, a company's value and the returns it earns based upon performance center heavily upon specific hopes attached to the next few years.

- *After this first three- to five-year period, the effect of the company's individual performance picture on its valuation becomes more vague.* The longer-term end of the forecast tends to be based upon more generalized assessments about the strength of the business franchise and about the industry's growth prospects. During this time, a reasonable forecast convention is to assume that any performance advantages will diminish as a result of competition.[17] Overall, DCF analyses of established companies rarely involve an acceleration of performance in later projection years, and their stock prices rarely square with such a forecast.

- *The residual term, typically beginning around Year 10, most often is governed by an assumption that the company's current set of competitive advantages by then will have run its course.* The business at that date is valued assuming zero growth (or zero value-creation) or upon a very low growth assumption equal to the level of long-run inflationary expectations impounded in the cost of capital.

Most company stock prices can be explained with this general pattern of assumptions. Individual companies with valuations differing greatly from this pattern tend not to stay that way. That means this pattern of results is very relevant to setting incentive targets. An example of such a DCF valuation appears, in a target-setting context, in Chapter 9.

Timing is Everything

The next few years are the most critical to value creation at any point in time. Performance during this period allows management to prove or disprove the viability of current strategies, skills and actions. Nearer-term results matter greatly to the stock market, as many companies find when they release disappointing earnings news. But companies often conclude, mistakenly, that all the stock market cares about is near-term earnings. Quite the contrary, the stock market values them based upon very long-term hopes about performance, a fact made clear by the large multiples of current earnings, dividends and returns customarily paid.

When a company's valuation falls due to bad earnings news, it typically falls by far more than the amount of the earnings disappointment itself. This is the long-run valuation mechanism in action. The stock market uses current information continuously to update its assessments of the company prospects and likely results. And as it does so, it focuses on the next few years. This is where specific expectations wait to be reinforced, invalidated or pleasantly surprised by actual results as they occur. This time frame is when the collection of strategies and initiatives of management come into play. The stock market uses near-term results to update its pivotal three- to five-year scenario and to set the level and trajectory of FCF for all the years to follow.

Most of the variation in stock prices among industry peers appears reconcilable to differences in the next few years' expectations. A company whose earnings are expected to double might be valued at 20 times historical earnings, while one with flat earnings might be valued at a multiple of 10. One whose earnings are expected to drop by half might be valued at five times its past earnings level. In each case, value as a multiple of projected earnings equals 10, so the differences in their historically-based valuation multiples are explained entirely by differences in near-term earnings growth. After the first few years, the forecast is mainly a matter of industry performance norms, with the individual company's results expected to converge toward them at some pace.

This is convenient. We don't have to wait 10 or 15 years to judge the success of a given management team and strategy. Rather, the usual time conventions of business planning — three- to five-year projection cycles updated periodically — will suffice as a benchmark against which to judge management's actual results and their contribution to value creation.

Turning from forecast term conventions to residual values, we note that FCF provides a prudent basis for computing them. In particular, it does a complete job of accounting for the use of capital by the business over time. That's particularly important where depreciating assets like buildings and equipment are concerned. Operating cash flows need to be sufficient not only to provide a return on fixed asset investments, but also to provide a return of those investments, generating cash flows sufficient to replace them over time as they wear out. FCF and many value-based metrics cover this issue by stating results on a net basis, after the economic effects of these replacement outlays.

Some other versions of DCF use an "exit multiple" approach to residual valuation, starting with perhaps a five-year FCF forecast and estimating residual value through a market multiple like six or eight times EBITDA (earnings before interest, taxes and depreciation[18]). A problem with this approach is that EBITDA does not take full account of capital's funding requirements. Being pre-depreciation, this measure reflects no reserve charge for replacement of wasting assets. Also, the "exit multiple" method does not require one to set out a forecast in which the company's specific results, and the value creation they imply, are made to account fully for the company's value. My view is that this less rigorous method does not meet the high standards needed when DCF is adapted to incentive design.

We've reviewed a number of aspects of the DCF model's typical forecast of results. Here are the implications for executive incentive design:

- *For incentive purposes, management's performance and its contribution to value creation normally can be assessed fairly completely over periods of three to five years.* This approach spans important gaps between the financial position of investors and those of management:

    - Most business initiatives are meant to generate results in this time frame, so it provides a working form of accountability for most of what management does. Incentive grants spanning this time frame, with new grants at regular intervals, will align management's income perspective with that of an investor, making use of a continuously forward-looking approach attended by high concern for results each year. This bridges a timing gap between investor valuations, which are denominated in future expectations, and value-based management rewards, which are based upon historical performance over time.

- It bridges an important information gap as well. Valuation of a company — public or private — is based upon the information held by likely investors in company shares. Management presumably knows more than owners, so this situation presents an example of the "informational asymmetries" that sometimes trouble the ties between investors and their management agents. A proper incentive structure simply encourages management to deliver the best possible results over the long term. This means paying management to bring to bear whatever advantages they have on behalf of investors, including any informational edge they hold.

- *"Capitalized operations value" isolates that part of enterprise value warranted by current results.* This is a reasonable basis for judging the value of actual results, one applied within many value-based incentive plans.[19] It is a "show me the money" approach since it bases rewards upon actual, current performance levels and sizes them based upon their valuation implications.

- *Stock prices imply that any performance advantages held by a company are expected to be reduced by competition and to fall toward market norms over time.* This has important effects on how performance demands are distributed among the specific years of a valuation forecast and on how ranges are set within incentive plans. For example, holding all else equal, weaker or shorter-term competitive advantages result in lower value. Such a company must deliver higher performance in the short to intermediate term to warrant a given valuation level.

The DCF Model Serves as a Proxy for Other Valuation Methods

We have relied upon one valuation method — the DCF model — to describe the general connection between business results and shareholder value. We are using it to compile a specific set of mandates for executive incentive design. We'd better be sure this method is valid because we are relying rather heavily upon it.

The DCF model does a good job of explaining company share prices. For most companies, the total value of capital invested in the enterprise can be reconciled, using the DCF model, to reasonable assumptions about its future income, capital usage and comparative investment risk. A couple of notable exceptions that come to mind are the run-up in Japanese equity values in the late 1980s and the high tech and communications bubble of the late 1990s. In each of these cases, financial analysts and commentators called into question DCF and other common, consistent valuation indicators. A crash followed each of these bubbles just as in the South Sea bubble and tulip crazes of hundreds of years before. The general rule is that valuations don't diverge much from what a reasonable DCF model would indicate, and when they do, it is not for long.

It is true that many acquisition prices are hard to explain using a traditional DCF model. However, acquisitions often are overpriced in relation to realistic performance expectations. The synergies driving many high deal prices appear particularly elusive. Business headlines and studies have made clear for years that most big acquisitions fail. The fact that the DCF model has to be "stretched" to make a bad deal look good is evidence of the model's validity.

The stock market, for its part, appears to keep its eye on the ball when evaluating likely acquisition success, undistracted by terms like "strategic" and "synergy." In fact, the market appears to be using a DCF model — its anticipatory nature, particularly, and its demand for future free cash flows to figure out the current valuation consequences of deals. Just as a DCF model would predict, the market regularly offsets the acquisition overpayment by subtracting it from the buyer's stock price as soon as it gets wind of the deal.

Among legitimate valuation methods, the "market comparison" approach is paired with DCF as the two most typical. Under the market comparison approach, companies often are valued based upon various multiples of earnings, volume or capital. These are drawn from study of public company peers or of acquisitions of comparable companies. Results of these valuations tend to reconcile to the DCF model:

- Using industry peers as valuation indicators works well because it reduces valuation assessments to matters of relative performance and value. Peer companies are in the same industry and have important things in common with the company being valued. Making sound calculations doesn't require coming up with isolated, independent assumptions about expected performance and risk and so on; a good bit of that already is baked into the peer share prices and their valuation multiples. If you simply apply those, you're already in the ballpark. The difficult thing is deciding what earnings multiple your company warrants. To do that, you're obliged to figure out where you ought to be in the range of multiples and why. The answers to those questions turn on:

  - The companies' relative prospects for income growth

  - The extent to which income is more or less "free" from re-investment demands

  - Comparative risk and the price investors charge for bearing it.

  That means that applying market comparison approach properly is a matter of applying DCF criteria properly.

- Holding all else equal, a DCF valuation of a company with higher earnings growth, more highly distributable income or lower risk will be higher in relation to current income. Market comparison methods pick up on this. The Wal-Marts of the world, for example, when compared to most of the casual dining sector, have economically profitable growth profiles that are not offset as heavily by higher capital requirements. That's why they attract higher valuation multiples in the marketplace just as they would in a DCF valuation. Overall, the DCF model is complete, resilient and well-suited to the tasks at hand.

Cost of Capital and Expected Returns

A company's cost of capital is driven by its risk level and by the prevailing yields for investments with similar risk. In Chapter 5, we will look closely at how costs of capital are computed, as well as other ways in which risk interacts with company incentive structures.

For now, we will look at some very specific implications that the cost of capital makes when judging business performance. One of the characteristics of the DCF model that is most useful to incentive design is the way that it links the cost of capital with future performance. If business results turn out as forecast (and capital market criteria and expectations do not change), the DCF model predicts total returns for investors at a level equal to the cost of capital. Consider the zero-growth example at the beginning of this chapter:

- The company's cost of capital is 10 percent. If performance goes as forecast, it will generate $100 in FCF at the end of Year 1. The value of the company remains at $1,000 since, at that date, it is a zero-growth $100 perpetuity ($100 per year, valued in infinity at a 10 percent cost of capital, is equal to $100/10 percent, or $1,000).

- Total investor return (TIR) for a particular period of time consists of the free cash flows (FCFs) received by investors plus any increase in the value of the enterprise they own. Investors get $100 in FCF in this scenario and no increase in value, so their TIR is $100. The value at the beginning of Year 1 is $1,000, so TIR amounts to 10 percent, equal to the cost of capital.

The same identity holds true under many different performance scenarios. See Figure 4-9 for an example of a company with growing income and capital levels.

The company is valued at the end of each year based upon the present value of FCFs remaining in the forecast. This company's performance was equal to targeted levels. Other valuation conditions — later years' FCF forecasts and the cost of capital — remained the same. Under these conditions, the DCF model specifies that investor returns equal the cost of capital, just as they would in the case of a fixed-income investment:

FIGURE 4-9: EXPECTED PERFORMANCE AND TOTAL INVESTOR RETURN

Year	0	1	2	3	Residual Value
Operating Income		$150	$170	$200	$200
Total Capital	$1,000	$1,200	$1,400	$1,600	$1,600
Increase in Capital		$200	$200	$200	0
Free Cash Flow (FCF) (Income Minus Capital Change)		($50)	($30)	0	$2,000
Cost of Capital 10%					
Present, End-of-Year Values:					
FCF for Remaining Forecast Term	($70)	($27)	$0		
Residual Value	$1,503	$1,653	$1,818	$2,000	
Enterprise Value	$1,432	$1,626	$1,818	$2,000	
Valuation at Beginning of Year		$1,432	$1,626	$1,818	
Value Gain		$193	$193	$182	
Free Cash Flow		($50)	($30)	0	
Total Investor Return		$143	$163	$182	
Return as a Percent of Beginning Value		10.0%	10.0%	10.0%	

- This company is worth $1,432 as of the beginning of Year 1 based upon its forecast FCFs and residual value. Its valuation at the end of Year 1 is $1,626,[20] so the value increase during year one is $193.

- Free cash flows are negative at $50.

- Total return is $143, or 10 percent of beginning value.

Later years work out the same way as FCFs are collected each year, and the present value discounting unwinds at the same pace.

Here are the implications for incentive design:

- *The performance/return linkage specified by the DCF model can be very useful when setting targets for company performance.*

Its inferences about performance and value creation are based upon external investor criteria. The process most companies use to set targets is based, in contrast, upon internal budgeting. Rather than using budget-based targets, companies can center their incentive plan award schedules on the performance expected by investors. If, for example, 5 percent annual income growth and 10 percent ROIC are consistent with shareholder expectations, these may be used fairly as targets within a bonus plan or long-term performance plan irrespective of the company's budget.

- *The DCF model also can be used to define business scenarios in which TIR is higher or lower than targeted levels.*

This enables companies to specify not only performance targets, but performance ranges. A typical award schedule would link pay with TIR across a broad range of outcomes. If 2 percent income growth and 8 percent ROIC imply TIR of zero percent, for example, that might be set as the incentive plan's threshold performance level. This approach — basing incentive payouts upon the valuation implications of financial performance — is not an unusual or novel one. On the contrary, it is the basic arrangement underlying stock-based incentive plans already; those plans deliver higher or lower gains over time based upon stock price movement, itself a function of expected results. As we'll see in Chapter 9, value-based target setting allows this basic connection between results and investor returns to be extended into other kinds of incentive plans; ones that offer greater line of sight and efficacy than stock-based pay. This approach brings the best of both worlds — the high line of sight and well-crafted performance metrics possible in an operating incentive format and the valuation criteria and outcomes featured by stock-based pay.

- *When making inferences about performance and stock price reactions to it, holding capital market conditions constant is a pretty big assumption. Valuation criteria and expectations shift constantly.*

We've already seen how changes in the weighted average cost of capital can cause the company's stock price to go up and down. Long-run expectations for performance of the company and its sector might shift as well, affecting FCF forecasts for many more years than the three used in our simplified example. Uncertainties, though, will affect any forecasting method. They are a normal part of any business planning process, whether the results happen to be used for incentive pay, capital allocation, financing or anything else. The way to deal with them within an incentive structure is through the mechanism of creating new incentive grants each year. If the cost of capital changes materially, or if expectations for company results do, these factors can be taken into account when setting targets for future bonuses and long-term incentive grants.[21]

The most important finding of this chapter, however, is the most basic assertion of the DCF model — value is a function of expected performance *over the long-run*. One of the most troubling aspects of the executive incentive structure at companies today is the outsized concern with short-term results. The scenario of investor returns just demonstrated that the next year's results account for only a small fraction of company performance — 10 percent in the case of a company with a 10 percent cost of capital. When near-term changes in performance have a big impact upon stock price, it is only through their effects upon long-run expectations. Shifting the incentive structure toward the longer term will align it more closely with management's essential task of value creation.

Taking that key point and the other insights accumulated so far, we can now compile a complete set of principles for effective incentive design and be confident about each of them. Those principles are value rules, and they are presented next.

Value Rules

Value rules are the basic principles of business governance, performance measurement and valuation that should shape incentive pay at the senior management level.

1. **Management serves as the agent of the company's owners — its shareholders.**
   Management's job is to govern the enterprise in such a way as to maximize the wealth of shareholders. All of the enterprise's other stated pursuits are signposts along the path to value creation.

2. **People in senior management are in the "decision" business and their product is value creation.**
   Their unique charge is to make long-term commitments of the company's resources and to manage its ongoing operations in the hope of earning returns for shareholders.

3. **Within the corporate governance structure, senior management is the group that holds the bulk of the important information and prerogatives.**
   Shareholder influence on business matters is comparatively fractional, anonymous and distant. The board does not run the company and therefore cannot act in an intensive and timely way upon business problems or opportunities. The general governance structure of business — board and shareholder oversight, relevant laws — cannot by itself encourage high performance consistently in the many actions that management can take.

4. **Management can be counted on to act in their own financial self-interest, so companies must be sure that maximizing shareholder wealth is in the interest of management.**
   Management incentives are that part of the rewards system that is meant to link executive pay and performance in a particularly explicit and compelling way. Companies must use incentives as a pro-active instrument of corporate governance, one that stands a continuous vigil in pursuit of high performance.

5. **To be effective, incentive plans must create a high degree of line of sight from actions to results to rewards.**
   They must be clear and specific, encouraging business decisions that create value, and discouraging those that don't. Shareholder wealth is created over time when the enterprise generates returns — when the company's stock price rises and when it pays out dividends. Stock price increases plus dividends equal the "total return" earned by shareholders. To serve shareholders, incentives must directly encourage management to maximize long-run total shareholder return.

6. **Incentives must take account of investor valuation criteria and performance expectations.**

   The stock market judges business performance in relation to its own valuation criteria and expectations — expected levels of cash flow that can be distributed from business operations in the future and the risk of those cash flows. These external benchmarks determine whether a given set of business results is likely to create value. Internal budgets and financial plans at companies have no direct role in value creation; they simply provide one source of information for the market to use in forming its own expectations. When judging what is and is not good performance, the stock market is the controlling authority. To properly connect executive rewards with value creation, incentive plan goals must take clear account of the set of expectations held by investors and the criteria they use to value expected performance.

7. **Investors hold financial claims upon business performance that are unlimited, long-term, concrete and continuous.**

   Investors enjoy the full range of upside in business performance as well as the downside. Their claims are long-term in nature and contractually strong, so they are concerned not only with the near term, but with the long run. Even if they sell their interests and don't stay for the long term, they know the price they receive will be driven by the long-run performance expectations prevailing at the time of sale. Their claims are unbroken, so every dollar the company uses, every bit of income it generates, and any resulting increase in value will affect their returns over time. A company's incentive structure should be similar in every regard.

8. **Effective incentives must focus upon matters that management can control.**

   Much of the movement in enterprise valuations lies outside of the scope of management's control, particularly during the three- to five-year time frame that is so critical to executive performance assessment and rewards. The focus of management's efforts should be on the controllable parts of value creation. Investors can't expect management to influence exogenous stock price drivers like interest rates or the overall economic climate. They clearly do expect them to improve business results to the greatest extent possible. Pay should be based heavily upon actual business results and not upon the uncontrollable elements of investor return. Company stock cannot be used effectively as the centerpiece of the incentive structure for many executives.

9. **To align pay with value creation and to create line of sight, executives at the business unit level must have a decisive stake in the businesses they run.**

   A glance at a typical company's annual report shows enterprise income, capital and risks dispersed into reasonably separable business units. Substantial opportunities for value creation are found at the business unit level along with a large part of the senior management workforce and important degrees of decision-making authority. To match stake and account- ability properly with authority, companies must create a substantial stake in success of entities like groups, divisions, profit centers and joint ventures.

10. **The effective time horizon of incentive pay must be shifted to the longer term to align it with shareholder interests.**

    The incentive structure should create a continuously forward-looking reward mechanism with high concern for results each year. Contrary to popular belief, enterprise value is based upon long-run performance. Near-term expected performance accounts only for a small part of a typical company's value. The stock market looks closely at performance in the near term, of course, but only as a source of information used in the constant process of updating the long-run performance expectations that drive stock value. Re-orienting incentives toward the longer term means issuing long-term incentives highly connected with things management can do to create value. Incentive grants spanning a longer time frame, with new grants at regular intervals, will align management's perspective on business results with that of an investor. Bonus plan parameters can be improved and stabilized as well, creating a more enduring financial stake for management.

11. **Within this structure, three to five years is the proper maturity for most long-term incentive grants.**

    Most of what differentiates one stock price from the next, particularly among industry peers, stems from differences in the expectations about performance over the next few years. The general mechanism of business performance and investor expectations plays out in a continuously forward- looking three- to five-year time frame. Also, as a practical matter, most of the things management does will produce measurable success or failure within a few years. This means the usual timing conventions of business planning — three- to five-year projection cycles that are updated periodically — suffice as a benchmark to judge management's actual results and its contribution to value creation. This approach also addresses important differences between an investor's perspective and that of management, working to remedy informational asymmetries, risk-related biases and gaps in accountability.

12. A company's overall incentive "spend" should be concentrated on the time frames, business results and organizational levels that match management authority most closely.

Companies should reinvent their incentives to address each of these dimensions decisively. The traditional incentive structure imposes a short time frame, entangles business results with stock market noise, and largely ignores the pivotal role of business unit management.

13. Three basic financial variables determine the value of a business enterprise: long-run operating income, capital usage and risk.

Most methods for business valuation boil down to these three drivers. They are the financial doors through which all business results, prospects or other factors must pass if they are to have an effect upon value. Each must be represented in proper proportion in incentive plans.

14. The traditional metrics used in most incentive plans — yardsticks such as earnings per share (EPS), net income, revenue, operating income and return on equity (ROE) — don't drive value creation consistently at all.

They don't reflect the three basic value drivers in proper proportion, so they allow many kinds of value-destroying business decisions to be rewarded. They also discourage many value-creating decisions. Income typically is represented strongly in incentive plans, but capital and its cost are not. This particular deficiency creates quite a number of problems. The pay mechanism must in one way or another attach a proper cost to incremental capital usage, with materially riskier businesses facing a higher cost of capital and vice versa.

15. Market valuation principles are agnostic about which metrics to use for incentive purposes.

Value rules are derived from specific linkages between performance and value, but they do not prescribe which measures to use in management incentive plans. They simply encourage any approach that supports value creation, just as they encourage any other business initiative that is likely to create value for investors. The task of value-based incentive design is to ensure that the principles of valuation are reflected consistently in incentive pay. This can be done in a range of ways involving plan targets and ranges, traditional and value-based metrics, the calibration of performance/ reward schedules, and the specifics of plan administration, communication and training.

16. **There is no single combination of value drivers that maximizes value creation.**

    Many different kinds of companies with different performance profiles can generate a given amount of value creation for investors. Low-growth companies may generate more cash flows for distribution to investors, while higher-growth ones may increase shareholder wealth as they increase in value. Traditional plans are biased in favor of businesses with higher growth. This is a source of unfairness in company incentive plans, one that often encourages the pursuit of economically unprofitable growth. To work properly and fairly in various businesses over time, incentives must take account of the bigger picture — the "total return" that an enterprise delivers to its owners.

17. **In business valuation, the past is relevant only as prologue.**

    Value is driven by expectations about the future. The metrics and standard-setting procedures companies employ in incentive plans, in contrast, often are distorted by the irrelevant part of past results. This affects assessments of performance against industry standards, over time, or among business units of a company, or after some transactions like acquisitions. Proper designs dismiss the irrelevant part of past results.

18. **Financing decisions may have some impact upon company value and returns, but any such effects are uncertain, modest and outside the control of most people in senior management.**

    Companies that wish to align incentives with value creation should immunize them, by and large, from the effects of financing decisions, like whether to repurchase shares or how much debt to use in the capital structure. Companies should not undertake financing transactions like an initial public offering, the full or partial sale of a subsidiary, issuance of tracking stock or a leveraged buyout primarily in pursuit of incentive effects. Such effects can be created without the transaction.

19. **Accounting doesn't matter.**

    Business value is based on economic results, not on the accounting portrayal of those results. Performance metrics should be based upon economic performance. And accounting rules should not affect the choices companies make about how to structure incentive pay. Companies should design their incentive plans in pursuit of business efficacy, not bookkeeping expediency.

20. The stock market continuously fine-tunes a company's valuation based upon changes in performance expectations and valuation criteria.

Stock prices move around a lot, and for a lot of reasons. Interest rates change constantly, for example, and so do other parameters like expectations for economic growth, long-term prospects of a particular industry, and the general price of equity investment risk. These and many other factors could affect marginal value creation and the decisions made in pursuit of it. Incentive plans are comparatively blunt instruments. The basic value drivers, time intervals and organizational levels involved in a company's incentive structure do not allow it to track all of the dynamics of market value. This means value rules should only be taken so far. Companies should not attempt to use incentive plans to micromanage every dimension of business decision-making. To be effective, value-based incentive plans must focus on the basics. They must create a clear, enduring stake in value creation and not be adjusted or revised heavily. Even in basic form, however, proper incentives can be remarkably resilient in the way they address the details of business decision-making.

Value rules indict current practices in the area of executive incentives, but this is spectacularly good news for companies. A typical company is getting little differential performance effect from most of the money it spends on incentive pay. Companies can change what they do and get substantial returns on these outlays. The balance of this book shows how to use value rules to reinvent executive incentives.

Endnotes

1   A more detailed approach is not helpful to our task. Trying to engineer an incentive plan to address all of the complex economic and business issues facing an individual organization is not worthwhile, as a general matter. That approach attaches a governance mandate to the incentive structure that is at once too broad and too detailed, making it hard to communicate and administer. It is one of the main reasons why value-based incentive plans, including many based upon the metric "economic value added," have failed in the past. Instead, we'll take the basic principles that link results to value and apply them consistently and broadly.

2   Chapter 12 outlines how proper incentives can help the company implement financial principles more effectively through effects upon budgeting, long-range planning, financial training and other activities.

3   Details of the DCF model, its underpinnings in areas like the theory of the firm, its application to many business decisions and the many academic contributors in this area are set out in many graduate textbooks on corporate finance including Brealey and Meyers.

4   Here is a quick refresher on the basic math of present value discounting of single cash flows. If $90.91 were invested today at a 10 percent expected rate of return and this return were realized, it would be worth $100 one year from now. That is computed as the $90.91 we begin with plus a 10 percent return equal to $9.09 for $100 in total. The present value of $90.91 and the future value of $100 are, in a sense, the same thing. They each are representations of the expected future FCF of $100, but the $100 is stated at a time one year from now and the $90.91 is stated in present terms. The equation involved in compounding the $90.91 investment to future value is $90.91 * (1 + 10 percent) = $100. To determine the present value of $100, on the other hand, we rearrange the equation and solve for present value: $100 / (1 + 10 percent) = $90.91. A sum to be received two years from now involves two years of compounding. $82.62 invested now will be worth $90.91 at the end of one year and $100 at the end of two years. The compounded future value of the investment is computed as $82.62 * (1 + 10 percent) ^ 2 = $100. We can re-arrange these terms to get the corresponding equation for discounting the second-period cash flow: $100 / (1 + 10 percent) ^ 2 = $82.62. Computations at year three involve three years of discounting.

5   As we'll cover in more detail in Chapter 7, this has implications for common financial performance measures. Operating income after tax divided by capital, which often is called return on invested capital (ROIC), is the same thing as RONA (return on net assets), return on investment (ROI), return on capital (ROC) and return on capital employed (ROCE). Return on assets (ROA), on the other hand, is a mixed construct. Typically used by financial companies, it normally is defined as net income (measured from an equity perspective) divided by total assets (or total capital plus non-interest bearing liabilities). Return on equity is equal to net income divided by stockholders' equity; its income and capital elements each are defined from an equity perspective.

6   The company's capital structure may have a strong impact upon its estimate of the cost of capital and therefore upon a given valuation scenario. We will argue in Chapter 5 that costs of capital do not actually vary that much, in practice, based upon company decisions about capital structure. Overall, we will recommend that company incentive plans should consider costs of capital explicitly, but only in rough, reasonable terms and without allowing possible changes in the cost of capital to affect pay very much.

7   In companies with high levels of debt, creating incentive claims based upon total capital may result in plan costs that are very dilutive in relation to the small amount of equity in the enterprise. This is one of the cases in which it may be prudent to

consider the equity perspective at least when sizing and testing the plan. Most incentive pay actually is based upon equity-based incentives and performance measures constructed from an equity perspective — like EPS and ROE.

8   Capital expenditures, net of disposals, constitute the gross increase in the net fixed asset account. Depreciation is the increase in accumulated depreciation (again net of the effects of asset disposals), a contra-asset account, so the increase in net fixed assets is equal to capital expenditures minus depreciation. The overall increase in net assets can be computed by taking the increase in net fixed assets and adding to it the increases in net working capital and other assets (like intangibles resulting from acquisitions).

9   Including most LBOs and private equity deals. Contrasting the buy-ins involved in most such deals with grants of cash or stock-based incentives, the executive gets capital gains treatment on stock sales, but the corporation loses the tax benefit of pay expense.

10 Management has some influence over the riskiness of business activities it pursues and therefore upon the company's cost of capital. Relevant risk effects are addressed in Chapter 5.

11 Changes to the cost of capital might have similar effects.

12 The version of the basic DCF model used in these simulations is the one described in Chapter 2. Simulations yield a statistical distribution of results that resembles that of a typical company's stock price; the natural logarithm of annual returns follows a generally normal distribution with a mean around 10 percent and a standard deviation of about 30 percent.

13 A limited, reasonable set of standard adjustments is described in Chapter 8.

14 Even when applied to businesses in which capital is highly relevant — ones with regulatory capital requirements like banks and insurance companies, for example — the change in capital is most important. For example, the DCF model deals with any capital deficiency or excess based upon its prospective impact upon capital needs and cash flow.

15 The TBR-based target-setting approach described in Chapter 7 provides an example of how to make reasonable use of historical capital levels when setting targets.

16 In low-accountability situations, they have a tendency simply to inflate such forecasts. Another tactic sometimes observed is to continually defer business gains into the out years, creating the classic "hockey stick" projection.

17 Economic theory and empirical research indicate that securities are priced as if business advantages are expected to wear away over time. Michael Porter's book, *Competitive Advantage*, addresses this phenomenon. The assumption of finite competitive advantage as a forecast assumption is addressed in several books by Al Rappaport and in the "fade" forecast construct applied in analysis done by HOLT Value Associates.

18 The vestigial "A" refers to past practice when companies amortized acquisition costs over time.

19 The metrics TBR and SVA (discussed in Chapter 8) use a perpetuity valuation method to convert current operating results into value.

20 This is equal to the residual value and the Years 2 and 3 FCF, each discounted to present values as of the end of Year 1.

21 A system of TBR-based phantom stock grants like those described in Chapter 10 provides a good example of this dynamic.

5

Risk, Executive Behavior and the Cost of Capital

R isk is the next big thing. Companies that understand risk well and deal with it effectively are on course to outperform others in coming years.

Business risks of all kinds have become a more prominent concern for senior management and company boards. Risk is also an increasingly explicit part of common business decision-making. Many product and service offerings in business involve risk transfers. These go far beyond the familiar products of the financial services industry like insurance, swaps, and other hedging maneuvers. The leasing and mortgage sectors have changed the basic risk profile of many durable good purchases. High-profile business topics like outsourcing are replete with risk-shifting implications. Some companies have responded to school districts' risk aversion and funding uncertainties by contracting to take on the risk of school energy costs as part of the management services they offer. Restructuring of corporate retirement benefit policies is moving an enormous amount of risk from the business sector to households. Households, in turn, have become much more sophisticated in recent years about matters like risk reduction through portfolio diversification and how their own time horizons and risk tolerances should affect investment decisions.

It's a big world full of risky opportunities. Astute management teams understand that many business decisions allow them to buy and sell risk. Those who do it well will have a serious performance advantage. Inept players — those whose decision-makers aren't balancing risks well for their investors — will get burned badly; consider the performance of Gray Davis as an energy buyer for the people of California. In a business, it makes sense to think through the effects of executive incentives upon the critical risk dimensions of business decision-making.

So far, we've identified risk as a primary driver of the cost of capital. As we saw in Chapter 4, the cost of capital is one of the three primary drivers of business valuation. It sets the valuation scale of the other two drivers, income and capital usage:

- It translates income into value. A $100 level income stream is worth $1,000 at a 10 percent cost of capital but $1,250 at an 8 percent cost of capital.

- It determines whether capital deployed in a business creates value or not. An investment yielding 11 percent in total returns will create value if the cost of capital is 10 percent and destroy it if the cost of capital is 12 percent.

The cost of capital is the rate of return that investors need to compensate them for the risks they bear. As we saw in Chapter 4, expected business performance, if achieved, creates results for investors equal to the cost of capital (holding all else constant).

When companies make risk and its costs a visible element of their incentive plans, they do it most often by incorporating a cost of capital into the measurement or benchmarking apparatus. The value-based metrics covered in Chapter 8 do this explicitly. They either attach a formal, risk-based capital charge to business performance, perform a valuation of business results based upon the company's cost of capital, or attach notional risk-based capital requirements to the business when computing its level of return. Companies using the traditional financial metrics set forth in Chapter 7 may address risk by benchmarking measures of return on investor capital against standards that reflect risk in one way or another. Risk can have an explicit role in incentive target setting as well. As we will see in Chapter 9, generally, companies with higher risk need to generate higher business results to satisfy investor demands.

Those concepts are all about risk from an *investor* viewpoint and risk as an *explicit* element of the incentive pay structure. When assessing risk and its important effects on incentives, it would be a mistake to stop there. Risk has a range of *implicit* effects, permeating many aspects of the incentive rewards structure. And looking at risk effects from the *personal* viewpoint of executives is at least as important as from the more customary and predictable viewpoint of diversified, liquid investors.

This chapter deals with a range of risk-related matters affecting how senior management incentives work, including the central, big-ticket risk issue of the cost of capital.

Investors vs. Management

Investors set the cost of capital. It represents the time value of money and the price of business risk to debt and equity investors. Those guidelines are valid, but they're all written from the investor's perspective. Our task is to encourage management to create value, so we should consider their perspective. Well-designed pay plans create a stake for management in income as well as accountability for use of capital. Incorporating the third driver into their plans, the cost of capital and the related dynamics of risk, is a bit trickier. The cost of capital does not necessarily reflect the time value that executives place on money nor the price they attach to risk.

We shouldn't expect management and investors to see things in the same way. Investors hold generally liquid and diversified interests, so they are concerned about the risks that a particular company's stock adds to a diversified portfolio. Senior managers and executives have an interest in the company that is neither liquid nor diversified, and every bit of the overall variation in business results may affect them. Career risks are a big issue from a management viewpoint, too, and a non-issue to investors.

The executive pay commentariat recommends that senior management hold a lot of company stock to align the interests of investors and executives. Actually, investors and managers are in quite different positions. Stock, which is investor currency, does not always function that well as an incentive device for management. Unlike investors, management has direct control over company operations. Management also makes specific decisions as individuals or members of small teams. Investor criteria and their impact, on the other hand, are general outcomes of a capital market process. This means executives' inclinations may depart greatly from investors, being subject to individual judgment attributes and issues like risk aversion, illusions of control and impatience.

Individuals may compartmentalize risks. They may draw distinctions between playing with house money and putting their own skin in the game. For them, sunk costs may never really be sunk. Investors, on the other hand, likely see all these risks as transparent and fungible. For example, suppose you went to the theater with $200 in tickets in your pocket and lost them on the way. Would you pay another $200 to buy new ones at the box office if you could? Or, like many people, would you just go home? Now instead, what if you did not lose the tickets on the way to the theater, but instead lost $200 in cash. Would you cash in the tickets — they're refundable — for $200 and go home? Cash and tickets are fungible, but many of the people who say they'd go home due to lost tickets say they'd stay for the show had they lost cash. This failure to see fungibility is a common quirk in economic judgment. In a pay context, people often attach a lot of value to money they can withdraw from the company, becoming especially risk averse with any prospect that threatens that balance.

These attributes have implications for the many detailed choices involved when setting up incentive plans, so it is worth taking a look at how they play out. If you're not up on issues like these, many of which underlie the "behavioral school" of investing, you may end up being schooled by them.

A Bird in the Hand is Worth Two in the Bush

We've noted that option grants often are a bad trade. They're expensive, from the company's viewpoint, since a grant is quite likely to lead to gains for the executives and dilution for the corporation. When a company with a $10 stock price issues a typical option, the grant is worth about $4, and that is its economic cost to shareholders. The executive, on the other hand, might think it is only worth a buck or two. Why? It normally takes a long time for the executive to be assured of option gains. With typical stock market performance — annual gains around 8 percent or 10 percent per year on average with a standard deviation of 30 percent — you'd expect many option grants to be underwater for a time after grant and many others to generate low and variable gains for years. Long time frames, lots of complexity and risk — this is the kind of financial claim an individual will discount heavily.

If you buy something for more than it is worth to you, you lose value. If you give something away and get less value for it in return, you lose value. If you pay $6 for something you could have had for $4, you are worse off by $2. Let's say you are out shopping in the marketplace with $4 in company money. You need to use it to buy something that the corporation needs. Four dollars might buy you a half-pound of coffee beans, a ream of paper, or about one minute of labor from Homer based on his annual pay. What if, instead of giving Homer cash of $4, you handed over options worth $6? You'd have spent $2 too much and made a bad trade.

Options invite this sort of discounting and that makes them a bad trade much of the time. Cash does not pose difficult valuation problems or excessive risk discounting. Whole shares of stock are likely to be valued fully as well. Now that option accounting charges are imminent, companies are going to be more even-handed about how they deliver incentives and will be looking for greater efficacy. They will want more bang for the buck or the same bang for fewer bucks.

An obvious place to start is to use instruments that aren't discounted heavily by the recipient due to risk — plans denominated in cash and shares. Four dollars of likely cost in cash or shares would be valued near $4 by the recipient, while $6 in likely option gains might be valued at only $4. An obvious solution is to use fewer options and more cash and shares, thereby saving a couple of bucks, having plans with more upside than before, or some of both.

Some observers believe companies should create even more complex forms of options than the vanilla grants used commonly now, perhaps ones with exercise prices that compound or move with an index. These are discouraged under current accounting rules so we don't see many now, but they may function well under certain circumstances (see Chapter 11). Since they are even more complex and uncertain than regular options, though, they may invite even more discounting and create even worse pay trades. That should limit their use only to those cases in which their features are especially compelling.

A Bonus Bank is Not a Lock Box

Another example of a potentially bad trade is a "bonus bank" of the type commonly prescribed for use with plans based upon the metric, economic value added (or economic profit — EP). In this arrangement, the executive's entire bonus is not necessarily paid out currently. Instead, all or part of it is placed in a notional bank. The entire bonus might be banked or just the amount over some cap. Typically, one-third of the bank is paid out each year. So, the bonus payment each year is a function of three-year cumulative performance. It includes whatever part of this year's bonus is paid currently plus a third of the bank balance.

There's nothing wrong with the basic math of bonus banks. Banking is a *quid pro quo* for the unlimited upside often recommended in the one-size-fits-all EP plans commonly promoted. It also is a way of overcoming the short-term bias that bonus plans often seem to create. Lastly, it is an attempt at fiscal control over EP plans that sometimes have uncertain targeting, ranges, leverage and economic dilution.

But, as presidential candidate Al Gore learned a few years ago, people don't see a notional lock box as being the same thing as a real bank account. Companies offering notional bonus bank accounts learned something similar. In truth, money in a bonus bank is pretty safe; normally, it is quite likely to be paid rather than wiped out by big losses in later years. As a liability to the corporation, it might be worth 90 cents on the dollar. But it often is worth less to participants since they see it as riskier.

Let's value the bonus bank in an example based upon the proverbial, personal guideline for risk discounting: a bird in the hand is worth two in the bush. This means the risky prospect is worth half the sure one. If participants see a bonus bank in this particular way, they'll discount the banked dollar to 50 cents, creating a bad trade from the corporation's viewpoint and a pay structure seen as uncompetitive. The issue is particularly stark in the case of a bonus plan since market practice is to allow recipients to take their bonus money off the table without subjecting them to any additional jeopardy.

Liquidity Preference, Not Happy Hour

Investors, taken as a group, almost never get a bird in the hand. One investor may sell and lock in gains for certain. But that just means another investor has assumed that continuing stream of prospects and risks. Investors as a group — the group of people for whom management works — hold a perpetual, uncertain stake in future results.

That means we can't ever really succeed when we try to align their interests with those of management. Suppose we took the "alignment" prescription to an extreme by accelerating a career's pay, issuing all of it in grants of stock or options, and then preventing executives from selling their holdings (through ownership requirements or "career shares" arrangements). We'd have management at once comparatively wealthy, threadbare and starving. An instructor in a real estate valuation class I took years ago noted to me that he'd gotten himself into this situation with illiquid real estate deals, saying, "I was rich on paper, sure, but I had a bit of a liquidity problem."

Companies sometimes want to lock up lots of pay over time. A bonus bank is just one example. If executives were allowed to become fully liquid, they could accumulate enough money to walk out the door and start booking those weekday tee times. But policies of golden handcuffs, meant purely to retain key people, can move quickly past the point of diminishing returns. It's a question of balance.

It obviously is not sacrosanct to shield executives from some investor risk. The question is how much is right? A good place to look is market norms. The company does act as a risk intermediary in labor markets, even at the executive level. In a process resembling loan securitization, it takes a portion of its general, uncertain income stream and turns it into the various tranches comprising the executive pay structure. Management needs to be able to take some money off the table once in a while, and companies typically let them do this in the form of salary, bonus and long-term incentive grants that are cumulatively liquid over time. Salaries, benefits and perquisites are relatively sure; bonuses are iced at the end of each year, and long-term incentives are about as uncertain as shareholder wealth.

So where should you be in terms of mix? Well, the market mix has been set through lots of well-informed marketplace activity over a period of years, so it apparently represents an overall approach that executives and companies find workable and to mutual advantage. It probably is a fairly efficient outcome in terms of balancing the appeal to executives while getting a reasonable performance for the company. It probably is a good cost solution, as well. If the company wanted to make pay substantially riskier or more illiquid overall, it would have to increase pay greatly in order to be competitive. In the market solution, investors basically are selling insurance and liquidity to the executive on voluntary terms that both parties regard as favorable. That is a good trade.

Some companies hold salaries far below market and make up for it with a higher bonus. In these situations, a portion of the bonus is pretty much like a salary from the company's viewpoint and not genuinely at risk. Putting these sure costs into the putatively "at risk" pay bucket simply invites participants to discount them. This brings the pay structure into conflict with a common judgment flaw. People systematically over-assess small risks. That's why you can sell them flight insurance, and that's why nuclear power causes outsized concern. This also explains why it's not a good idea to subject an unusual amount of cash pay to risks, even ones seen as small. You'd have to increase pay a lot to make up for that.

Companies don't have to muddle through every issue to have effective pay programs. They can move rapidly toward good decisions about how to structure pay plans, basing them on solid principles that apply in the bulk of cases. They can do this by narrowing choices and dismissing some of them early in the process. In the instant case, that means they don't have to depart materially from the time frame and liquidity of the market's overall pay mix. They just need to redesign their elements using sound techniques.

To violate the market's proportions is to invite participants to see the whole pay program as a bird in the bush and discount it. This is a recipe for trouble. Companies that fail to meet competitive norms have to by and large bear the consequences. An equally questionable approach would be to create a pay package much more liquid than the market norm.

Was That a 'Put' Option or a 'Call' Option We Just Granted?

Let's examine how the structure of pay trades risks between the company and executives. Some observers have noted that management's claims upon business results do not align with equity holders' because management's cash financial claims are like debt. Salaries are cash annuities, like bonds. So are retirement accruals. Stock options, it is argued, bring the overall pay package in line with those of debt and equity investors as a group.

But a debt-plus-options financial claim is not equivalent to the interest that investors hold in the overall enterprise's value and returns. A basic option valuation identity — the put-call parity equation — can help us straighten this out when applied to enterprise financial claims:[1]

Debt plus call option = Stock plus put option

The typical pay structure is a debt-plus-option deal, with a relatively assured debt-like claim in the form of salary and benefits and incentive plans whose variability creates option-like upside or that just consists of actual options. But as the equation suggests, that doesn't add up to a stock-equivalent claim upon the overall enterprise. If the company's value falls, executives typically keep their salary and benefits and may even get some bonus pay. That's like having a put option on the company's value, one that amounts to insurance against a decrease in value.

The typical market mix of pay does create a reasonable overall set of financial interests. It is a claim on enterprise value plus a "put option" that actually protects executives from some of the downside that investors bear.

As noted earlier, controlling the risk involved in the pay structure is a reasonable outcome of a market process. It may create an advantageous trade of risk and value when compared to a riskier structure, so it is not something to be cast aside even in the restructuring of pay.

Drawing Risk Distinctions

Executives differ greatly as to their roles, but companies shouldn't make big distinctions among them when setting up incentives at the top of the house. Rather, management teams should be lumped together, either at the corporate or business unit level, and tied to operating results that create value over time. This is the simplest and most effective approach.

Executives also differ in their perceptions of and tolerances for risk. This calls for another simplifying prescription. Once you have people in an incentive plan, simply assume they are all the same in how they see and price risk. They're executives, after all, not people pulled at random out of the line at the Department of Motor Vehicles. They typically have some wealth and, apparently, some appetite to play in the top levels of enterprise. They'll have a proper fear of risk, but the very concept won't leave them quivering in a corner. Competitively and practically speaking, they'll see some risk as unavoidable.

Let's just treat this issue in the blanket way we treat other matters — like whether they respond to money incentives (yes, let's assume), whether they will quit if we are cheap on pay (a risk prudent to avoid) and whether they will cheat if the pay plans allow (probably some of the time, so let's be careful). How can the pay structure accommodate risk differences among executives? Here are some examples:

- **With exercise features of long-term incentive plans.** These allow executives to take some money off the table when needed for liquidity or risk management purposes.

- **With stock purchase and deferred compensation programs.** These allow executives to elect to put their pay back into the company, perhaps allowing it to continue to ride based upon corporate or business unit performance.

- **With incentive plans that encourage management, as co-investors, to pursue the best paths for their businesses.** These are based on their own best assessments of business prospects and risks.

- **Using a "buy-in" deal, like bonus give-ups, as part of a new long-term incentive plan.** (See phantom stock example in Chapter 8.) This encourages the confident and entrepreneurial types to self-select into higher levels of plan participation.

From the Illusion of Control to Actual Control

In the bull market of the 1990s, stock option grants gave many executives an unusual sense of control. Company financial successes seemed to boost stock prices directly. High performing business units often saw coincident gains in the corporate share price as a reliable example of cause and effect and as direct credit for their contributions. Executives looked at their rising market valuations and in them saw reflections of their personal competence. The ability to exercise options, and to "time" the gain based upon an assessment of the stock's future direction, seemed to firm up a sense of mastery of the universe. The system was working just fine, and executives were in charge.

Lottery tickets did pretty well in the 1990s too. Huge, multi-state pots were in the headlines. People waited in long lines, envisioning riches to come. States found that enabling people to call out their own lucky numbers gave them a sense of control that made these products even more appealing. Lotteries are still going strong, but, where the stock market is concerned, people now have a greater sense of market risk and less a sense of control.

The notion of control allows us to look at business risks and see which ones are productive within an incentive plan and which are not. We can separate risks into those that are good and bad. Entrepreneurial risk is relatively comfortable for management, at least those who are competent and confident. Being subjected to a lot of risks beyond one's control, on the other hand, is a bad thing. If someone runs a big business unit, business unit results contain acceptable risks, for the most part. Results of other business units and market vagaries are not. Risks that are opaque — those affecting payouts in a confusing incentive plan, for example — are unfavorable on this scale.

Increasing the line of sight within incentive plans — the actual control over results — is a good trade for the company to make within its incentive structure. It can do this by putting in operating incentive plans in full or partial replacement of stock-based pay and by pushing plan metrics down to the levels of various business units. In such plans, the risks that executives bear are concentrated around a reasonable source — actual financial performance of a business unit over which they have some control.

Risk and the Term Structure of Incentive Pay

For most senior managers, a bonus plan offers high line of sight — from business actions to results and rewards. But designs and metrics often change, and future targets and opportunities always are up for re-negotiation, so focusing upon future results rather than current ones often is just a bad bet from a pay viewpoint. And, again, option grants aren't really incentives at all since they are mainly based on a stock price one cannot affect. That means the working end of the incentive structure is short-term.

This is a problem. Many business opportunities that senior management may pursue involve not only a balanced view of risks, but also a longer-run profile for return. A short-term bias in the incentive structure will encourage executives to chase only those business initiatives paying off within the crimped time frame and performance interval of the current bonus plan. This almost certainly discourages good longer-run initiatives at many companies, simply because so many profitable business initiatives have a multi-year timeframe for generating high returns.

That would be a problem even with no business risk at all. An investment yielding zero return in its first year and very high, certain returns in all subsequent years would not pay in most bonus plans. Because the investment does not increase income in the current year, the executive would get no bonus. Expected returns on the investment in future years, being certain and obvious, would be built into the budget-based targets used in most plans. So, in exchange for making a good investment, the executive gets no current reward and higher performance goals that offset gains in future years. Bad investments work similarly. Their substandard income levels normally work to reduce future budgets.

Risk adds more problems when trying to figure out whether a given incentive structure will encourage high returns or not. This has to do with the nature of risk and long-run results. Business decision-making is done under conditions of uncertainty and therefore is the same thing as betting, to a certain extent. Business people, for their part, are good intuitive statisticians and hold superior knowledge about the specific prospects and risks of their businesses. As investors, we pay them to make good bets on our behalf.

Here is the statistical problem with short-term thinking. Many business bets become safer when their returns are allowed to run for a few years, but they look risky nontheless to anyone who has a short view. Operating income of a typical business — measured around a trend line or a given target — has a standard deviation between 15 percent and 20 percent per year and follows a reasonably normal distribution. Take a business investment (a good, value-creating one, let's assume) with a $50 expected level of operating income per year and a 20 percent standard deviation. The standard deviation is $10 in dollar terms, so the business would expect to have operating income between $40 and $60 around two-thirds of the time. Expected income over three years is three times higher at $150 but the expected risk is not three times higher; the standard deviation is $17.30, only 12 percent of expected income. Having a financial claim upon three years of performance means having, in essence, three rolls of the dice. Three years of performance causes a risk reduction similar to the diversification effects of holding three securities in a portfolio rather than one. The annual expected return remains $50, but it becomes more predictable — safer — when measured over three years.

This makes an executive with a longer-term time frame more likely to accept it based upon his or her own personal risk tolerances. An executive with a short-term perspective will see it as riskier — because it is, within the shorter time frame — and will be more likely to turn down this deal. And remember, this is a good deal and not a particularly risky one.

Typical incentive ranges compound this problem. Another reason to turn down this decision in the near term is that it might bring income above the plan's maximum, rendering at least a portion of the returns ineligible for reward in the current year. Longer-term results are more predictable and therefore more likely to be rewarded within a given performance range. (Setting performance ranges properly is a good solution here, too; see Chapter 9.)

Overall, near-term results are a crapshoot while longer-term results are more predictable. If the incentive structure is short-term, it will make many good business actions appear intolerably risky and at least partly ineligible for reward.

The incentive structure can be moved toward the longer term using these approaches:

- Performance shares earned based upon consolidated results, for corporate-level officers

- Performance share, unit or phantom stock plans based upon business unit results, for reasonably separable business units

- Enduring, adaptive methods for measurement and standard-setting in the annual incentive plan, creating a concrete, multi-year claim upon future business results

- A restructured incentive mix, particularly if short-term when compared to the market's short-term incentive/long-term incentive mix.

Structures like these can create a situation in which all members of management feel they have a stake in medium- to long-term financial results. They have a financial stake resembling ownership; clear, concrete, continuous, and unlimited. In a structure like this, risk-related incentives in the plan effectively piggyback on the executives' personal risk tolerances. If they take risks on the part of investors, they share in those risks and stand ready to share in the gains, as well.

Even though executives' views of risk are not exactly like investors', piggybacking on their personal risk tolerances can be a good idea. The typical plan structure does not allow fine-tuning the risk aspects of business decision-making. It does not allow the practical implementation of project-specific costs of capital, for example, or deal- or initiative-specific costs. You can adjust the cost of risk by business unit, but that will not get concerns about differential risk onto the table consistently at those times when it matters.

A more consistent method is to make it clear that all business gains and losses will affect executive pocketbooks over time. Once executives understand that they share all risks and gains from their actions, they are much more likely to balance risks against gains sensibly. A drawback is that this may lead to risk aversion, which makes it critical for plan communication to emphasize risk/reward tradeoffs.

Capital-Related Risk Issues

The metrics used in many bonus and performance plans simply underweight the amount of capital used by the business, placing disproportionate emphasis upon profit and revenue. This encourages many value-destroying decisions, irrespective of risk, since one can be paid for putting capital into low-rent uses as long as they generate at least a modest improvement in income.

Capital measurement also carries some risk-related consequences. Since capital is priced too cheaply within many plans, it can encourage management to gamble more than it otherwise would. Business gambling often involves putting up capital as stakes and getting income and cash flow as the payoff. Income almost always is recognized as such in financial statements. Capital usage — or the foregone income opportunity it carries — usually is not apparent in the metrics used in incentive plans. So a structure that is light on capital means management gets all the upside of the gamble but suffers a disproportionately small cost if it is wasted.

I noted earlier that company incentive structures often are short-term and may under-reward longer-term investing. Companies sometimes adjust for this by granting "relief" for the capital costs of bigger investments like acquisitions or plant construction and immunizing financial results, in full or in part, for their effects. The problem with this is that it dilutes accountability for big decisions. It either strikes their capital costs out of the incentive system entirely or attempts to defer them into future years' incentive targets. Future bonuses are uncertain, and so is the accountability for any such deferrals, so the incentive structure may encourage excessive risk taking. You get whatever gains the bet produces now. Later, you pay, at most, only the partial costs of the bet.

For solutions, companies should use metrics or other plan terms that account fully for income and the use of capital over time, such as:

- Total business return or economic profit, which take into account income, capital and risk

- Combinations of traditional metrics (e.g., ROIC and operating income) that reflect both capital usage and income, with the balance between their respective effects being driven by the cost of capital

- Target-setting approaches that take account of capital usage.

In all cases, there should be a clear emphasis on capital usage in plan-related communication.

Growth Bias, Capital Usage and the 'Total Return' Plan Format

Total-return-based solutions are worth separate discussion. A total return measurement format covers the main moving parts of value creation and can be useful as a solution to many performance measurement issues in companies. Risk is one. Under these approaches (various forms of total business return or total shareholder return), business financial performance is measured based upon the two main ways in which it serves the financial interests of shareholders:

- By increasing the value of the business they own, and

- By generating cash flows from operations that can be distributed to them (free cash flows).

If the incentive plan pays for growth only — ignoring the cash yield from a business irrespective of its growth rate — then it will favor the pursuit of high growth rates all of the time, in all business conditions, without full regard for the costs and risks involved. Total return plans create an explicit reward for business growth on the one hand and cash yield on the other. They clearly express the notion of balance rather than the more typical message that growth, no matter the risks and costs, is the only thing that pays. They make it clear that there are rewards under a range of different business conditions, not just in strong markets. This helps reinforce the message that management has a plausible long-run stake in results, not one that will automatically be invalidated if business conditions change.

Risk Management Policies, Stock-Based Incentives and Top Officer Rewards

No matter what public companies do with incentive structure for the broad senior management group, they surely will end up with the few top officers having a lot of exposure to stock price movement. Even if they reduce stock option usage, there will still be a lot of stock-based incentive pay in the future for people at this level (e.g., performance shares, restricted stock). This, combined with past grants and stock holdings, means that differential rewards for these people will continue to be mainly about share price movement. So, for the few top officers, the stock market will stay in the driver's seat where their incentive rewards are concerned. It will dictate — to the extent the stock market can be said to communicate, in a rewards context — how these people get paid for risk management just as for every other dimension of what they do.

If the company uses particularly distinctive risk management or hedging policies, the incentive system will encourage it to do so to the extent it increases share price. Similarly, it will encourage any risk-related aspects of diversification, business integration, restructuring, or arrangements with suppliers or customers to the extent such activities create value.

The market's understanding and valuation of senior management's actions should motivate executives to do a proper job of risk management. Understanding is a big element of the mechanism. For many dimensions of performance at many companies, the stock market understands business policies and discounts them very well into the stock price. It does this so well, incorporating information in such a complete and instant way, that markets are largely "efficient" and stock price movements are largely a "random walk."

I would not rely on the market to do this properly in all cases, though. In the case of a publicly traded mortgage industry client, for example, hedging practices appeared complex and opaque to the market. In this case, it appeared that getting proper market recognition for risk-adjusted performance would depend heavily upon the specific dialog between its CEO and investors.

Whether the market understands all of a company's risk management dealings or not, it will be making valuation judgments about them, and those could go one way or the other:

- The market may regard a particular company's risk management practices as valuable. More intensive management of risk does create a demonstrably more stable stream of earnings returns. This may appeal to investors. They may see the costs of the various hedging tactics as cheap in relation to risk reduction.

- On the other hand, investors may not attach much value to a company's risk management regimen. They may see many of a company's unique risks as largely diversifiable ones within their own portfolios. They may regard the likelihood of financial distress as being low, so they are not comfortable with the company going to unusual lengths to insure against it. They may see the overall costs of risk management practices as unfavorable in relation to their benefits.

Public company systems will rely inescapably upon the stock market to reward top officers for proper risk management. The stock market's feedback to the company and its top officers — investor and analyst dialog, the overall level of valuation of its shares, the valuation response to specific news — should be very rich in terms of risk assessment.

The dynamics of stock-based incentives can affect certain business practices at a level as specific as this. How much cost a company is willing to bear to be immunized from certain risks should be affected by the extent to which the stock market appears willing to pay for that sort of insurance. Relying on the stock market to fulfill this kind of specific role within the incentive structure is not that unusual. I often suggest that companies look to the market's valuation mechanism as the way to get rewarded for capital structure policy (immunizing plan goals from such changes, in contrast, since few people affect them). More companies are likely to parse their incentive performance standards in this way in the future as they move away from heavy stock option usage. They are likely to give more thought to which aspects of performance they are encouraging by using stock as an incentive currency and which they are encouraging through the formal goals that will appear in more and more long-term incentive plans.

The Wages of Risk: Estimating the Cost of Capital

Whether the cost of capital is at one level or another has strong effects upon business value. Going back to the discounted cash flow (DCF) example at the beginning of this chapter, a decrease in the cost of capital to 8 percent has the effect of increasing the value of the enterprise by 25 percent.[2] An increase in the cost of capital to 12 percent reduces value by 17 percent. In many other, more typical DCF model scenarios — ones with moderate growth, capital increases and longer forecast terms — the effects of changes in the cost of capital are even greater.

Getting the cost of capital right clearly is an important matter in valuing the enterprise. In a valuation context, the stakes on precision are high. Risk estimation and the cost of capital are not only important matters in the valuation arena, but also complex, ambiguous and sometimes controversial ones. That's true in some other areas of corporate finance as well, like investment evaluation and financing policy.

It is not true, for the most part, when designing incentive plans. The current situation is that most incentive plans impose only weak and vague accountability for the use of capital and opportunity cost. For companies wishing to use incentives to create value, this blind spot obscures two of the three main value drivers: both capital and risk. Companies should fix this issue, and they can do so in a wide range of practicable ways within their incentive structures. But costs of capital need not be set for incentive purposes with nearly the precision required for other applications.

The cost of capital for a business is the rate of return required by investors in order to compensate them for the risks they bear. The cost of debt to the company is equal to the overall interest rate paid on borrowings. Since debt is deductible from income taxes for a taxpaying corporation, debt financing has certain tax benefits commonly assumed to contribute to the value of the business. By convention, these tax benefits are taken into account by stating the cost of debt on an after-tax basis. A company with an overall borrowing cost of 6 percent and a tax rate of 33 percent would have an after-tax cost of debt capital of 4 percent (6 percent * [1 – 33 percent]).

Let's just assume for the moment that the cost of equity capital is 10 percent. To figure out the company's overall cost of capital, the costs of debt and equity are averaged together based upon the levels of debt and equity used. If the company's value consists one-third of debt and two-thirds of equity, its weighted-average cost of capital (WACC) is 8 percent. (See Figure 5-1.)

This actually is a typical figure for a medium to large public company with average risk. So, what does the 8 percent cost of capital represent? Three main things:

FIGURE 5-1: WEIGHTED-AVERAGE COST OF CAPITAL EXAMPLE			
Capital Source	Weighting	After-Tax Cost	Weighted Cost
Equity	67%	10%	6.67%
Debt	33%	4%	1.33%
Total			8.00%

- When the company makes a typical investment within its business, it needs to get a rate of return on investment over time of 8 percent in order to satisfy its investors. If it gets a higher rate of return, the investment creates value for shareholders by generating residual, or excess, income. If it gets a lower return, the investment destroys value. Many incentive plans fail to reflect this economic fact. Remedying this basic issue is one of the main ways in which we can improve company incentives.

- To value the business, we should discount future cash flows at an annual rate of 8 percent. This will be a key parameter later in this book when we are setting performance targets in incentive plans. It will allow us to examine a company's stock price and unlock the information it holds about what performance needs to be in order to satisfy investors. It also allows us to compute the capitalized value of current operations. That, again, is the value made apparent by the company's actual financial results, and it is a reasonable basis for scaling rewards under certain incentive structures.

- As we saw at the end of Chapter 4, if the company's results in the future are equal to expected levels, then, holding all else equal, the company's total return to investors will equal 8 percent.

Beta Coefficients and the Capital Asset Pricing Model

The actual cost of equity for a company is trickier to determine than the cost of debt because expected returns on stock investments cannot be observed as directly as debt interest rates. Companies have to use estimation methods to attach a reasonable cost to equity. The capital asset pricing model (CAPM) is the technique used most often by companies to judge the overall risk of a business and to attach a cost to the capital it uses.[3] CAPM is derived first by making certain assumptions about investor attitudes and the structure of capital markets. Then, investor behavior is predicted, as well as the mechanism investors will use to price risk:

- CAPM assumes that investors are risk-averse. For a given level of expected return, they prefer investments offering lower risk. Diversification reduces risk. A combination of risky securities — a portfolio — will have lower overall variability in return than the average of the individual securities in the portfolio. This is because the gains on some securities will offset losses on others as long as their returns aren't perfectly positively correlated.

- Capital markets offer a wide range of investment choices. Investors, in their search to reduce risk, can be expected to hold broadly diversified portfolios. Investors can improve their investment risk/reward profiles even further by combining their risky asset portfolios in various ways with "risk-free" investments like U.S. Treasury securities. Following CAPM's strict assumptions, investors are actually found to hold the same "market portfolio" of risky securities. They combine such holdings with risk-free investments in various ways to suit their individual risk tolerances. This strategy allows investors to get the highest returns at every risk level and to create a portfolio whose risk/return trade-off suits them best.

- In that situation, the relevant measure of risk for a particular security is how much risk it adds to the market portfolio of risky securities, the one that everyone who owns any risky securities is likely to hold. That risk contribution is measured by seeing how much the security's returns co-vary with returns on the market portfolio. The rest of the security's variability is unrelated to the market portfolio's movements, so it disappears in the diversification process. In a CAPM world, investors demand a return only on the covariant part, since that is the only part that increases their portfolio's risk and therefore subjects them to any incremental risk.

This covariant risk metric is called the beta coefficient. A company with average risk will post a beta of 1.0. Beta runs mostly in the range of 0.6 to 1.4, with 0.6 being low risk and 1.4 being high risk. If a company's own beta cannot be observed (because it is a private company or a business unit, for example) then betas of peer companies may be consulted as an indication of risk level.[4]

CAPM uses beta to figure out the cost of equity. A typical formulation expresses the expected rate of return on an equity security (Ke) as a function of the company's beta coefficient (b), the risk-free rate of return (Rf) and the market equity risk premium (Rm – Rf):

$$Ke = Rf + b\,(\,Rm - Rf\,)$$

The market equity risk premium is the higher return that market investors demand on an average stock investment, over a risk-free investment like a Treasury security, to compensate for the additional risks involved.

The risk-free rate in the United States typically is taken to be the yield to maturity on long-term U.S. Treasury bonds. Long Treasury bonds are hardly risk-free. They are subject to principal value risk if they aren't held to maturity, reinvestment rate risk if they are, purchasing power risks depending upon inflation rates and even default risk in the unlikely event of a global economic meltdown. Nonetheless, they provide a baseline estimate of the real rate of return for investments with little risk plus the yield premia associated with a long-term maturity and inflationary expectations.

Normalizing the risk-free rate at 5 percent and adding the risk premium for equity investments, typically estimated in the 4 percent to 6 percent range, provides an overall equity rate of return centered on 10 percent for an average company. A low-risk company with a beta of 0.6 would have an equity cost of 8.0 percent, while a high-risk company beta of 1.4 would warrant a rate of return of 12.0 percent. This range covers the landscape for most medium to large companies under typical market conditions.

Financial Leverage and the Cost of Capital

Start-ups, particularly those with venture financing, sometimes cite higher equity rates of return. Depending upon the nature of the investment, venture capital and private equity firms cite expected portfolio rates of return from 15 percent up to the 40 percent to 50 percent range per year.

Financial leverage explains some of these higher yields since it affects the risks built into the costs of debt and equity. Whether it affects the cost of capital overall or should affect incentive pay is another matter. For example, expected returns on equity in the 15 percent range would be reasonable in a leveraged buyout of a mature, moderate-risk company. If the company's purchase was financed 80 percent with debt at a relatively high pre-tax cost of 9 percent and a 33 percent tax rate, the debt portion of the capital structure would represent a cost of about 5 percent of the deal price [80 percent debt * 9 percent cost of debt * (1 – 33 percent tax rate)]. With a 15 percent equity rate of return, the overall cost of capital works out to be the run-of-the-mill 8 percent computed earlier (15 percent cost of equity * 20 percent equity weighting is 3 percent of deal cost, plus 5 percent debt component of cost = 8 percent).

The math in these examples shows that financial leverage does not necessarily affect the cost of capital or the value of the business. In this case, a big change in capital structure simply redistributed risk between equity and debt investors. Whether or not leverage affects value, and to what extent, are subjects of ongoing investigation by academics, experimentation by companies and marketing by financiers. Historically, companies assumed that an optimal capital structure should be pursued, one balancing the risks and interest rate costs of higher financial leverage with its tax benefits.

Nobel Prize winners Modigliani and Miller identified conditions in which firms might be indifferent to capital structure, how tax policy might encourage firms to maximize debt financing, and how costs of financial distress would act to moderate levels of financial leverage actually used. Further work has looked into ways in which investor arbitrage might eliminate any discounts in the stock prices of the under-leveraged. If there are significant valuation gains to be had by changing capital structure, after all, many actors in capital markets will try very hard to make any such changes happen. Investors don't leave that kind of money lying in the street. They might substitute personal leverage for corporate leverage, for example, continuing to the point where they've bid up the company's share price and eliminated any discount. Or they might simply take over under-leveraged firms, re-capitalizing them and pocketing any gains. The mere threat of this would narrow any discounts in advance. Overall, one must conclude that any effects of financial leverage on the overall value of an enterprise are modest and uncertain.

Other Methods and Evidence for Attaching a Cost to Capital

Methods other than CAPM can be used to measure and price business risk. For those uncomfortable with CAPM's dismissive treatment of diversifiable risks, there is the method of looking at overall risk rather than just its market-covariant "beta" element. Another method involves focusing on that part of risk that really frightens the risk-averse — the downside — by looking at the semi-variance. It also is possible to disaggregate risks in various ways — splitting overall risk into business and financial leverage components, for example — or foreign investment risks into business, currency and expropriation elements. This allows pricing of risk by element, either through present value discounting or through risk charges like synthetic insurance or hedging costs.

Bond yield premia are a good source of information about the prevailing prices for various elements of risk. The risk premiums among junk, high quality corporate bonds and T-bonds say a lot about how much risk investors are willing to bear for another point or two of yield. T-bonds convey information about the base level of returns needed on any long-term investment, and inflation-adjusted bonds expose inflation's contribution to them. One method known as arbitrage pricing theory, or APT, specifies numerous drivers of the cost of capital. A less sophisticated method, but one that effectively remains in wide use, simply takes a risk-free rate or cost of debt rate and adds a rough risk premium to it based upon the judged risk of the deal or the investment. New methods surface periodically in the financial press.

Don't Split Hairs

Capital markets and enterprises exist in a big, complex, risky world. There are lots of ways in which risk is measured, bought and sold. It does not have to be all that complicated for our purposes, though. For a wide range of companies, I have used costs of capital mainly in the 7 percent to 15 percent range. Readily observable risk levels typically have placed companies clearly into one segment or another of the range.

In business valuation, costs of capital do matter greatly. Small differences in expected returns do have big impacts upon security prices. In the incentive design arena, in contrast, simplicity is more powerful than precision. Here, it is counter-productive to argue about a few basis points. Using a rounded figure for the plan's cost of capital — like 10 percent, for example — has the material advantage of allowing break-even returns on investment to be calculated easily. Within incentive plans, simply giving rough justice to the cost of capital is a huge improvement over the current state of economic lawlessness. Over-detailing the cost of capital complicates the plan and makes it less effective. It is one of the areas in which value-based incentive plans sometimes fail.[5]

This advice differs strongly from the views sometimes taken by company financial management and from many consultants specializing in value-based solutions, so let us provide some supporting observations.

Incentive plans, even ones adhering to important valuation principles, typically involve rough procedures for performance measurement, grant administration and adjustment of results. These terms affect the cost of capital and the monetary risk truly faced by the participant, with much larger impacts than any small differences in the formal cost of capital.

Business risk affects the cost of capital. This chapter described some of the conventions used by investors when assessing business risk. An executive may price the risk of business decisions very differently than shareholders. The financial interests of executives, unlike those of shareholders, are undiversified, illiquid, long-term and often more strongly tied with the prospect of career advancement than anything else. In an incentive design context, addressing these is more important than getting the cost of capital just right from an investor perspective.

Labor markets, like capital markets, involve risk intermediaries. Companies offer relatively safe compensation and benefit packages to most of the workforce, providing valuable income security. Investors as a group bear greater risk in terms of their compensation from the enterprise. Top management's compensation structure is highly variable as well, but nothing in the equation dictates that it must be the same as that of owners. It actually would be an enormous coincidence if the normal hodgepodge of incentives, salaries and benefits worked out to resemble an investor's financial claim. Attempts to fine-tune the price of risk through some incentive plan's cost of capital would pale in relation to these considerations.

Costs of capital are driven by prevailing yields on capital market investments, to some likely but modest extent by capital structure, and by business risk. Executives have no impact upon the first of these factors and only a few can affect the second. We identified the third factor, business risk, as a poor candidate for incentive micro-management. This does not mean that these factors should not be priced fully within the workings of an incentive plan. They definitely should be, otherwise the plan will not attach a proper cost to new capital and will permit many value-destroying actions to be rewarded. But changes in the cost of capital should not be driving the variation in overall incentive awards particularly strongly. Otherwise, uncontrollable variables are in the driver's seat of incentive pay, and that is almost always bad for efficacy. Costs of capital should be set at rough, reasonable levels and not amended frequently.

The economic guidance provided by incentive plans does not replace the company's other tools of financial governance. Almost all corporations evaluate large investments and other initiatives with a fairly close eye on the risks involved and returns needed. That is the company's opportunity to apply precise, up-to-date, project-specific costs of capital, fine-tuning business decisions to create the most value. Incentive plans, in contrast, are blunt instruments. Their overall effects upon the company's investment evaluation process can be very positive, to be sure. They can create new accountability for capital outlays and their general opportunity costs. To achieve these effects, though, incentive plans need not use exactly the same costs of capital used for project evaluation, treat them with nearly as much precision, or apply them in a variable, piecemeal way to each of a company's business initiatives. Incentive plans can provide consistent thematic and directional guidance to business decision-making and they can do so in a way that is comprehensive and compelling. Just don't ask them to take you to the third decimal point on each initiative.

Overall, in most incentive design applications, the cost of capital need not be a troublesome matter.[6] My general prescription for the cost of capital is to use a reasonable, rounded figure for the entire company, allowing it to vary among business units or over time only when material differences emerge. And, to be clear, incentive plans do not have to feature an explicit cost of capital. They merely need to impose an income hurdle consistent with the cost of capital when the enterprise uses new capital. They can accomplish that in lots of ways, which we'll see in later chapters.[7]

At the same time, company incentive mechanisms must recognize that investor returns are strongly affected when costs of capital change. Accordingly, costs of capital should not be made so inflexible that executive gains are discon-nected with those of investors. Instead:

- Keep the cost of capital construct fixed for the duration of individual grants like bonuses, phantom stock grants or performance share or unit grants.

- If the cost of capital changes materially, take this into account when setting up future long-term incentive grants and bonuses.

Management can pursue high- or low-risk business strategies and thereby affect the cost of capital. If such actions cause a material change in it, some aspect of the incentive structure should be adjusted to reflect this. Targets can be amended to demand higher or lower returns, for example, or metrics or award schedules can be adjusted to attach updated costs to new capital usage. However, as the front section of this chapter suggested, the plan's terms themselves can address much of what is relevant about business risk. They can subject executive pay to the full set of ups and downs in business results and encourage participants to balance these risks personally. In their agency role, executives decide many things on behalf of owners. The hurdle rates applied to business decisions are among those things. The incentive structure can improve business governance by placing consistent, reasonable costs on capital usage.

Endnotes

1   See *Options Markets*, John C. Cox and Mark Rubenstein, Prentice Hall, 1985.

2   The initial example is a zero-growth perpetuity, so it can be valued by taking the annual FCF and dividing it by the cost of capital. At a 10 percent cost of capital, the enterprise is worth $1,000. At an 8 percent cost of capital, it is worth $1,250 ($100/8 percent).

3   See the article "Best Practices in Estimating the Cost of Capital: Survey and Synthesis," Robert F. Bruner, Kenneth M. Eades, Robert C. Higgins. Robert S. Harris, *Financial Practice and Education*, Spring/Summer 1998, excerpted in *Harvard Business Review*, September 1996. The authors found the capital asset pricing model is by far the method used most commonly by companies to set costs of equity capital.

4   Financial leverage affects betas. More highly indebted companies have more variable equity returns, so they have higher measured betas. Peer betas may need some adjustment if the peers have capital structures differing greatly from those of the subject company. In those cases, the observed betas on peers can be "un-levered" to a zero debt equivalent beta (an asset beta), then levered back up to the level of the subject company.

5   A similar, common issue is the procedures used to adjust targets and results for various business events. That is another area in which a preference for financial precision simply overcomplicates the plan and reduces its efficacy. This issue is detailed in the discussion of metrics in Chapter 8.

6   The main exception to this rule is in the area of expectations-based target setting. These techniques, detailed in Chapter 9, involve "fitting" a DCF to a company's stock price in order to extract information about the performance expectations that support it. That procedure is essentially the reverse of the business valuation process and requires some precision in risk assessment and cost of capital estimation.

7   Techniques presented in later chapters include applying a "capital charge" within a residual income metric or using a capitalization rate within metrics like SVA or TBR (Chapter 8). Companies also can set up award schedules that trade off income and capital effects in accordance with the cost of capital by, for example, using combinations of metrics like operating income and ROIC (Chapter 7). They also can use a range of target-setting methods that take account of shareholder criteria for returns on new capital (Chapter 9). Granting levels under incentive plans of all kinds can be benchmarked for their overall dilution effects, taking into account the effects of cost of capital on shareholder resources (one example appears in Chapter 10).

6

Pay for The Right Stuff — Do's and Don'ts of Performance Measurement at the Senior Management Level

Stock-based grants, particularly stock options, blur the lines of sight that run from management's actions to performance to rewards. In light of that, companies should make a lot fewer vanilla option and stock grants, and instead:

- Make much more prominent use of operating incentives; incentives tied to operating performance rather than exclusively to stock price movement

- Concentrate much more incentive potential at the business unit level

- Focus incentive plans on shareholder value creation.

This means using more performance unit plans — ones that deliver cash when long-term business goals are achieved. It also means using performance goals to a greater extent within stock-based incentive plans — through performance share grants, for example, or stock grants whose vesting accelerates based upon performance. It means making sure that all incentive plans deliver pay only when company performance warrants — when it supports value creation. And it means rewarding success decisively whether it is found at the corporate, group, division or profit center level. Do you know what all these solutions have in common? They take formal goals and metrics, place a lot more weight on them and bring them much closer to home, making company processes for performance measurement and goal setting an even bigger deal than they are now.

The new system of metrics and incentives will be more challenging to run than the one in place at most companies. In the structure used commonly now, there are no formal business goals or metrics behind the bulk of top management's incentive pay. Rather, most of the money comes from stock options and restricted stock grants. Income from those depends simply on the number of shares granted and the price they later attain. In that system, it is the stock market that sets expectations for performance and decides what gains have been earned. The market is remarkably astute and efficient, to be sure, when it values company shares. But, to most, its mechanism is mysterious, distant and unsteady. It doesn't work as an incentive for many people.

Running stock-based incentive plans is a little too easy. Here is how it works much of the time. First, you figure out how many options each person should get, mainly by studying competitive data. Along the way, some thought may go to the question of how company culture interacts with the breadth of plan eligibility. The plan might address some other specific factors purported to drive the pay mix as well. But, as noted in Chapter 3, the design process produces remarkably similar results across very different types of companies. There may be a lot of talk about executive incentives being driven by the specifics of company strategy and setting, but there isn't a whole lot of customizing discernible in the end results.

If companies are going to do a better job with their incentive plans, they're going to have to turn off the autopilot. They will have to stop outsourcing the most difficult work of senior management pay administration to the stock market. In particular, they must take control of the standard-setting and measurement processes that deliver the bulk of incentive pay and transform them into real business performance tools. And here is the rub: they can't use the metrics and target-setting processes they have now. They can't just load more incentive potential on budgets and earnings per share (EPS). Current methods are like an unstable vehicle. If you put these additional burdens on it, it will end up in the ditch.

To understand how incentives should be structured for people in senior management, we start with a couple of baseline ideas:

- People in senior management have a material impact, either by themselves or by working within a management team, upon the financial results of the overall company or a business unit within it.

- Here, we are talking about that element of the executive rewards structure called incentive pay. *It should be based preponderantly upon financial performance — particularly on the controllable elements and those linked most closely with value creation.*

At most companies, senior management incentive pay should not be based much, if at all, upon individual goals or other nonfinancial yardsticks. It should be based on well-constructed measures of actual financial success. This is a key assertion, one going to the heart of management's role in the enterprise. This book's discussion of incentive metrics is concerned mainly with measures of financial performance. That's where the money is in operating incentive plans, and that's where it should be most of the time. It is also where there are big problems that, if remedied, hold the promise of improving business results significantly.

It's often thought that bonus plans are a good medium for rewarding individual performance, but, at the senior management level, most companies do not make this choice. For one thing, many bonus plans attach no part of awards to individual performance, departmental goals or any nonfinancial metrics. In long-term operating incentive plans like performance plans, nonfinancial goals are even more unusual.

Many bonus plans do attach some part of awards to individual or depart-mental results. However, we actually disregarded the role of individual performance when we conducted the statistical simulations in Chapter 2. That was because, among those companies that do attach some award potential to individual performance at the senior management level, the effects on actual payouts tend to be very muted:

- When included at all, individual performance is assigned a low weighting. About one-third of the companies in Towers Perrin's annual incentive plan design survey assigned a specific weight to individual performance. Among these, the median weight for top officers is 25 percent.

- Individual or departmental performance sometimes is used as an award modifier and therefore is valued or devalued explicitly based upon financial results rather than being rewarded as an independent matter.

- The overall bonus often is subject to financial performance thresholds, making it even more unlikely that other kinds of goals pay much when they differ in outcome from financial results.

- The individual part of awards often is administered less generously when financial results are poor (and rarely is it increased as an offset).

When bonus time arrives for someone in top management of a corporation or a business unit, there simply isn't much money payable based upon individual performance as a truly separate matter from financial results. That means zero is a workable approximation of the typical weighting of bonus pay on individual performance — of the sway that it actually holds when plans pay out at one level versus another.

Accountability vs. Immunity

The incentive metrics presented in the next two chapters all focus on overall financial results of a company or its business units. This is a very deliberate focus.

It is based on some general assertions about what part of business performance should be used to create the proper levels of financial stake and accountability at the senior management level:

- *Individual results.* When incentive pay is delivered preponderantly based upon financial results, it is driven by the combined performance of a management team. This approach recognizes the strength of contributions by individuals, to be sure, but does not place much value on individual performance beyond its contribution to financial results over time in the business. Considering the scope and nature of management jobs, companies can reasonably approach incentives in this way. They can tell a typical executive, in effect, that if someone in his or her position is spending a lot of time on things that don't preserve or improve financial performance over time, then something is wrong in their priorities. I think most investors would agree with that assertion.

  This isn't the end of the line, of course, for paying the stellar individual or department. Companies pay out a lot of money each year for non-incentive pay programs. The company can give the executive who excels a big increase in salary if it thinks his or her ongoing individual merit is quite high, typically ratcheting up the value of retirement benefits as a result. The company can reduce the individual's salary and all other pay by 100 percent if it holds strongly contrary views. And the company can focus on individual performance in a myriad of other ways that don't actually involve formal pay plans. Peer pressure is a big factor here, one felt strongly by under-performing members of a management team. So is pressure from a boss and, for that matter, from subordinates. The dynamics of a typical management team and its CEO — particularly when the group holds a compelling financial interest in business success — amount to a continuous performance management program. If, on the other hand, the company is one that lets individual performance problems go unchecked, then attaching bonus potential to individual performance won't help because the company won't use that tool decisively. It appears that those companies using heavier weightings on individual and departmental goals are doing so in response to valid aspects of their organizational structure (e.g., centralized structures with large functional and line organizations rather than a set of mostly separable units, product lines or regions).

- *Nonfinancial goals.* Fifty-six percent of respondents to Towers Perrin's survey indicated they assign bonus weight to a nonfinancial measure, with customer satisfaction and employee satisfaction cited most often at 8 percent and 4 percent, respectively. Weightings placed upon these goals tend to be low, so their overall influence in pay delivery is a fraction of their prevalence.

Nonfinancial goals present some of the same issues that make individual performance such a non-starter as an incentive goal at the senior management level. Management's actions, if successful, should show up in remunerable financial results within a reasonable period of time, like one to five years.

Nonfinancial goals are interesting only to the extent that they drive financial success of the business over the long run. Valid nonfinancial goals are subsumed by, and properly represented in, measured financial success in the business. Nonfinancial goals such as customer satisfaction, employee satisfaction, brand recognition and market share may be very rich in concurrent business insight and very worthwhile to measure and pursue. They may be critical elements of broad-based business literacy efforts and even effective in pay delivery in the broader workforce. But they don't broaden the basic system of goals and accountabilities at the senior management level.

Nonfinancial metrics often have a timing advantage. They may be valid leading indicators of future business health and financial success. Surveyed companies cite a desire to support future value creation 38 percent of the time when using such goals. But their "leading" aspect is not necessarily needed at the senior management level. Using general, historical measures of financial performance, senior management's incentive structure can be used to create a continuously forward-looking, long-term claim upon business success. Senior executives, for their part, can be expected to commit to the business and see their actions through before cashing in. At this organizational level, nonfinancial goals do not stem any important time gap.

- *Immunity from "uncontrollables."* Basing pay more heavily on actual financial results partially immunizes senior management from the largest source of pay variation they face now, which is the large movements in stock price — unrelated to actual business results — that drive most gains on stock-based incentives from one year to the next. That is a pretty strong form of immunity, but it is proper for senior management whose strongest impacts are upon business results.

Many companies want to take their plan designs farther down this road, however, putting in place an extensive apparatus of immunization or indexing. They might use performance share plans based upon the indexed metric "relative total shareholder return," for example, or use peer-based metrics of other kinds.[1] They also might use metrics that adjust, at least in part, for strong exogenous drivers: market share rather than revenue, for example, or the customer value-added metrics sometimes applied in electric and gas utilities. To immunize results from uncontrollable matters (e.g., fuel costs, interest rates, exchange rates, housing starts, commodity prices), they sometimes up-weight the more controllable aspects of business performance within their incentives or adjust their metrics or targets outright depending upon the level of these external drivers.

Many businesses have a lot of exposure to outside factors, to be sure. However, the basic structure of operating incentives deals with much of this source of variation. Paying based upon medium- to long-term financial results — through more enduring and adaptable target-setting approaches in annual incentive plans, for example, and through greater use of long-term incentive plans based upon operating goals — increases the "signal to noise" ratio within the incentive structure.

When companies are tempted to immunize or index their results for pay purposes, they often are reacting to garden-variety cyclicality or uncertainty in their business conditions, not to the presence of specific exogenous factors that take business results largely out of management's control. The general target- and range-setting and measurement dynamics of a longer-term incentive structure provide plenty of opportunity to deal with the first two of these factors.

The case of the third factor, exogenously driven results, can be examined statistically. We find the level of inter-correlation in industry stock prices and financial results to be substantial in many sectors. This certainly indicates that results are about opportunity as much as performance. It also indicates the strength of exogenous drivers. However, individual company performance varies strongly within such samples. Overall, there aren't that many sectors in which results really can be said to be out of management's hands — ones in which inter-correlation is far above norms. Those would seem to be the only legitimate cases for indexation or immunization, and they are a mixed prospect even there. For one thing, investors may expect management to take actions to reduce some exogenous risks, through formal hedging operations, for example, or through actions like business diversification, integration, shifting risks to customers or suppliers, or insuring certain risks more strongly.[2] Some very strong exogenous factors (the home construction outlook, for example) are predictable enough that they can be handled through annual target setting.

Lastly, note that relative and immunized metrics can be more complex and can amount to moving targets, likely creating less compelling incentives than those involving absolute business goals. They all work against the important value rule of clear stake and accountability. Overall, these approaches should be used as a last resort, only after exhausting the other, clearer and more effective solutions.

Twenty-five percent of respondents to Towers Perrin's survey indicated consulting peer data when setting performance targets, and 7 percent said they do so for all their metrics. Not all of these use peer results to adjust results after the fact in a formal indexation scheme. This finding suggests that indexation probably is concentrated in those cases in which the concerns about exogenous factors are most valid. That situation could change quickly, though. Changes in option accounting will compel companies to deliver more long-term incentive pay based on formal goals, and difficulties in setting longer term goals will cause them to look again at indexed metrics, particularly relative total shareholder return (TSR). When they do, caveats and considerations like these warrant a look.

Value rules clearly demand that you don't leave your incentive structure largely in the hands of the stock market. They also insist that you don't atomize it into a lot of compartmentalized and subjective goals. Lastly, they don't endorse the general notion of a moving target. You'll be setting new targets each year when you establish new bonus and long-term incentive plan opportunities. For most, that provides all the opportunity needed to adjust goals to new business conditions. Companies should recognize that the new market situation requires them to do a better job of setting performance goals for incentive pay purposes. The bulk of them should address that challenge directly rather than making material use of indexed metrics. Target-setting methods are discussed in Chapter 9.

The prescription about peer-based metrics really applies to all three of these areas: individual goals, nonfinancial goals, and indexing or immunization schemes. If any are used significantly in senior management's incentives, it should be because of clearly distinctive things about the company and its structure. To do so in more typical cases simply insulates management from consequences of their own decisions. The enterprise may act as a risk intermediary for the broader workforce, creating employee rewards packages that insulate them from most business risk in exchange for their valuable work commitments. This can be a very sensible strategy in the broader workforce. When over-applied at the top management level, it risks being counterproductive.

It's better for important decision-makers to stay focused on long-run results, while evaluating all initiatives — product quality improvements, customer service levels, acquisitions and cost reduction efforts. That ought to have a naturally prioritizing effect. Money does talk, after all.

Indeed, one of the most promising things to a typical company, when implementing value rules, is this opportunity to concentrate senior management's incentive rewards upon long-run financial results they can affect. That is where the line of sight is greatest and most compelling, where the power to remedy decision-making biases is held most strongly, and where specific, proper alignment with shareholders is most sensibly pursued. It is the power alley of the executive incentive structure.

The Rich Are Different

Nonfinancial goals may be quite useful in a range of analytical and communication efforts and sometimes even in broad-based pay delivery. Management should adhere to these goals if they are used prominently in communication and variable pay initiatives in the broader enterprise. And they should make the investment in tracking and reporting such business indicators as long as this activity improves business decisions and outcomes. But that doesn't make these goals suitable as the primary basis for rewarding senior management or judging its success. Accountability is defined differently for senior management than for the broader workforce, and this is best kept in mind when looking at their pay.

Let's say management invests a lot of effort in improving the quality of products and customer service, but these efforts don't ever improve financial results. It is not clear that company leadership should be paid for attainment of product quality and customer service goals by themselves. The broader employee base, on the other hand, may be entitled to variable pay delivered on this basis if those were the terms of their plan. They succeeded, after all, in hitting the goals they were given.

Senior management is different. They came up with the goals. If the initiatives devised by management weren't successful, then either they were wrong from the outset or the company got burned by business uncertainties. If they were wrong, executives should not get paid. And if they made a good decision that was thwarted by a bad turn in the business situation, they should not get paid (and vice versa). This is the deal they signed up for. It is one whose risks executives are accustomed to bearing and that they would not escape to any real degree if they quit and took a management job at some other company. It is a risk they are in a financial position to bear as well, so companies don't have to go to a lot of trouble to insulate them from it. The very concept of upside and downside is not going to leave them quivering in a corner.

It is only fitting that senior management should be subjected to the bulk of the risks and rewards of the businesses they run. *Ultimately, management is not in the job of devising strategies and initiatives and seeing them through to completion. Management is in the business of making decisions that actually deliver results over time.* In this example, they did not. In these circumstances, in more successful ones and in all others, the charge of incentives is easily met. All they must do is create a clear and decisive stake in long-term outcomes.

This Scorecard is Balanced, How?

Nonfinancial goals are sometimes held out as leading indicators of value or of ways to add balance to the overall system of metrics in a company. But we don't have to devise leading indicators of future results in order to deliver senior management pay productively. We can wait to see if those results actually occur and then reward them. Managers have to commit to see things through. In exchange for this, the company must commit to reward them decisively when they do. Moreover, we have already seen how a company's share price takes in investor expectations for future performance, reflecting the contribution of customer satisfaction and of other indicators of success in the market. Stock-based pay no doubt will continue to weigh heavily in corporate-level management's incentive structure, so we can expect it to reflect, in roughly discernible terms, those leading indicators the stock market finds most interesting.

Advocates of heavier use of nonfinancial goals — balanced scorecards and the like — tend to see systems that emphasize financial performance as being heavy-handed and rigid, focusing inflexibly upon the bottom line. Actually, the bottom-line approaches are more flexible than alternatives:

- A company that simply ties rewards to persistent, good quality financial results has a system that can pay out well under many, many different business scenarios as long as they create a lot of value. A reality of business success and stock valuation is that many different business profiles and results can bring about a particular level of value creation. That is true across industry peers, among business units of a company and over time in a given business.

- A balanced scorecard, on the other hand, is a script for a specific business drama. Scorecards and other elaborate schemes that take a nonfinancial approach to goals allow very little deviation from the path prescribed. Bonus potential is atomized into a series of different goals, and each is given its own measurement regime and weighting scheme. Management is obliged to hew rather closely to the path set out at the beginning of the year. Conditions may change, and the goals may get stale quickly. The goals, or some important aspect of the way they come together in the incentive scheme, may have been wrong from the outset. The business unit may be a relatively autonomous one but, as far as incentive pay goes, management's latitude has been taken away.[3]

A results-based goal is to ask a coach to win football games. A balanced scorecard would acknowledge the importance of winning, but also require that certain combinations of plays be involved, perhaps irrespective of how the game develops. The balanced scorecard seems to do something else, too. It seems to look down its nose at the coach's inelegant preoccupation with victory. Value rules, in contrast, are about winning persistently.

The scorecard approach is not only a heavy-handed, central planning method, but actually is a trap for the overconfident. We'll see in coming chapters how easy it is for typical, innocuous-looking bonus award schedules to end up with very inappropriate payouts. This is due to the way that metrics, weightings and award ranges can interact.

A system involving nonfinancial goals is obliged to get even more things right. It involves more metrics, more weightings and more interplay. Every nonfinancial metric is several steps removed from the basic drivers of value creation. It must get all these extra steps right and do so in an environment in which any perceived links among goals and eventual value creation are far more tenuous than they are when described directly in terms of long-run financial results. And remember, management is management. Once the game starts, executives hold all the cards. A system like that, used at the center of executive rewards, is just a sucker bet.

The dangers of bad metrics in pay plans are well worth pointing out in stark terms. Again, these goals may be very helpful when used in communication efforts and as part of broad-based variable pay. The process of coming up with them may be marvelously revealing and insightful. But, in many such settings, companies tend to put one measure after another up on the wall like paint chips. Then they don't hesitate to tack the results onto management incentive plans. In practice in many settings, a scorecard is an economically unprincipled device. And since management incentive design is already economically unprincipled, balanced scorecards are not helpful when added to the mix.

David Larcker and Christopher Ittner of the Wharton School surveyed 157 companies about their use of nonfinancial metrics, finding their systems poorly specified and inadequate to the task of delivering management pay.[4] Here are some of their anecdotes:

- Patent-based incentives encouraged managers to increase new filings irrespective of whether it made more sense to license someone else's technology or whether the patents ever earned back their cost or were even put to work.

- A bank based customer service scores on polling of actual visitors to bank branches. A manager coaxed in visitors and plied them with food and drinks.

- Quality targets of an automaker were reached when management reclassified certain flaws as acceptable.

Some companies are making productive use of balanced scorecards as general tools for measurement and communication. If such companies want to have top management and the broader workforce being paid based upon the same scorecard, they should conform the broad-based incentive plans to ones designed appropriately for senior management. That means running a rigorous design process, one correlating the scorecards' measures strongly to actual, value-creating financial results.[5] To do the opposite, to put a lot of typical nonfinancial goals into senior management's plans, is like the tail wagging the pit bull.

Look What They Done to My Strategy

Incentives can assist or endanger important business processes like budgeting, long-range forecasting, capital expenditures review and acquisition selection and pricing. Strategic planning is a serial victim.

Nonfinancial measures often spring from the company's strategic planning process in an attempt to "get focus and accountability." One *Fortune* 500 head of HR remarked on the phenomenon when he said, "Every time we come up with a new strategic initiative, we think we are going to implement it by tying it to comp." This is a common view, cited by 58 percent of surveyed companies that use nonfinancial goals. Companies sometimes use "strategic" goals in partial replacement for financial success in their senior management incentive plans.

How's that working out? Let's look at a couple of examples of the risks here:

- A housewares company prided itself on innovation, noting that a big chunk of its revenues came from new products. Revenue from new products probably was a valid indicator of success in product innovation and very legitimate subject matter for strategy discussions. However, this company made the mistake of setting it up as a goal in incentive plans. Factions of management then busied themselves discontinuing products and replacing them with modestly revised versions of the old ones. This activity did not create any value but it increased revenue from "new" products that counted toward the bonus plan goal.

- Another case didn't involve manipulation. Rather, the harm was done through direct pursuit of the goals. New product revenues were a strategic indicator of success in this example as well, along with high margins. Low margins were a cultural taboo, seen as a failure to innovate and get paid for innovation in the product price. The largest, oldest business unit actually had many mature products sold into markets that focused more upon price than anything else. Trying to keep away from the "third rail" of low margins, this business unit held prices too high, losing market share and, eventually, profit.

The biggest money lost as a result of strategic goals surely stems from the many overpriced acquisitions made in pursuit of strategic growth. News media accounts over the last few years are replete with examples of how large corporations destroyed, in total, hundreds of billions of dollars in market capitalization from ill-conceived, overpriced or badly executed mergers and acquisitions.

How might the company use incentive plans to get real support and accountability for its strategic plans? First, let's consider the case in which the company's strategic plan is a good one — credible, feasible to implement, likely to create value within a reasonable time frame. In this case, incentive plans that emphasize financial success over time will be very supportive of the strategic plan just as they are for any other value-creating initiative.

What if the strategic plan is economic nonsense? It could happen. A scan of any month's *Wall Street Journal* headlines makes it clear that big, bad business strategies are commonplace. Well-designed incentive plans will discourage those just as they do other actions likely to destroy value. This isn't a bad thing. If the idea really is a loser, then management and investors should be happy that the incentive plan is stopping the insanity.

What if there is just a credibility issue, a case in which the broader senior management participant group simply is mistaken about a good strategic plan's merits? In this case, the incentive plans encourage the strategic plan's sponsors to remedy this perception gap. If they fail to do so, the company loses. But they were on track to lose anyway, since a plan that lacks credibility isn't going to find its way properly through the organization. What were they going to do, shove the discredited strategic plans and their goals down everyone's throats by setting them up as gatekeepers in the incentive plan? That would make gamesmanship by participants seem like the high road, not just the easy one. Half-hearted, partial compliance with a new strategic mandate may be worse than repudiation.

Many business observers argue that the bigger problem is not strategy formulation but implementation. Companies can win again and again with less-than-perfect strategies, but they probably can't win with mediocre execution. Decisive incentive plans draw a straight, bold line from strategy formulation right through any successful execution.[6]

The fact that a company happens to have a set of nonfinancial indicators is not by itself reason to obfuscate the senior management incentives. Sure, a company and its board may agree on a particular set of strategies for their businesses. They may want to judge it using a closely defined and balanced set of indicators. They may want to encourage the whole organization to pay attention to details. They may be right in all of this, but they can pursue these wishes in many ways. An executive incentive plan is the wrong tool for the job.

Does This Matter in the Overall Scheme?

The overall incentive scheme consists mainly of stock-based incentives. Some companies believe that all those stock-based grants form an effective bulwark against the various risks we just recounted. Why would management do that kind of thing, they argue? The stock price would fall and they would lose some of their option gains. For reasons noted at length earlier, options do not man this barricade very well. Most option recipients believe, correctly, that they can't do much about the stock price and, in any event, stock and options don't come with instructions on how to create value. What is going to keep management, especially those in business units, from chasing the easy money tied to bad goals in their bonus plan? Some distant, vague threat of marginally reduced option gains? I don't think so. Management's own good judgment and inclinations normally are a strong form of protection here, but incentives should be well designed nonetheless to address those cases when they are not.

There is a serious line-of-sight issue in management incentive structure at many companies. The way to increase line of sight in executive-level incentive plans from their typical, weak levels is not to atomize them into a set of laughably "gameable" nonfinancial goals. If the company wishes to use nonfinancial goals in this effort, it should draw them from a rigorously set system of value drivers.

Shareholders don't have much use, in the end, for relative or immunized business results; their wealth is denominated in absolute terms. They can't spend strategies, either. Rather, strategy formulation and implementation are a means to the end — value creation. And scorecards aren't the frame for judging and rewarding senior management's success. Instead they are tools for management to use in its governance of the broader enterprise. At the executive level, almost all of the business benefit from increasing line of sight is to be gained by creating a well-designed, material money claim upon long-term financial results that participants can influence.

The strategic, nonfinancial, or individual details are best left to the senior management teams that know how to run the business. With pay plans based upon value rules, they have all the incentive in the world to get those details right and use them to encourage great performance from the company.

Endnotes

1 More remarks on relative total shareholder return and other peer-based methods appear in Chapters 9 and 11.

2 This does not assert that any of these is the proper general response to specific, exogenous risks. Whether or not companies should do any of these things is a debatable matter from a financial viewpoint and, in any event, something for them to decide. I'm simply pointing out that the presence of material, exogenous factors does not by itself mean that financial performance is outside the scope of control of management for purposes of incentive pay.

3 This is an example of an over-specified incentive plan. Value-based incentive plans that use too many adjustments have the same problem: trying to use the blunt instrument of an incentive plan to fine-tune business decision-making.

4 "Coming Up Short on Nonfinancial Measurement," *Harvard Business Review*, November 2003.

5 My Towers Perrin colleagues have addressed these issues with balanced scorecards, developing more rigorous "integrated" scorecard goals that are tied strongly to financial results.

6 Towers Perrin's 2003 broad-based (mainly nonmanagement) rewards survey found that high-performing companies create comparatively tight linkages between goals and business strategy. This finding highlights again the distinction between senior management and the broader work force; communication rather than strict cause-and-effect linkages being more important to incentive design in the latter case.

Motive, Means and Method — Evaluating Financial Performance Metrics

A colleague likes to remark that the difference between a good golfer and a bad golfer is that the good golfer knows where his bad shots are going to go. That's what this chapter is about. It shows the pros and cons of various metrics and clarifies the cases where their results depart from value creation. It makes sense that financial results generally drive the delivery of senior management's incentive pay. What doesn't make sense is that so many of the measures in common use today misdirect business decisions. This chapter will demonstrate how to apply value rules to the selection of metrics, and use them to identify deficiencies and consider remedies. This should help companies improve the state of their game, when it comes to incentives, by seeing where they run afoul of value rules and how they can get back in bounds.

Incentive pay is on course for big changes. Let's look at the effects upon Homer, the sample executive we discussed in Chapter 2. Homer is at a particularly important level in the organization where incentives are concerned, and the effects of our recommended changes would mean the most to people like him. This book centers on the Homers of the world: members of the senior management group who are not among the top few corporate officers. They're not only the biggest contingent within senior management; they're arguably the most important when designing incentive plans. Their number is large, so they hold more business knowledge and skill, in sum, than other top echelons. Their place on the organization chart means that they are closer to the details of business unit affairs than those higher up the ladder, and that they have more ability to identify the more pertinent risks or opportunities.

These are the executives who have a lot of discretionary power over things like what information to contribute to company planning efforts, what initiatives to propose, what others to support — where to spend their valuable personal capital, time and effort. They're distinct from the broader workforce because they are in jobs that specifically empower them to have a material impact.

Homer and his peers are found at too great a distance from the CEO, board or shareholders to be monitored directly by them or for stock-based incentives to be particularly effective as agency tools. That means corporate leadership has to lean heavily upon other governance tools — e.g., performance management, rewards systems and financial controls — to be sure these folks are consistently serving shareholders.

A Whole New Ball Game

For reasons set forth in earlier chapters, company incentive structures are going to change greatly over the next few years. When this happens, they're going to change hugely for the Homers of the world. Here is the math:

- As we discussed in Chapter 2, Homer's incentive pay totals $250,000, of which $90,000 is his potential bonus at target and $160,000 is the value of his option grant. Of this, we found that only $45,000 was plausibly within Homer's line of sight — the 50 percent of his bonus based upon his group's operating income.

- Let's say the company wants to increase the line of sight and efficacy of its incentives. It increases the business unit weighting in the bonus plan to 75 percent, so the portion of the bonus payable based upon business unit performance rises to $67,500. It discontinues the options and instead issues performance shares, ones based upon business unit performance. The grants are worth 80 percent of face value, so the $160,000 in long-term incentive grant value will require a grant of $200,000 in shares.

Based upon the particulars of plan design, these changes increased the line-of-sight score, in the statistical simulation of his pay structure that we did in Chapter 2, from 20 percent to 75 percent.[1] Seen another way, we now have $237,500 of incentive pay at risk based upon business unit results, or five times what we had before. This is a huge increase in the stakes the company has placed on the specifics of incentive design at the business unit level, particularly on the metrics. If the plans have encouraged economically profitable growth, they will do so five times as strongly after this restructuring of awards. If bad stuff has been eligible for rewards, on the other hand, these changes will encourage that just as strongly. Perhaps even more strongly since value-destroying actions — like making low-yielding investments and chasing economically unprofitable revenue — often are the easiest actions to take. Money talks, and these changes make it scream.

We can crank up the volume further if it makes sense to do so. The effects cited were attained with a rather moderate change, after all. Homer's incentive deal remains very corporate in appearance. A significant chunk of his bonus is still corporately-determined, and the long-term incentive grant is denominated in shares of the ultimate parent. What if the company had revolutionized pay even further for people at Homer's level? What if the company concluded that people like Homer aren't expected to participate much in corporate matters, can be relied upon to do so when needed, and have bigger fish to fry back at their own offices? In that case, the company might convert all of Homer's incentive potential into business unit plans. Companies sometimes do put business unit heads partly into corporate incentives but leave their direct reports in only the business unit plans.

In that case, we'd be delivering Homer's bonus entirely based on the business unit's results. We'd also be paying the long-term incentive in cash rather than corporate stock, taking the stock-related award leverage in the performance share plan and converting it to a more leveraged stake in business unit results. We'd do that by increasing the slope of the award schedule to provide higher additional pay for each unit of additional business unit performance (without changing pay at target). We'd quickly end up with incentives that vary six to 10 times more in value than before, based upon business unit success.

Let's Get Cynical

Either approach puts a much bigger bounty on business unit success, one that seems big enough to affect results. Does this approach bet too much on money and its influence? Perhaps incentive money doesn't matter all that much. Instead, perhaps most executives practice a kind of capitalistic altruism, always aiming to do right by shareholders even when it threatens their own rewards. If the world actually looked like this, there still would be very strong reasons to align incentive pay with the operant parts of value creation:

- As we've said, stock options don't come with instructions on how to create value. Bonus plans have a more didactic format, but their message often is erroneous since many allow pay to increase when investor returns are falling. Better-designed incentive plans clarify the real path to value creation. Most companies can get better economic yield from business opportunities by evaluating them more consistently in terms of their main value drivers, which are long-run operating income, capital usage and the cost of capital. Linking these concepts to pay is another way to increase their visibility throughout the enterprise and get better business decisions. A well-designed incentive plan is a bully pulpit indeed.

- From a purely fiscal viewpoint, competitive amounts of incentive pay bring a large cost. This cost behaves better if it is funded by value creation close to the source. In that case, measures of business results — ones used to make business decisions — are netted at every level by the substantial pay costs they entrain. A more complete portrayal of the net success of business units allows better judgments about them, better resource allocation and better results over time.

Incentives do matter for at least some of the people some of the time. A certain amount of diligence in these matters is required just as it is for other commitments made on behalf of owners. Just as companies do when forming legal contracts, companies should design incentives under the assumption that the parties will not act exclusively in their mutual interests in the future — and for that matter, that it will not always be sunny outside.

The problem with a broad-based assumption of altruism is that it is very often wrong. Recall the Michael Douglas character in a signature movie of the 1980s, *Wall Street*, and his tagline, Greed is good. For incentive purposes, greed is good. Greed is reliable as a motive while altruism is not. Companies can depend on it.

As for investors, they want competitive, money-focused people running their companies. When these people are using resources and chasing business opportunities, investors want them to covet gains and fear risks. If they didn't have a healthy interest in money, investors wouldn't trust them to apply the proper diligence to the many, many money decisions involved in their jobs. You want first-class executives in those jobs, not first-class philosophy professors.

The assumption of greed is proper and prudent to build into the design of incentive plans. And the reality of greed is just fine, too, if you want those plans to have an effect upon company results. In other words, we're going to assume the people in management have the motive to enrich themselves in whatever way their incentive plans allow. We're going to ensure we don't give them the means to do so, instead concentrating their financial interests to support those of owners. The presumptions of this kind of analysis will appear cynical at times. The details of many legal agreements may seem that way, too, but, in those contracts as well as these, looking for trouble is diligent and proper, while ignoring it is sloppy and hazardous.

Market Practice in Financial Measurement

Companies rely mainly on familiar, traditional measures to judge results and deliver rewards within their incentive plans. In a Towers Perrin survey of annual incentive plans, these metrics (defined and evaluated in this chapter and the next) were most often cited:

- Earnings per share (EPS) — 34 percent
- Sales, revenues — 25 percent
- Net income, earnings, profit — 22 percent
- Earnings before interest and taxes (EBIT) or EBITDA (additionally before depreciation and amortization[2]) — 14 percent
- Operating income, operating profit — 13 percent
- Cash flow — 12 percent

- Return on equity — 9 percent

- Pre-tax income — 9 percent

- Return on invested capital or investment (ROIC or ROI) — 8 percent

- Customer satisfaction — 8 percent

- Return on assets (ROA), return on net assets (RONA) — 8 percent

- Other operating measures (e.g., operating margin) — 6 percent

- Economic profit (economic value added) — 5 percent

- Employee satisfaction — 4 percent.

Note the percentages total more than 100 percent due to multiple responses. We'll re-categorize these shortly for purposes of our discussion, treating operating income and EBIT together, for example, and ROIC and RONA as the same thing.

Revenue, Volume and Gross Margin

Let's start our discussion with revenue, a measure of performance used often at both the corporate and business unit levels in many kinds of incentive plans, including those focused on senior management. Performance against revenue goals captures a lot about business health and success, since it reflects growth in the volume of business and the prices held in the marketplace. In a growing company, it often is a leading indicator of profitability.

Companies that see organizational scale or market presence as a strategic variable sometimes use revenue and volume as pay metrics. Consumer products companies are a good example. Incentive plans used by Coke have been based partly upon case volume, for example. Market share is always used as a performance indicator in such settings and sometimes enters into pay programs. Revenue growth versus peers gets at many of the same matters covered by market share, measuring the company's ability to expand along with the size of the market and to get a bigger piece of it.

Gross margin is an indicator of some aspects of business health, as well. It has particular interest for companies with up-market brands, for example, since it testifies to the strength of consumers' preference and their willingness to pay more in response. Companies whose products offer performance advantages expect higher gross margins as well when the market pays them for their innovation and technical prowess. BMW automobiles provide a good example of both the cachet and performance phenomena.

Using a metric to judge business success is one thing. Linking executive pay to that yardstick is another. When we start attaching pay to these metrics we see some potential problems:

- Too much focus on revenue can lead the organization to chase unprofitable growth. The basic issue is that revenue as a financial metric does not capture any of the expenses involved in generating operating profit, nor the costs of its capital. Revenue by itself misses most of the basic drivers of value creation, so we can hardly expect it to encourage their pursuit. Volume has the same issue. Too much emphasis on growth in and of itself surely is a driving force behind many of the failed acquisitions that companies experience.

- Gross profit is equal to revenue minus the cost of sales, so it does reflect at least one cost category. But it attaches no importance to other cost categories. It would not encourage a company to outsource manufacturing, for example, even when such a move would be greatly beneficial. The gains to the company from outsourcing would be felt largely in capital costs and operating expense, and these don't count in the gross profit computation. It might also encourage overspending on advertising or product development since these amounts don't count while any increased sales and gross profits do.

- A widely quoted business metric, gross profit, is not used much in incentive plans. But it sometimes is considered a candidate for this role. Gross profit normally is stated in percentage terms, and that is where it causes its greatest concern. Too much emphasis on margins can encourage price gouging that reduces revenue, profit and value creation over time. The general margin-related issue is that value creation is an absolute construct, so its business advice often conflicts with that of percentage-based margins.

Revenue is used to a significant extent in plans. On the whole, most established companies don't place much emphasis on revenue as an independent matter from operating profit or other, more complete measures of financial results. Rather, they tend to attach a weight of less than 50 percent to any revenue goal for a senior management team.

That is a good thing. But it is not enough to keep companies entirely out of the trouble that can attend the practice of basing incentive pay on revenue. In a typical incentive attaching some separate weight to sales goals, management can make more money by increasing sales without increasing profit, through sales that bring zero incremental profit. Figure 7-1 is an example of a plan that includes a revenue goal and some scenarios of performance and reward it implies.

Let's say that it is a bad year and performance appears to be on track toward threshold levels: $90 in revenue and $8 in operating income. The scenarios show three ways to get performance up to targeted levels:

- *A hard way, involving winning profitable new sales.* Sales end up at $100 and profits at $10, so this performance scenario involved getting $10 in new revenue with incremental profit margin of 20 percent.

Figure 7-1: INCENTIVE PLAN WITH REVENUE AND OPERATING INCOME GOALS

	Bonus Award Percent of Target			Weighting	Scenarios		
	0% Threshold	100% Target	200% Maximum	Percent of Target	Hard Way to Target	Middle Way	Easy Way to Target
Revenue Range	90	100	110	50%	100.0	105.0	110.0
Operating Income Range	8	10	12	50%	10.0	9.0	8.0
Payout					100%	100%	100%
Management's Order of Preference					3	2	1
Investors' Order of Preference					1	2	3

- *An easy way, cutting prices to the point where marginal profit is zero.* In this case, revenue increases to $110 but profits stay at $8.

- *A middle-of-the-road answer, one involving $105 in revenue that increases profit by $1, or 7 percent.*

Consistently profitable new revenue is best for investors. It results in higher income and value. The scenarios bring equal pay for management, so they encourage the easiest one first: unprofitable new revenue. This plan puts investors' interests at odds with those of management. The same is true to a lesser extent in plans placing lower weightings like 40 percent or 25 percent on revenue.

This basic example of plan testing exposes the kind of issue we encounter in many incentive plans. Before rolling out plans, companies should test them to see how they reward good and bad business decisions.

Solutions
Revenue as an Award Modifier

Revenue growth is seen very often, and quite validly, as an important business challenge, a strategic goal and a leading indicator of future profit. Figure 7-2 is one example of how revenue can be featured in a plan without putting management at odds with investors.

Figure 7-2: INCENTIVE PLAN WITH REVENUE GOAL AS AWARD MODIFIER

	Bonus Award Percent of Target			Scenarios		
	0% Threshold	100% Target	160% Maximum	Hard Way	Middle Way	Easy Way
Operating Income Range	8	10	12	10.0	9.0	8.0
Award on Operating Income				100%	50%	0%
Revenue Range	90	100	110	100.0	105.0	110.0
Revenue Award Modifier	0.8	1.0	1.25	1.0	1.125	0.8
Payout				100%	56%	0%
Management's Order of Preference				1	2	3
Investors' Order of Preference				1	2	3

Revenue is a big factor in this plan, but operating income is in the driver's seat. Operating income places a value on management's performance, which is then modified by revenue performance. The effect of revenue is important, but it plays out in a way more consistent with value creation.

Revenue as a Basis for Future Income Targets

A more devilish solution is to take management's "revenue is a leading indicator" assertion and make it put its money where its mouth is. The company can do this in the context of target setting. This year's revenue growth increases next year's operating income goals based upon a standard overall margin. In that case, if the company took in $10 in unprofitable sales this year and the standard margin next year was 10 percent, its operating income goal next year and every subsequent year would be $1 higher than otherwise. We used this method as part of the procedure used to set targets for a diversified manufacturing company, creating a pro-growth incentive plan, but one in which it would not make sense for the business to expand with unprofitable volume. A typical budget-based target-setting process guarantees no such *quid pro quo*.

This target-setting example shows how mechanical algorithms sometimes function better than budget-based goals by creating financial stakes and account-abilities that have both a memory and a shelf life.

Revenue and Other Milestones in New Business Ventures

In many high-growth, high-investment settings, none of the solutions cited work. A start-up business or a new joint venture often bases bonuses on milestones that are hit from startup to market. Using a revenue goal might not make sense for a year or more.

For example, my neighbor started up a joint venture that developed a new soymilk product for Dupont and General Mills a few years ago. He recounted to me how the product made it through the approval process and was brought to market. He concurs that placing a lot of emphasis on short-term profits — making them prominent and urgent goals within incentive plans — would be dangerous for this type of startup. How? The company could just spend a bit less on promotion and other growth costs, quickly attain the top of the pay range against its modest current income goals, and grow the top line more slowly. This slower sales growth is of little pay consequence in an income-heavy plan. Again in this example, management's interests would run counter to those of investors, who would be looking for rapid movement up the sales curve in the early years on the way to greater value creation over the long run.

Profit can be a counterproductive measure in such cases, but the relevant issue is mainly one of timing. The success of the venture, like any other business, can be judged perfectly well based upon financial performance over time. However, incentive plan goals in the early years likely will be based upon enterprise milestones, many of them nonfinancial, and probably upon discretionary judgments about success to date.

Such a system is hardly strict in a financial sense, though. The leaders of such an enterprise should be rewarded for focusing upon long-run value creation, in the meantime minding every dollar consumed by the venture. You probably can't accomplish this using only the bonus plan in this situation. And, of course, customary long-term incentives like corporate stock and options won't reflect a small venture's success reliably.

Many start-up ventures like these are meant to break through the corporate bureaucracy and pursue success more nimbly. Their incentive solutions should do the same thing. A good choice is to put in a long-term incentive plan — phantom stock or a performance unit or share plan — based upon the venture's cumulative financial results. A range of such solutions appears in later chapters, including a couple in which revenue is used as the basis for valuing a business during the early growth years. One start-up company denominated a portion of bonus awards in long-term incentive (phantom stock) grants. This got two messages across at the same time:

- Revenue and other early milestones are critical to the longer-run success of the business; the bonus plan provides serious upside based upon attainment of these goals.

- However, bonuses are paid partly in phantom stock whose value is based strongly upon cumulative financial results over a period of several years. So, all this encourages taking actions during the start-up and high-growth phases with an eye toward longer-run, sustained profitability.

Using Value Rules to Choose Metrics

The earlier discussion focused on problems with revenue, volume and gross margin as metrics, and what can be done about them. These are just a few of the dozens, even hundreds of measures that a company might consider. Companies bat around new measurement ideas all the time. What's needed is a general method for reviewing measures and their suitability for use in incentive plans, and in particular in plans directed at senior managers.

Value rules are perfectly suited to this task. Let's use them as our method to assess revenue as a metric for use in a management incentive plan:

- **Step 1.** *Compare the metric to the primary value drivers in the discounted cash flow (DCF) model: income, capital usage and the cost of capital.*

Revenue reflects only part of the first driver and neither of the next two. So it's a very incomplete metric and, in many cases, it will conflict with value creation. We can test this by moving other variables around. What if revenue rose while profits were flat (the unprofitable sales growth example)? What if revenue and profits rose, but capital outlays wiped out any valuation gains (the bad acquisition example)? At this point, the company's anecdotal experience is very useful in deciding which cases are feasible.

- **Step 2.** *Ask this question: as a practical matter, are plan participants in a position to take material advantage of the gaps in the metric?*

  If the revenue-based incentive plan is a sales commission arrangement, one dealing with equally profitable products over which participants have no pricing control, then it may not conflict at all with value creation. If the whole top management team is in it, it very likely is a problem.

  Notice here that we do not ask whether participants would actually manipulate company results and harm shareholders. Rather, we simply identify whether they could. If they can, it is a problem that needs solving in one way or another. Basic standards of diligence in this important area require that incentive plans connect with value creation. Again, a little bit of cynicism is more appropriate in these matters than a lot of naïveté.

- **Step 3.** *Look for solutions based upon value rules. In the case of revenue-based plans, that means looking for an offsetting emphasis upon expenses, capital usage and the cost of capital — upon the elements of DCF value not covered by revenue.*

  These already may exist within the incentive structure. If the plan features revenue as a modifier rather than as a separate goal, then it may not need adjustment. The plan already may synchronize well enough with income, while still giving strong emphasis to revenue as the company desires. In the start-up company situation, the existence of a well-designed phantom stock plan might offset deficiencies in the bonus plan metrics, particularly if the phantom stock plan is large in relation to bonus pay. Procedures for setting performance/award schedules offer another solution. If the problems aren't to be offset in any of these ways, then the plan just needs new metrics. Many companies don't see it this way. They dismiss the deficiencies within their plans as matters not needing explicit remedy within the incentive structure. One reason is that they do not realize the extent of the potential problems. Another reason, though, is that they believe the issues aren't serious because the company's financial controls — investment and acquisition analysis, for example — don't permit big problems in business decision-making. A closer look at company experience, however, often suggests that gaps between pay and value creation do warrant a remedy. Punting to the finance function is not one.

Context for Evaluating Financial Metrics

Financial metrics have a range of important roles when creating incentive plans at the corporate, group, division or profit center level. They may act:

- As the basis for all or part of award potential, independently of other metrics, within a goal-based annual or long-term incentive plan

- As a basis for the valuation formula used in a phantom stock plan

- As a basis for setting targets denominated in other measures (e.g., setting targets for operating income and return on investment [ROIC] based upon total business return [TBR])

- As a multiplier or modifier of performance or awards stated principally in other terms

- Within a performance/award schedule that determines awards jointly as a function of several measures — a "matrix" format based upon EPS and return on equity (ROE), for example

- As a threshold condition on overall award payment within plans — a "circuit breaker" often set at the corporate level

- As the basis for setting the number of shares or options granted in a stock-based incentive plan, for accelerating grants already made, or for determining the number of shares earned in a performance share plan

- As part of a method of judging dilution related to incentive plans.

Let's assume the metrics we are reviewing are used in the first context cited above — as a basis for earning material amounts of award within an incentive plan. That is the role in which metrics must meet the highest standard.

Operating Income, EBIT and Return on Invested Capital

Operating income is gross margin minus operating expenses. The after-tax version is net of taxes. In an uncomplicated company — one without much in the way of non-operating sources of income and expense aside from interest expense — operating income is the same thing as earnings before interest and taxes. Operating income is a commonly quoted measure of business performance and size that is used more often than any other when devising incentives for business units. It is the "sweet spot" of the income statement for our purposes, being stated after subtracting the operating costs that most management team members can influence, but before the financing costs they can't.

Return on invested capital (ROIC) is equal to operating income divided by capital. It is stated in percentage terms and, like operating income, it comes in pre- and after-tax versions. ROIC is the same thing as return on capital employed (ROCE), return on net assets (RONA) and return on investment (ROI).

Are these good incentive plan metrics? Let's roll out our three-step procedure using value rules and see:

Step 1: Operating income after tax is one of the three main drivers of valuation, along with capital usage and the cost of capital. Operating income differs from operating income after taxes only to the extent of taxes. So, taxes, capital usage and the cost of capital are the only structural differences between this metric and a full description of value creation.

The tax issue normally is addressed by stating the measure after taxes, or by using a pre-tax measure when tax policy and effects are seen as being outside of the participant group's main focus. It also can be addressed by including tax effects in a free cash flow element of the plan (e.g., in incentive plans based upon the metric total business return, to be discussed in the next chapter).

So, assuming there's no big issue with taxes, a reasonably good incentive plan based upon operating income ought to do a good job of encouraging the income growth that drives value creation. So far, so good. Now, how about capital and its cost? These drivers take us to the heart of problems with operating income as an incentive plan measure.

- Operating income does not by itself take capital usage into account. If operating income after tax in business unit A rises from $100 to $110 with no change in capital, then the value of the company's operating performance goes up. If the business unit used $2,000 in new capital to increase income by $100, on the other hand, the low return of 5 percent surely destroyed value. Operating income alone does not tell you whether actions taken in its pursuit created value or not.

- The other blind side of operating income is the cost of capital. If the investment in the earlier example had been $1,000 rather than $2,000, the return on the investment would have been 10 percent. Is this enough of a return to create value? It depends upon the cost of capital. Investors need to get a return on the investment in the business to compensate them for the risks they bear in funding it. That "hurdle" rate of return is the cost of capital.

If the cost of capital is 8 percent, a $1,000 investment needs to generate a return of at least $80 to create value. This investment generated a return of $100 so it did create value. Operating income by itself doesn't tell us anything about the cost of capital, so it again is an insufficient basis to judge success in the value creation realm. Other income-based metrics we'll see shortly — pre-tax income, net income, EPS and cash flow — have various degrees of blindness to capital usage and its cost.

Return on invested capital, on the other hand, does take into account the capital involved in business initiatives. ROIC on new investments like these can be benchmarked directly against the cost of capital. However:

- The ROIC measurement alone does not include the cost of capital, so it does not by itself signal whether or not value creation occurred.

- ROIC is based upon historical capital. Differences in company histories and accounting practices can greatly affect the amount of capital reported. These differences could cause Company A to have ROIC of 5 percent of historical capital while Company B might report 20 percent, even if it has exactly the same income prospects and valuations. So ROIC, like operating income, does not by itself identify value creation in a consistent way.

Each factor can be a problem depending upon the role of ROIC within an incentive plan. If the plan bases awards on ROIC improvement, for example, then Company A would take on an investment that offers ROIC of 5 percent or better, including many value-destroying investments with ROIC under its cost of capital of 10 percent. Company B would turn down any investment offering ROIC below 20 percent, including many with value-creating yields above 10 percent. We ran into this exact problem during a project with a manufacturing company a few years ago. The plan's goal-setting procedures for ROIC, like those at many companies, required business units to improve ROIC from existing levels, whether they started at 35 percent or 3.5 percent. The value creation rule, in contrast, is that new investments must earn yields in excess of the cost of capital. The beginning level of capital, and therefore the existing level of ROIC, is irrelevant.

Differences in capital measurement often are serious enough that ROIC cannot even be used to benchmark results among peers or business units, much less against absolute standards of value creation. And speaking of absolutes, note that ROIC is not one. It is stated in percentage terms. Value creation is stated in terms of absolute value. Two business performance scenarios may involve the same ROIC, but one may be far larger than the other and may have created much more value. This indifference to quantity leads to problems like those ascribed earlier to margin measures. In pursuit of ROIC by itself, companies may wish to sell off assets and shrink the business to where it consists mainly of ones with high yields in relation to historical capital, even if this course of action creates no value. We'll look at some other return-based metrics later — ROE, CFROGI — that have the same set of problems.

Step 2: Are these problems with operating income and ROIC a concern, considering who is in the participant group? If senior management is in the plan, then you bet it is. They make the decisions about capital and these two measures pose a range of problems in that area.

Step 3: So, how do we address these problems? In the same way that we recommend addressing it within all incentive plans, by getting income, capital and its costs represented in proper proportion within the plan. That means amending the plan's metrics, target-setting methods, award schedules, or all of these.

Operating Income and ROIC Solutions

Here are some solutions to the issues associated with operating income and ROIC:

- As in the revenue-related example noted earlier, we can cover this matter through target-setting methods. Let's take a company that uses operating income as its sole measure of business performance. If the company increases capital by $1,000 and it has a 10 percent cost of capital, it does need to get after-tax operating income on the new investment of at least $100 to create value. Jacking up the operating profit target for the next year by an additional $100 creates accountability for this goal and encourages the company to make only value-creating investments. As we'll see in the next chapter, this is the equivalent of an incentive plan based upon the metric economic profit.[3]

- Where ROIC is concerned, we simply recommend not using it as the sole measure within an incentive plan, but instead combining it with absolute measures of business scale or income. It is combined most often with operating income. In these cases, the emphasis upon growth in operating income provides scale to the ROIC criterion. The presence of ROIC in the plan addresses the fact that operating income does not reflect capital usage.

Two Wrongs Can Make a Right

The second of those two alternatives is a somewhat common general approach, but it often is flawed at the detail level, so it needs to be constructed carefully.

Figure 7-3 is an example of an incentive plan format based upon operating income (after-tax in this case) and ROIC.

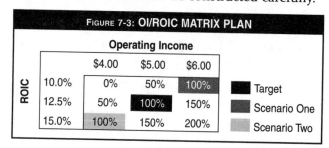

FIGURE 7-3: OI/ROIC MATRIX PLAN

		Operating Income		
		$4.00	$5.00	$6.00
ROIC	10.0%	0%	50%	100%
	12.5%	50%	100%	150%
	15.0%	100%	150%	200%

■ Target
■ Scenario One
■ Scenario Two

The plan is typical, using performance ranges of +/− 20 percent on each metric, a 0 percent — 200 percent award payout and a symmetrical award schedule. This plan has metrics constructed from an "operating" or "total capital" perspective as recommended in Chapter 4. It has wide award ranges with no kinks or discontinuities. The ROIC performance range uses the cost of capital, 10 percent, as its minimum level, so it appears to discourage lower, value-destroying ROIC levels. The matrix format hints at certain valuation dynamics, too, according less return to income growth when associated ROIC is lower. Overall, it appears to reflect many value rules. Let's test it.

The center cell of this award matrix pays awards at 100 percent of target if levels of income and capital are at $5 and $40, respectively, so that ROIC is 12.5 percent. Last year's income was $4 and capital was $40. This target scenario and each to follow involve a $1 increase in income from the "base" business. Let's examine some other outcomes that reward management equally:

- **Scenario One.** What if performance ends up in the upper right hand corner of the matrix, with operating income at $6? Last year's income was $4 and there was a $1 increase in base business, so there is an additional $1 income gain here that came from some initiative that we can set apart and evaluate. Let's say it is a wholesaler stocking up to carry a new line of products.[4] With ROIC at 10 percent, ending capital must be $60 because $6 is 10 percent of that. Capital last year was $40 and the base business had no additional capital demands, so this separate investment apparently amounted to $20. A $1 income gain on a $20 investment is a poor return at 5 percent, yet the plan pays out at target.

  How bad was the investment decision? The $1 income increase — assumed to be level and permanent and therefore valued as we learned in Chapter 4, when divided by the cost of capital — is worth $1/10 percent, or $10. The investment outlay was $20, on the other hand, so the company is worse off by $10, net. The plan nonetheless pays out 100 percent at target because it does not recognize this destruction in value. Investors would have been better off if management had not made the investment, but the incentive plan treats the two outcomes equally.

- **Scenario Two.** Target awards also can be earned with ROIC of 15 percent and $4 in income. Income at $4 is a dollar off the base case of $5, while ROIC at 15 percent suggests that capital fell to $26.67 ($4/15%). These could be effects of shutting down a line of business, for example, and liquidating the net assets tied up in it. That performance level pays out at 100 percent as well. But it actually involves value creation of $3.33. Liquidation proceeds apparently were $13.33 since net assets fell from $40 to $26.67, but the reduction value from the $1 income loss was only $10 ($1/10%).

This award schedule appeared reasonable at first glance. When we got into the details — the level at which the incentive plan actually operates — we saw some serious flaws. That is very often the situation. As we saw in Chapter 2, it is important to be very careful when setting up incentive plans to look for holes in the

FIGURE 7-4: OI/ROIC MATRIX BASED UPON VALUE CREATION

		\$4.00	\$4.50	\$5.00	\$5.50	\$6.00	
ROIC	10.00%	0%	0%	0%	0%	0%	
	11.25%	44%	50%	56%	61%	67%	
	12.50%	80%	90%	100%	110%	120%	■ Target
	13.75%	109%	123%	136%	150%	164%	■ Scenario One
	15.00%	133%	150%	167%	183%	200%	■ Scenario Two

Operating Income (column header spanning \$4.00–\$6.00)

measurement scheme, fix them if needed and to test the overall plan before rolling it out. In this case, a solution would be to change the award matrix so awards are aligned with value creation. Figure 7-4 is such a matrix.

Value creation or destruction at each cell in the matrix is compared to the company's \$50 base case value, with the difference used to set up the award schedule. These percentage deviations from target are leveraged up by a factor of five in order to create 200 percent upside. The value-destroying scenarios in the matrix are zeroed out and made ineligible for reward. In this matrix, scenarios 1, 2 and all others simply pay out in relation to their valuation effects.

This is a good general solution for incentive plan award schedules, one that we cite several times in later chapters. The matrix format allows the dynamics of value creation — the tradeoff between capital usage and income gains — to be specified at many different performance levels. It is generally under-used, however, noted by only 10 percent of respondents to Towers Perrin's annual incentive design study.

On the Importance of Being Earnest

The matrix format may be used less often because it is relatively complex. And a value-based matrix like the one we just reviewed is particularly so when compared to the usual cookie-cutter metrics and award schedules. But the extra complexity is worth bearing in exchange for the more consistently proper incentive effects. This level of complexity won't make the plan ineffective. The executive teams that get paid by plans like these look closely at the details. They examine the circumstances and maneuvers that are most rewarding. They often regard the specifics of the award schedules as a set of ground rules that endorse some kinds of business conduct and set others out of bounds. Even if they're less literal than that, when reading corporate intentions into the plan, they're often inclined to do what it takes to get paid. If corporate rolled out a plan with a bunch of economic loopholes in it, they often figure, it makes sense to find out what those loopholes are, so, at least in a pinch, they might be pursued.

We're buying management performance with these plans, and the market situation is *caveat emptor*, or "buyer beware." We need to take a close look at the business guidelines that we're issuing in the form of incentives. If we are not diligent, we'll create a bunch of performance loopholes and encourage our key decision-makers to exploit them at least some of the time.

We do a lot of this kind of detailed analysis in later chapters dedicated to incentive design, as opposed to this chapter dealing with measurement. However, this initial example warrants a look here because the OI/ROIC matrix is an example of a system of financial measurements, one that makes up for the deficiencies of single metrics by combining them in productive ways.

We've noted traditional financial metrics like operating income and return on invested capital tend to be incomplete. That is, they fail the tests posed by value rules because they do not place sufficient emphasis on each of the main drivers of value: income, capital usage and the cost of capital. Most of the value-based metrics, in contrast, stand up well. Traditional metrics hold the serious advantage of being simpler and more familiar than value-based ones. If you're going to use them in a prominent, high-stakes way, though, you have to pay close attention to how you tie them to pay. You'll be obliged to combine them in various ways and take care with the award schedules and the many scenarios they reward. Under either approach, though, you'll have to do more work than you would with traditional designs and deal with more complexity.

Pre-Tax Income, Net Income, EPS and ROE

This is the mainstream of corporate performance measurement. These are the traditional metrics used most often to deliver bonus pay to top officers of public companies:

- Pre-tax income is earnings before interest and taxes (EBIT) minus net interest expense and other sources of non-operating income and expense.

- Net income is pre-tax income minus income taxes.

- Return on equity (ROE) is equal to net income after tax divided by stockholder's equity.

- Return on common equity is equal to net income after taxes and preferred dividends (that is net income available to common shareholders) divided by common equity.

- Earnings per share, or EPS, is equal to net income available to common shareholders divided by common shares outstanding. EPS has two versions under current U.S. GAAP depending upon how outstanding shares are calculated:

    - Basic EPS is based upon the number of shares actually outstanding.

- Diluted EPS reflects the net increase in outstanding shares that would occur if in-the-money stock options and other contingent, equity-equivalent claims were converted into new common shares.[5]

EPS is the main yardstick of financial performance cited by analysts and the business press. Companies believe that shareholder expectations are denominated in near-term EPS, forcing them into a constant game of next-quarter capitalism that compels them, in turn, to tie pay to EPS. As we saw in Chapter 4, EPS has no monopoly on investor attention; the stock market consistently looks past EPS toward longer-run expectations for free cash flow. Much of the mystique and prevalence of EPS as an incentive metric is undeserved.

The term EPS actually can take on a range of identities. Companies with material, non-recurring influences on their financial results may distinguish EPS that comes from ongoing activities from the effects of things like discontinued operations, extraordinary items and accounting rule changes. In recent years, companies and analysts have released many additional *pro forma* EPS calculations, basically amounting to EPS *without all the bad stuff.*

Basing pay on these heavily adjusted measures runs strongly counter to the incentive design advice we made in Chapter 4 — to reflect every bit of company performance when measuring performance of top management. Our general rule for performance measurement is not whether the bad stuff should be included — it always should — but whether, if it is a big distortion, it should be capitalized or run through current income. Likewise for good stuff.

Discretionary definitions are not the biggest problem with these mainstream measures. The biggest problem, actually, is capital structure, and the list goes on from there. From here, make that. A review from the viewpoint of value rules provides these major findings:

- These incentive metrics differ from the operating income driver of value in that they all reflect non-operating sources of income and expense. Aside from net interest costs, which are a very big deal, we are not paying much attention to non-operating items. The general situation with these non-interest, non-operating items is:

  - If they're material, they may require some adjustment to the income and capital constructs used in incentive plans.

  - What to do with them depends heavily upon line-of-sight issues, but generally the assets and results involved are someone's responsibility and should not escape the company's apparatus of measurement and account-ability. That means the default version of pre-tax operating income actually is EBIT for most companies.

- Sales of non-operating assets are clearly one-time in nature, making them candidates for capitalization into the "capital" construct used in incentive plans. The default treatment of one-time proceeds of $10 for example, would be to reduce invested capital by $10.

- Large levels of non-operating assets — excess cash, for example, or land held for resale — can distort measures like ROIC, particularly when ROIC levels are used in a rigorous way in target-setting or benchmarking. Companies may remove their effects in such cases, following the general rule of stripping out big "uncontrollable" items from performance when they are so large as to subvert the incentive plan's intended effects.

- Incentive plan targets can be set taking into account the standing or expected levels of non-operating assets and income.

- Minority interest, if material, may require some adjustment to place income and capital levels on a consistent basis (see example in Chapter 10).

- The pretax income measure that initiates the computation of these metrics is stated net of interest costs. This violates the "total capital" perspective that describes value creation in the DCF model. As we saw in Chapter 4, it leaves measurement and pay arrangements wide open to manipulation and distortion. It is a big issue in measurement, and here is how it can play out:

  - These incentive metrics favor any investment with a yield above the after-tax cost of debt. If the company invests $100, and it has an overall cost of capital of 10 percent, then we know it needs to generate after-tax operating profit of at least $10 to create value.[6] An investment with after-tax operating profit of $5, for example, would destroy $50 in value; the income is worth only $50 based upon current operating performance ($5/10% = $50).

  - Net income and its siblings do not see it that way. If debt interest rates are 6 percent, taxes are 33 percent, and the whole $100 deal is financed with debt, then interest expense after tax rises by $4. Any income in excess of this threshold causes all the metrics to rise. The five dollars in operating income would add one dollar to net income.

  - It would also add $1.50 to pre-tax income and a penny to EPS if 100 shares were outstanding. It would increase pay based upon any of these metrics while destroying shareholder value.

  - There are "denominator" issues to consider as well. The $1 income increase adds a percentage point to ROE if book equity is $100; the denominator, equity, did not expand since the deal was all debt.

TABLE 7-1: REPURCHASE EFFECTS WITH ZERO GROWTH AND DEBT

Year	0	1	2	3	Residual Value
Operating Income After Tax	$100	$100	$100	$100	$100
Total Capital	1,000	1,000	1,000	1,000	1,000
Increase in Capital		0	0	0	0
Free Cash Flow (Income Minus Capital Change)		$100	$100	$100	$1,000
Cost of Capital 10.0%					
Present Value as of End of Year:					
FCF for Remaining Forecast Term	$249	$174	$91		
Residual Value	751	826	909	$1,000	
Enterprise Value	1,000	1,000	1,000	1,000	
Valuation at Beginning of Year		1,000	1,000	1,000	
Value Gain		0	0	0	
Free Cash Flow		100	100	100	
Total Investor Return		$100	$100	$100	
Return as a Percent of Beginning Value		10.0%	10.0%	10.0%	
Book Value of Equity (Capital Minus Debt)		$1,000	$1,000	$1,000	
Share Price:					
Debt % of Ending Value	0.0%	0.0%	0.0%	0.0%	
Ending Debt	$0	$0	$0	$0	
Equity Value	$1,000	$1,000	$1,000	$1,000	
Number of Shares Outstanding	1,000	909	826	751	
Stock Value per Share	$1.00	$1.10	$1.21	$1.33	
Earnings per Share:					
Interest Expense (4% cost after tax)	$0	$0	$0	$0	
Net Income	100	100	100	100	
EPS	$0.10	$0.11	$0.12	$0.13	
Outstanding Shares:					
Equity Cash Flow (Free Cash Flow – Interest + Debt Change)		$100	$100	$100	
Equity Value Before Repurchase (Including Equity Cash Flow [ECF])		1,100	1,100	1,100	
Stock Value per Share Before Repurchase		$1.10	$1.21	$1.33	
Number of Shares Repurchased with ECF		91	83	75	
Number of New Shares Outstanding		909	826	751	

		0	1	2	3	3-Year Avg. or Growth. Rate
TABLE 7-1: REPURCHASE EFFECTS WITH ZERO GROWTH AND DEBT (CONT'D)						
Effect of Debt and Repurchases:						
Operating Income Growth			0.0%	0.0%	0.0%	0.0%
EPS Growth			10.0%	10.0%	10.0%	10.0%
Growth in Enterprise Value			0.0%	0.0%	0.0%	0.0%
Total Investor Return			10.0%	10.0%	10.0%	10.0%
Growth in Stock Value			10.0%	10.0%	10.0%	10.0%
Total Return to Equity holders			$100.0	$100.0	$100.0	$100.0
Return on Invested Capital			10.0%	10.0%	10.0%	10.0%
Return on Equity			10.0%	10.0%	10.0%	10.0%
Shares Controlled by Management		10.0%	11.0%	12.1%	13.3%	1.1%

As noted earlier, these income- and return-based metrics carry some problems cited in the cases of operating income and ROIC. Income-based metrics are not sensitive to capital usage. Return-based metrics do not explicitly comprehend the cost of capital, can be affected by inconsistencies in historical costs of assets, and can distort some target-setting methods.

Debt, Share Repurchases, EPS and Stock Option Gains

We've seen some but not all of the ways financing decisions can distort metrics and pay. There still is big money to be made on share repurchases. In the first scenario (Table 7-1), a company with zero debt and zero growth in operating income can produce EPS growth of 10 percent per year with share repurchases. Table 7-2 involves 5 percent income growth and capital increases based upon 20 percent incremental ROIC. In this case, debt is held at 33 percent of enterprise value. This scenario turns 5 percent income growth into EPS growth averaging 16.4 percent. This is not a bad game, and it is one that can be played year after year.

Management's control of the enterprise grows each year in the first two scenarios. Table 7-3 shows an example like the one in Table 7-2 except with rising debt levels. IBM's share repurchase policies were labeled a "slo-mo LBO" in 2002 — which seems a fitting title for this scenario since management doubles its percentage control of the company's equity. It also takes 5 percent annual growth in operating income and turns it into 31.6 percent average EPS growth.

Recent U.S. tax law changes may reduce the incentive for companies to pursue repurchases. So may changes in stock option accounting if they compel companies to use full-share forms of equity incentives, ones that reward not only repurchases but also dividends. Still, whether a given company hits its EPS targets and pays its senior management can have as much to do with corporate-

TABLE 7-2: REPURCHASE EFFECTS WITH MODERATE GROWTH AND DEBT

Year	0	1	2	3	Residual Value
Operating Income After Tax	$100	$105	$110	$116	$116
Total Capital	1,000	1,025	1,051	1,079	1,079
Increase in Capital		25	26	28	0
Free Cash Flow (Income Minus Capital Change)		$80	$84	$88	$1,158
Cost of Capital 10.0%					
Present Value as of End of Year:					
FCF for Remaining Forecast Term	$208	$149	$80		
Residual Value	870	957	1,052	$1,158	
Enterprise Value	1,078	1,106	1,133	1,158	
Valuation at Beginning of Year		1,078	1,106	1,133	
Value Gain		28	27	25	
Free Cash Flow		80	84	88	
Total Investor Return		$108	$111	$113	
Return as a Percent of Beginning Value		10.0%	10.0%	10.0%	
Book Value of Equity (Capital Minus Debt)		$656	$674	$693	
Share Price:					
Debt % of Ending Value	33.3%	33.3%	33.3%	33.3%	
Ending Debt	$359	$369	$378	$386	
Equity Value	$719	$737	$755	$772	
Number of Shares Outstanding	737	669	607	549	
Stock Value per Share	$0.97	$1.10	$1.24	$1.41	
Earnings per Share:					
Interest Expense (4% cost after tax)	$14	$14	$15	$15	
Net Income	86	91	96	101	
EPS	$0.12	$0.14	$0.16	$0.18	
Outstanding Shares:					
Equity Cash Flow (Free Cash Flow – Interest + Debt Change)		$75	$78	$81	
Equity Value Before Repurchase (Including Equity Cash Flow [ECF])		812	833	853	
Stock Value per Share Before Repurchase		$1.10	$1.24	$1.41	
Number of Shares Repurchased with ECF		68	63	58	
Number of New Shares Outstanding		$669	$607	$549	

TABLE 7-2: REPURCHASE EFFECTS WITH MODERATE GROWTH AND DEBT (CONT'D)					
Year	0	1	2	3	3-Year Avg. or Growth Rate
Effect of Debt and Repurchases:					
Operating Income Growth		5.0%	5.0%	5.0%	5.0%
EPS Growth		16.6%	16.3%	16.5%	16.4%
Growth in Enterprise Value		2.6%	2.4%	2.2%	2.4%
Total Investor Return		10.0%	10.0%	10.0%	10.0%
Growth in Stock Value		13.0%	13.0%	13.0%	13.0%
Total Return to Equityholders		$93.4	$95.9	$98.2	$95.8
Return on Invested Capital		10.2%	10.5%	10.7%	10.5%
Return on Equity		13.8%	14.2%	14.5%	14.2%
Shares Controlled by Management	10.0%	11.0%	12.2%	13.4%	1.1%

level choices about debt and share repurchases as it does with underlying operating performance. The examples show that it is remarkably easy to take a given level of performance and, using debt and repurchases, supercharge its EPS implications (in example, debt cost was held at 4 percent for simplicity).

The Great Game?

This is a game, but companies may not always know they're playing. Businesses aren't necessarily manipulating their incentive metrics. To some extent, the metrics may be manipulating them. The conventions of traditional measurement skew economic performance. If they're used as guidance for business decisions, they're sure to encourage bad ones at least some of the time. In this case, the market's seeming impatience for EPS may have driven the repurchase policy. In an earlier example, a bad acquisition caused income and EPS to rise. Companies may not look far beyond market share and revenue concerns to put a company on the acquisition screen. If the deal is accretive to EPS within a reasonable time frame, as many bad ones are, it often looks like a go.

We've seen that capital structure is a big part of the issue, troubling the effective use of net income, EPS and ROE in incentive plans, though these are the yardsticks used most commonly.

When companies make choices regarding how to finance investments, whether to restructure their capital sources, whether to pay, stabilize or increase dividends, or whether to repurchase shares, they are doing two things:

- Doing something that almost no one in an incentive plan can influence
- Affecting incentive pay for most members of company management.

Year	0	1	2	3	Residual Value
TABLE 7-3: REPURCHASE EFFECTS WITH RISING DEBT: "SLO-MO LBO"					
Operating Income After Tax	$100	$105	$110	$116	$116
Total Capital	1,000	1,025	1,051	1,079	1,079
Increase in Capital		25	26	28	
Free Cash Flow (Income Minus Capital Change)		$80	$84	$88	$1,158
Cost of Capital 10.0%					
Present Value as of End of Year:					
FCF for Remaining Forecast Term	$208	$149	$80		
Residual Value	870	957	1,052	$1,158	
Enterprise Value	1,078	1,106	1,133	1,158	
Valuation at Beginning of Year		1,078	1,106	1,133	
Value Gain		28	27	25	
Free Cash Flow		80	84	88	
Total Investor Return		$108	$111	$113	
Return as a Percent of Beginning Value		10.0%	10.0%	10.0%	
Book Value of Equity (Capital Minus Debt)		$693	$598	$500	
Share Price:					
Debt % of Ending Value	20.0%	30.0%	40.0%	50.0%	
Ending Debt	$216	$332	$453	$579	
Equity Value	$863	$774	$680	$579	
Number of Shares Outstanding	774	623	486	363	
Stock Value per Share	$1.11	$1.24	$1.40	$1.59	
Earnings per Share:					
Interest Expense (4% cost after tax)	$9	$9	$13	$18	
Net Income	91	96	97	98	
EPS	$0.12	$0.15	$0.20	$0.27	
Outstanding Shares:					
Equity Cash Flow (Free Cash Flow – Interest + Debt Change)		$188	$192	$196	
Equity Value Before Repurchase (Including Equity Cash Flow [ECF])		962	872	775	
Stock Value per Share Before Repurchase		$1.24	$1.40	$1.59	
Number of Shares Repurchased with ECF		151	137	123	
Number of New Shares Outstanding		623	486	363	

Year	0	1	2	3	3-Year Avg. or Growth Rate
TABLE 7-3: REPURCHASE EFFECTS WITH RISING DEBT: "SLO-MO LBO"					
Effect of Debt and Repurchases:					
Operating Income Growth		5.0%	5.0%	5.0%	5.0%
EPS Growth		31.0%	29.1%	34.8%	31.6%
Growth in Enterprise Value		2.6%	2.4%	2.2%	2.4%
Total Investor Return		10.0%	10.0%	10.0%	10.0%
Growth in Stock Value		11.5%	12.6%	14.0%	12.7%
Total Return to Equityholders		$99.2	$97.3	$95.1	$97.2
Return on Invested Capital		10.2%	10.5%	10.7%	10.5%
Return on Equity		13.9%	16.2%	19.5%	16.2%
Shares Controlled by Management	10.0%	12.4%	15.9%	21.3%	3.8%

The funny thing is what they may not be doing. They may not be affecting the valuation of their enterprise overall very much. Capital structure probably works mainly like the book-keeping choices also set forth in Chapter 4, producing huge effects on financial reporting in the near term and modest or zero effect upon investor returns over time. Company financing moves may simply trade risks and cash flows among investor classes at market transaction prices.

For now, though, let's assume a company's financing decisions do make a big difference to shareholders. Examples:

- Maybe a company is "under-leveraged" and, by using more debt, it does a better job of exploiting the corporate tax benefits of debt finance and helping shareholders avoid double taxation on the equity side. Maybe these effects aren't already being accomplished in a macro sense by investors through arbitrage or adjustments in their own portfolios.

- Before U.S. tax law changes, repurchase programs were thought to allow a company to deliver the results of operations — free cash flows — to investors in a more tax-efficient and flexible way. Capital gains brought about by repurchases still allow shareholders to withdraw taxable income from the company when timing is best for them rather than at quarterly dividend intervals. And the company may be able to do this without unduly dis-appointing the dividend-hungry investors, who may not see future stock prices as a lock box in which their foregone dividends are preserved with interest. Shareholders can vote with their feet, as they say. Let's assume few of them do.

- Maybe share repurchases and taxable distributions signal that management is paying closer attention to the use of capital within the enterprise, judging more closely whether all the company's opportunities for reinvestment of operating cash flows really are opportunities from a value creation perspective. In the view of many investors, that would be a nice development and maybe even a buy signal.

- Maybe a company's high bond rating isn't all it is cracked up to be. The interest cost savings stemming from a high rating are modest, but the foregone tax advantages and related valuation effects are large. All else being equal, a company could conclude it is better off with more debt.

Let's step around the debate about whether financing policy adds value from an enterprise viewpoint. Instead, we'll stipulate for now that there is some better policy regarding capital structure and distributions for a company and, if management moves toward it, the shareholders will enjoy abnormally high stock returns for a time. We suggested in Chapter 4 that such gains are modest and uncertain, but for now let's assume they're worth chasing.

In that case, shareholders should want these things to happen. But, from an incentive structure standpoint, they don't need to do much to encourage management to act. The few corporate types actually involved in these decisions (the CEO, CFO and a few other financial managers) will always have a lot of money riding on the stock price. Anything they can do to increase the stock price will pay them well. If anyone else in incentive plans has their pay driven much by capital structure, they're just free riders or victims of policies they can't control.

Stock-based incentives for the top corporate officers probably are about all that needs to be done to encourage pursuit of the best capital structure. Companies could stop here with capital structure-related incentives, but they almost never do.

- For now at least, most of the incentive money is in options. Options reward management for producing capital gains, but not dividends. (These two parts of total shareholder return interact in an area called "shareholder expectations," but let's put that aside until Chapter 9). This means that share repurchases are favored over dividend increases. Even if repurchases do nothing for shareholders in terms of total shareholder return (TSR), they do have the convenient effect of converting TSR otherwise receivable in dividends into capital gains. And the latter pays off for option holders.

- The second biggest chunk of incentive cost is delivered based upon EPS. In Tables 1, 2 and 3, we observed a rather strong EPS play involving more debt, more repurchases and no dividend increases. Most companies can add a few points of EPS this way. Investors as a group didn't necessarily benefit in our earlier examples, but persistently higher EPS growth likely would have salutary effects upon cash pay.

Remedying Issues with Pre-tax Income, Net Income, EPS and ROE

We've identified the issues with these metrics. Let's move on and look at some solutions:

- Make greater use of operating measurements like operating income and return on capital — rather than their equity-based counterparts, EPS, net income and return on equity. Do you feel it is hard to disconnect folks from EPS, given what a big deal it seems to be for shareholders and the board? Put in plans that encourage the best possible operating results for the enterprise over the long haul — that encourage the greatest return to all holders of enterprise capital — and these plans will encourage optimal EPS performance over time.

- At the same time, make heavier use of operating incentives generally by putting in medium-term plans and shifting the operating incentive structure from an exclusively annual one to one with a longer horizon. This increases line of sight for most people. It also increases the weights on the operating measurements used.

- When necessary, immunize plans formally from capital structure changes. A financial services subsidiary of a major manufacturer does this in a phantom stock plan profiled in Chapter 8, restating net income each year based upon a normalized equity capital-to-assets ratio. Some corporate bonus plans compute EPS before repurchases.

There are other approaches. Return on equity and EPS can be combined in a matrix format like the one presented earlier in terms of operating income and ROIC. Metrics in this category also can be combined into systems of drivers, down-weighting the effect of capital structure on the metric's outcome.

Cash Flow Metrics

Next we address a range of cash flow metrics: EBITDA, operating cash flow, cash flow per share, cash flow return on gross investment (CFROGI) and free cash flow. These metrics often are used in industries in which heavy depreciation charges and debt financing make reported earnings low, negative or in any event difficult to benchmark. They are common in the broadcasting, real estate and power generation industries, for example. High-debt companies, including leveraged buyout (LBO) companies, often use them since they focus closely on the critical matter of cash flow coverage of debt service.

Part of the performance play in an LBO is to take a stable business with low reinvestment requirements and commit much of its cash flow to external debt service. Proponents assert that this forces new discipline on management of company costs and capital outlays, improving efficiency and value and funding high returns for holders of the company's sliver of equity. Cash flow measures sometimes are used to try to synthesize these LBO-like incentives within other types of companies. Companies also implement measurement systems based upon cash flow because they consider them to be better indicators of the ongoing earning power of an enterprise. Here are definitions of the major cash-flow-based metrics (excluding the value-based ones like CFROI and CVA that are covered in the next chapter):

- EBITDA is earnings before interest, taxes, depreciation and amortization. Since U.S. accounting rules no longer require companies to take periodic amortization charges for intangible assets they acquire, this measure might more properly be called EBITD. It is EBIT plus depreciation, or pre-tax operating cash flow. This metric is used very often as a valuation yardstick, since it focuses more clearly upon persistent earning capacity, in comparison to the more heavily accrual-based metrics found farther down in the income statement. Some phantom stock plans use EBITDA for valuation purposes, a practice we evaluate with some skepticism shortly.

- Operating cash flow is equal to operating income (usually after tax) plus depreciation. It is the starting point of the free cash flow (FCF) computation defined in Chapter 4. FCF is the amount of cash flow that can be distributed from operations after satisfying the company's capital reinvestment requirements. It is computed as operating cash flow minus net capital expenditures and additions to net working capital and to other assets. (More briefly, it is operating income after taxes minus the overall change in capital.)

- Cash flow per share is EPS plus depreciation per share. There is another metric called cash EPS, but that is a bit different. It is EPS plus amortization per share. It was rendered obsolete by the discontinuance of intangible amortization under U.S. generally accepted accounting principles (GAAP).

- Cash flow return on gross investment (CFROGI, or "see froggy") is a cash version of ROIC, computed as operating cash flow divided by gross capital (the customary definition of capital or net assets, plus accumulated depreciation). Since the income metric used in the plan — operating cash flow — is gross of depreciation, the capital construct is as well.

To apply value rules to cash flow metrics, we need to learn about something called "recapture." To create value for owners, a company must generate enough cash flow not only to provide a return *on* its net assets, but a return *of them* to the extent they wear out and need replacement over time.

A company might hold land parcels for investment, for example, leasing them out for use as parking lots while waiting to sell them for development. This company does not need cash flows to fund the replacement of these assets. Land does not wear out and require replacement in the way that buildings and equipment do. Investors in this company have certain expectations for return, but they expect to receive these returns mainly in the form of value gains on company investments.

The developer who buys the land and puts a hotel on it, on the other hand, needs cash flow from operations sufficient to replace depreciating assets as they wear out — things like furniture, equipment, room decorations and fixtures, HVAC systems, windows and, eventually, structural elements of the building. If instead of hotels the company has shorter-lived assets — if it operates a fleet of taxicabs or leases out photocopiers, then it needs to devote even greater cash flows to asset replacement before it can be said to earn any return on investment for owners.

The fact is that all cash flow is not created equal. The measures considered until this section deal with the issue in a simple way; they are all net of depreciation charges. The common cash flow measures, in contrast, are all stated after the "add back" of these charges.

In the context of an incentive plan, the recapture issue may cause companies to waste capital or overpay incentives. EBITDA, for example, can be a very useful yardstick for expressing value. However, it can have adverse consequences when used with an incentive plan. In an example of a phantom stock plan of a general type described in Chapter 10, a company is valued at six times EBITDA. The plan subtracts new investments from the FCF element of a "total return" computation (value gains plus FCF). This means the plan imposes a break-even EBITDA-yield requirement of 16.7 percent on new investments. That's $1/6$, or one divided by the valuation multiple. The problem with the 16.7 percent yield requirement is that it is economically inadequate for many investments, particularly those involving depreciating assets that need to be replaced over time. By the time you subtract taxes from the gross yield of 16.7 percent, then the recapture or depreciation cost — another 10 percent, roughly, if the asset lasts 10 years — then actual yields surely are below the cost of capital and may even be negative.

This suite of cash-based measures poses some other issues as well, but they are not new ones. Cash-based income metrics do not provide for a complete overall return on the capital used in the business, just as operating income and net income do not. The return-based metric, CFROGI, poses the same issues as ROIC.

There are solutions to issues associated with the metrics based on cash flow:

- A practical solution is to apply them only in cases where asset composition and life are largely fixed, like the real estate business or cable television. In this case, criteria for return simply need to be set at levels high enough to reward only those investments that create value.

- Another solution is to accompany the measures with some accountability for gross capital usage. Over time, gross capital requirements will reflect the recapture criterion. The award schedule used in an independent power producer's phantom stock plan, for example, balanced operating cash flow against gross capital invested in the enterprise. As an alternative, cash flow and CFROGI can be combined in a matrix format in much the same way as ROIC and operating were earlier in this chapter.

In other examples in the next chapter, the CVA and RVA metrics each involve capital charges that include both return and recapture elements. The CFROI metric addresses the problem through an internal rate of return computation.

The Big Choice

The metrics debate has a lot of moving parts. Many of the commonly cited "metric" problems in the incentive structure actually stem from its short-term nature. When you shift the operating structure to the medium-term, you're addressing a lot of what is wrong with senior management's pay. We've also seen in this chapter that many of the problems with traditional metrics can be addressed without abandoning them as a group. We'll see more solutions later. Companies no doubt will continue to evaluate dozens of variations on financial metrics as they set up incentive pay plans.

It's possible to address the flurry of issues involved in this area without memorizing all of its moving parts. The moving parts of value creation are set out in value rules. None of the incentive metrics discussed in this chapter comprehend those moving parts entirely, so they need to be used with care and some means of correction needs to be applied. Most of the metrics discussed here are familiar and commonly quoted ones. That is a strong advantage, so it often is worthwhile to examine their deficiencies and patch them up in various ways for more productive use. Another choice would be to ditch traditional metrics and use value-based ones, and that is what the next chapter is about.

Endnotes

1   Simulation is done under the same general assumptions as the one in Chapter 2, except that annual incentive pay is based 75 percent upon business unit operating income and 25 percent on corporate EPS, while long-term incentive pay is a performance share plan under which shares are earned based upon a value-based measurement approach.

2   Current U.S. GAAP does not require companies to amortize acquired intangible assets, so the "A" in EBITDA is vestigial.

3   It is equivalent to a plan using the "beginning capital" version of economic profit in particular.

4   Large business investments like new plant construction, development and rollout of new products or acquisitions also would work as examples, but these normally don't generate performance at intended levels within a year.

5   The gross number of new shares issued is netted by items like the exercise price to be paid or the value of bonds to be tendered, transaction tax effects, and any unamortized balance of past grants.

6   As set out in Chapter 4, the more general rule of value creation is that the future free cash flows from the investment, discounted at the cost of capital, must exceed the investment's cost. In this example and many others, longer-run free cash flow effects are estimated based upon current operating income. Any large gaps that arise between operating income and free cash flow are addressed within the overall time frame of a well-designed incentive structure and its adjustment procedures.

8

Value-Based Performance Measures

What if you held a war and nobody came? In the mid-1990s, business journal headlines trumpeted new metrics like economic value added and cash flow return on investment. *CFO Magazine* covered the "Metric Wars" among promoters of these two metrics and a few others, and *Fortune* began to force-rank corporate America based upon economic value added. It looked then as if big changes were afoot in the performance measurement arena. Most companies seemed on course to dump the primary methods they used to judge and reward business success and to adopt wholly new ones.

It didn't happen. Companies continue to use traditional metrics like earnings per share (EPS), return on equity (ROE) and operating income (OI) to deliver cash incentive pay. The best-known value-based metric, economic value added, was cited as a bonus plan metric by only 5 percent of the companies polled in Towers Perrin's annual incentive design survey. And, with much larger stock and option grants, companies now outsource an even larger part of their executive rewards system to the stock market, diminishing the relative importance of pay-related metrics. Ten years after the "Metric Wars," value-based metrics account for very little of senior management pay in corporate America. And, if a company is not using a value-based metric as a performance measure in its executive pay programs, it is not really using it at all. The metric wars are over, and traditional metrics won.

Do you remember where you were when the metric wars broke out? Of course not. Only a few wonks were paying attention. But most companies did take a reasonably close look at value-based metrics — and in particular, economic value added — in the 1990s. Almost all of them balked at running value-based metrics through the organization in the ways their promoters insisted.

Why? I still answer as I did back in the mid-1990s, when a typical exchange on the matter occurred during a compensation committee meeting. In the meeting, I disappointed the committee chair whose own company was heavily invested in the economic value added metric. He predicted that most companies would be going down that path within a few years and asked for my view. I replied that I favored value-based metrics (I still do), but that I didn't think they held any monopoly on solutions in the area of value-based incentive design. Rather, it seemed to me, many of the things really being accomplished with elaborate value-based metric systems could be accomplished in a range of other, simpler and more effective ways.

My prediction was that some companies would adopt the economic value added system wholesale as his company had done, and some would pursue its benefits in other ways. I noted, as many observers did at the time, that many companies were likely to look at a big rollout of economic value added, see complexity, risk, cost and unfamiliar incentive constructs, and just pass. Some, not being aware of the alternatives to the more doctrinaire value-based plans, would muddle, defer the matter and eventually put it aside and continue with a traditional approach. This assessment turned out to be accurate.

It did not look back then as if value-based metrics by themselves were going to take over the world. Rather, the interest in these metrics derived from a bigger trend that has been in place for decades. That story concerns the ascendancy of basic, powerful principles of corporate finance. It is about their advantageous use in more and more areas within businesses and in their markets for commerce and capital. I learned a bit about this kind of thing while a graduate student in the business school at University of Chicago and during my 20 years as a financial advisor to industry. I have been thrilled to see the string of Nobel prizes awarded to the leading lights in this movement. I think the story is still going strong. The value-based management (VBM) movement of the 1990s is a chapter in this bigger, ongoing story.

Now again, the selection of performance metrics is becoming a high-profile matter. Companies now face rational accounting treatment for options, which will encourage them to re-examine their habits in the area of incentive design. They're going to have to rebound in some way from these accounting changes, simply because their incentive policies were pulled so far in one direction by the current rules.

The options numbers are huge, so any reversion from heavy option usage will involve huge numbers. If an all-option company changed to granting performance shares, as many are considering, it would quickly triple or quadruple the amount of senior management's incentive pay that depends upon formal metrics, targets and ranges. Any problems with incentive plan terms then would become all the more troublesome. Arguing for less ambitious goals, for example, could become a much more rewarding tactic. So could the many types of acquisitions that increase revenue and income while destroying value.

When companies move, they will do so in the context of a less ebullient stock market than they saw in the 1990s. Statistically speaking, that simply means we should plan for a more normal market, one in which stock prices fall almost as often as they rise and, in many cases, fall and recover only years later. There is nothing wrong with this as a capital market situation. The stock market takes good account of business performance, but it also discounts a lot of other factors and has its own timetable. That is sorely troubling to companies that use the stock market to run their executive pay systems.

Well-functioning incentives should state clearly how to create value and get paid, but options are silent on this critical matter. One thing they definitely can say is, "I've fallen and I can't get up!" This is sure to happen more often in more typical market conditions than those that prevailed in the 1990s. Stock prices that move sideways for years will be another common scenario, along with the many cases in which some business units are going like gangbusters, but not getting any gains on their parent company option grants.

For several years, companies have been in an era of stock option malaise. A more typical stock market than the one we saw in the 1990s is one that inspires less confidence. Market recoveries, for example, are assessed against very recent memories of decline. Many members of senior management discount stock options more heavily now. Growth and success disguise many problems, and the problems with stock-based pay have become more transparent and compelling: random, seemingly incomprehensible movements, little connection with executive actions, zero directive power, utter disengagement from business units and their high business stakes.

The new setting also demands greater diligence. All through the 1990s, corporations and their boards were moving toward a new stage of evolution in corporate governance, particularly with regard to senior management pay. Large corporate failures, accounting abuses and the stock market collapse then caused an evolutionary leap. We talked in the last chapter about "the importance of being earnest." Unlike Oscar Wilde, we did so without irony. Earnestness is the new standard.

Companies are going to take the huge pile of resources they use for senior management incentive pay and put it into some very different buckets, ones with more "operating" measurement constructs, more focus on long-term results, and more business unit stake. This will intensify the focus on metrics and goal-setting and the stakes involved in getting them right. Getting them right means applying the relevant value rules:

- Focusing the organization upon long-run, genuine operating performance, rather than short-run performance results distorted by traditional metrics

- Focusing upon external, value-based standards as a way of judging success, rather than upon internally negotiated budgets and plans

- Eliminating the more common sources of bias and manipulation that plague traditional metrics and plan designs without adjusting the plan to the point of incomprehensibility

- Paying close attention to the overall use of capital by the enterprise because it is a decisive matter — and one addressed poorly in many plans — in determining whether business decisions create value

- Applying a consistent cost of capital to business decisions, one taking reasonable account of business risks, because the effective cost attached to the use of capital in most incentive plans is unclear, either too high or too low, and often very inconsistent

- Emphasizing that management has a tangible ownership stake in every dollar of enterprise income and investor capital — rather than the vague, weak accountabilities normally present in a company's incentive structure

- Providing a proper, fiscally prudent basis for delivering executive rewards based upon value creation — whether it is at the corporate, group, division, profit center or venture level.

To do it right, companies are going to have to take another look at their habits, which puts value-based metrics right back into the mainstream debate. But the debate will be a very different one now. The narrow "should we do economic value added or not" frame of much of the 1990's VBM movement was not adequate at that time. It is even more inadequate to the higher stakes of the current debate.

Value rules do not require the use of any specific metric. Nor do they go so far as to endorse the specific target-setting algorithms or incentive plan formats that some advisors suggest. Proper standards do require reasonably complete fiscal control over the use of incentives in the business. They do require that incentive plans adhere to consistent financial criteria and be administered with integrity. Where the choice of metrics in senior management's pay is concerned, that means taking account of the basic financial drivers of value: income, capital usage and the cost of capital. Criteria like these can be satisfied in a wide range of ways.

Value-Based Measurement

Value-based metrics? Here's what I'm talking about. A value-based measurement approach is defined strictly by the following:

- It can be reconciled with business value. Normally, this means that the present value of a given scenario for company performance, when measured by a value-based metric, can be reconciled directly to results of a discounted cash flow (DCF) valuation of the same scenario.

- When used in an incentive plan, it encourages management to make business decisions that create shareholder value. This boils down to three conditions:

  - It encourages management to maximize long-run operating income.

  - It encourages business investments offering returns in excess of the cost of capital. At the same time, it encourages management to sell off assets if net proceeds are higher than the value they would contribute to the enterprise over time.

  - It encourages management to reduce risk and the cost of capital to the extent they can.

We know from the last chapter that traditional metrics like EPS, operating income and ROE do not consistently encourage value creation. Rather, incentive plans based upon those metrics tend to allow many scenarios in which value-destroying decisions are rewarded and vice versa. That standing tenet of the 1990's VBM movement is about to come back to the forefront.

Value-Based Metrics

We'll be reviewing six value-based metrics in this chapter:

- Economic profit (EP, a.k.a. economic value added)

- Total business return (TBR)

- Shareholder value added (SVA)

- Cash value added (CVA)

- Cash flow return on investment (CFROI)

- Real value added (RVA).

A seventh metric was introduced in Chapter 7 as the basis for an award matrix driven by operating income and ROIC. This metric, "net value added," is a derivative of EP, so it is not presented among the separate metrics we evaluate over the course of this chapter. However, the matrix technique that was used does add a seventh genuine alternative. Rather than using an explicitly value-based metric, a company can combine traditional measures into *systems* that consistently align results with value creation. This general technique assembles traditional measures into combinations that sync up with value drivers, and it can be accomplished based upon other metrics, such as TBR or SVA. Several incentive plans in Chapters 9 and 10 base award schedules on TBR, for example. In this chapter we'll also describe a metric called return on economic capital, one based upon the risk-based capital concept used in the financial services industry.

Each of the value-based metrics reflects income, capital usage and the cost of capital in proportion to their effects upon valuation. These connections are depicted in Figure 8-1.

Figure 8-1 might look a bit like the Rosetta Stone at first glance, but we can decipher it more readily. A few things are apparent on its face. The first four metrics are computed using just the three drivers of the DCF model: income, capital usage

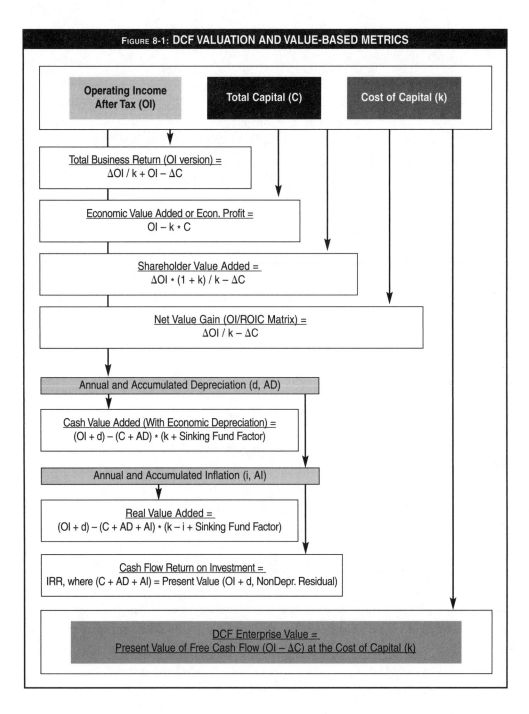

FIGURE 8-1: DCF VALUATION AND VALUE-BASED METRICS

Operating Income After Tax (OI)   Total Capital (C)   Cost of Capital (k)

Total Business Return (OI version) = $\Delta OI / k + OI - \Delta C$

Economic Value Added or Econ. Profit = $OI - k * C$

Shareholder Value Added = $\Delta OI * (1 + k) / k - \Delta C$

Net Value Gain (OI/ROIC Matrix) = $\Delta OI / k - \Delta C$

Annual and Accumulated Depreciation (d, AD)

Cash Value Added (With Economic Depreciation) = $(OI + d) - (C + AD) * (k + \text{Sinking Fund Factor})$

Annual and Accumulated Inflation (i, AI)

Real Value Added = $(OI + d) - (C + AD + AI) * (k - i + \text{Sinking Fund Factor})$

Cash Flow Return on Investment = IRR, where $(C + AD + AI) = \text{Present Value } (OI + d, \text{NonDepr. Residual})$

DCF Enterprise Value = Present Value of Free Cash Flow $(OI - \Delta C)$ at the Cost of Capital (k)

(that is Δc, or the change in capital) and the cost of capital. The measures below are based upon operating cash flow, so they require that depreciation (d) be added back to income. Consistently, cash flow metrics include capital on a basis gross of depreciation, so we add back accumulated depreciation (AD) in those computations. The only other general factor considered is inflation, and that affects the inflation-adjusted metrics, RVA and CFROI (i denotes the inflation rate, while AI refers to inflation's accumulated effect).

These value-based metrics are all drawn from the same well. The chart, dense as it is, does make it clear that if we simply consider the three drivers of DCF, and sometimes set apart the effects of depreciation and inflation, we can construct the full range of value-based metrics. This should help in demystifying this subject matter. Now let's walk through definitions and initial computations and see the best uses of each approach.

Economic Profit (EP) or Economic Value Added

EP is defined as operating profit after tax, minus a charge for the use of capital. It measures the extent to which operating results exceed basic investor demands for return on their capital. It is a form of the "residual income" or "economic rent" concepts in longstanding use in business and economics. SternStewart & Company developed the economic value added version of this metric and trademarked it as EVA®.

The basic idea of EP is that a business creates value for owners if it is able to generate returns on invested capital that exceed the opportunity cost of capital. DCF makes the same implication, as do other value-based metrics. Economic value added takes this maxim of value creation and converts it into an operational, periodic measure of performance.

The example in Table 8-1 on page 183 shows Year 1 operating income after tax of $150. The capital charge is $120, based on a 10 percent cost of capital and $1,200 in capital. EP is equal to $30, or $150 in income minus the $120 capital charge.[1]

Economic profit in its basic form is a simple, complete metric that can be used productively in annual and long-term incentive plans. It is the simplest way in which income, capital and its cost can be combined into a single metric. EP should be used when companies want to take a decisive step toward value creation and break away entirely from traditional measures. EP and other residual measures also make sense in other cases. For example, we implemented EP at a gas turbine manufacturer. It already had ROIC as a measurement and had allocated capital costs as part of predecessor plans, so moving to EP represented little change and added complexity. Also, EP was an intuitive solution to some of that company's target-setting issues.

Even in most basic form, residual income metrics do have some communication problems. Measured residual income is low or negative at many companies, rendering "percent change" comparisons meaningless. Residual income metrics also have a format that just does not resemble the most familiar modes of business judgment, troubling not only growth assessments, but other familiar frames of judgment like margin, yield or turnover. Though simple and accurate, residual income simply does not reconcile easily to the typical suite of quantitative metrics executives are used to applying. For these reasons, award schedules using metrics like income and return, but calibrated in value-based terms, typically provide a better solution than EP.

Capital charges in EP plans often are subject to distortion based upon issues affecting the measurement of beginning capital. Another general alternative to the basic formula of EP is to base the capital charge upon the change in capital. This overcomes two issues with residual income metrics: capital measurement inconsistencies and low or negative levels of residual income that throw off percentage change comparisons. A large energy company chose to implement a residual income metric but based its capital charge only upon the change in capital as a way of avoiding this problem.

Like the other metrics, EP accretes performance at a distinct periodic rate. Basically, dollar one of any income increase is a dollar's gain in EP terms, and dollar one of capital increase reduces EP by a dime, at a 10 percent cost of capital. Whether any particular interval of EP gain pays anything to senior management, and how much, depends upon the independent matters of plan design and standard setting. A plan that shares a percentage of any EP with the management group will pay out based upon that same dollar year after year. A plan based upon EP improvement, or one using some other ratcheting device as part of standard setting, will tend to reward it only once. This is a design choice, not an outcome dictated by the metric itself. The percent-of-EP plan will render a negative EP company — that's around 50 percent of the population in any given year — ineligible for reward. That obviously has to be addressed in some way. It can be done using the standard-setting methods covered in Chapter 9.

Economic value added is the best known of the value-based metrics. Market research shows that it is synonymous in the minds of many corporate executives with the broader subject of VBM. This testifies to the marketing prowess that has been behind economic value added for many years. It also says something about the power of having a simple, easily recalled format.

Use the Metric, Lose the Rest

Usually, companies using the EP metric should adopt it in its basic form with only a few, obvious contingent adjustments for things like acquisitions and divestitures, ones that apply to just about any value-based metric. This means that the basic metric is not subject to any adjustments as part of its routine computation. Rather, it consists entirely of income, capital and the cost of capital.

There are complex methods for metric adjustment stereotypically linked with EP or economic value added. Promoters of residual income metrics have cited over 100 possible metric adjustments, often advising companies to adopt a great number of these. For example, a large German manufacturer adopted about a dozen such adjustments in connection with its global, EP-based annual incentive plan. That company's culture is very centered on its high-quality engineering. Accustomed to working with very low tolerances, it has a high tolerance for complexity and a high interest in precision. When it comes to pay plans, most companies don't. Such adjustments usually render EP plans incomprehensible to most participants. For those people, the incentive plan simply cannot work in any clear or direct way.

Many of the EP adjustments are unnecessary when the incentive structure rests upon value rules. Metric adjustments sometimes involve reversals of basic accruals like the company's bad debt reserve. Most such reversals simply move a bit of income from one year into another. This approach simply takes too much trouble to isolate performance in any one year, perpetuating the troublesome preoccupation with near-term results. A better approach is the value rules prescription to lengthen the effective time frame of the company's incentive structure.[2] That creates an incentive stake in longer-run results, rendering small issues like reserve manipulation pointless. Ironically, EP's many accrual adjustments do not include the reversal of depreciation expense, which is the mother of all accruals.

Some companies spread out expenses incurred in areas like R&D and marketing, running them through the P&L over a period of several years. From a motivational perspective, this is meant to stem any temptation to cut back on discretionary items like advertising or certain R&D outlays in an attempt to make the numbers at the end of a particular bonus year. As we saw in Chapter 4, such moves have no impact upon free cash flow or upon longer-run earning power. This is a reasonable adjustment to consider in a bonus metric, but again, the more complete response is to create a serious stake in longer-run results. Also, many matters can be reflected in the target-setting process rather than as metric adjustments. For example, expected results of acquisitions can be built into incentive targets in ways that can improve accountability and decision-making. The metric is then left in a clearer state.

In these ways and others, value rules provide a simpler and more effective way of addressing important incentive matters than the adjustment-heavy, bonus-centered paleo-VBM tactics of the mid-1990s. A company may still find it needs to adjust for a few items in its results. But the companies that apply a lot of adjustments aren't necessarily those with business circumstances really warranting them. Rather, the pattern seems to be that the true believers in VBM, the companies that want to use metrics and their specific adjustments to rule many details of executive behavior, are the ones more likely to pile on a lot of EP adjustments. Though well meant, the result is a classic example of mission creep: using incentives to police too many aspects of executive decision-making.

EP plans often involve their own methods for plan structure and target setting. Examples include bonus banks, multi-year targets set by inflexible formulas, and award ranges centered on EP improvement rather than EP in absolute terms. They are meant to overcome many of the EP issues cited so far. However, these features often simply add up to an unworkably complex apparatus. The HR head of one of the world's largest retailers properly asserted this about the EP plan he inherited, "Hey, I'm a smart guy and I don't understand this thing."

In general, companies should discard the stereotypical EP apparatus and adopt value rules. They should not adopt a *circa* 1994 version of value-based management.

Total Business Return (TBR)

TBR is the term for any of a range of metrics that track the increase in the value of a business plus the income or free cash flow it generates.[3] This two-part measurement approach is like computing total shareholder return — dividends plus capital gains — on a stock investment. The version of TBR presented in the graphic is one based upon after-tax operating income. Another version that is at least as common is one based upon earnings before interest, taxes, depreciation and amortization (EBITDA). EBITDA-based versions, as commonly applied, have deficiencies that mean they do not comply with value rules (noted initially in Chapter 7).

Working with a project team at Carlson Companies, I developed an income-based version of TBR for use in the company's phantom stock plans. In constructing it, we drew upon the format of other TBR metrics, my experience with measurement and valuation principles like those in the DCF model, and the underpinnings of the EP and SVA metrics.

Value, in this version of TBR, is based on the perpetuity valuation methods and assumptions mentioned in Chapter 4. In the example in Table 8-2 on page 184, this company's income is $600 at the outset so its value is $6,000, or $600 divided by the 10 percent cost of capital. In Year 1, income rises by $150, so the value gain is $1,500. Free cash flow (FCF) is negative at -$450, resulting in total business return of $1,050.

This version of TBR, when used to measure multi-period results, simply adds up FCFs for a period of time like three years irrespective of their timing. The DCF model, in contrast, is highly concerned with the timing of FCFs, with positive ones that occur earlier being worth more, and so on. A version of TBR that is more precise in this regard is shown on the next line of Table 8-1, and that is the one that we will reconcile to the DCF model shortly. Most often, the simpler version of TBR works better despite its imprecision. Simplicity is a powerful thing in these matters, after all. And any issues with valuation imprecision normally are offset within the usual workings of the incentive plan (e.g., overlapping multi-year grants, phase-ins of large capital outlays into TBR results).

A dollar of forecast-term income or capital reduction has a like effect upon FCF and so upon TBR. Increases in income over the forecast term have a multiple impact based upon the cost of capital. The multiple is 10 when the cost is 10 percent, for example. A basic TBR phantom stock grant on 1 percent of a company entitles holders to 1 percent of income over the forecast term, charges them for 1 percent of any capital increases, and gives them 10 percent of any increases in income.

TBR provides an annuity claim on the initial income level so it begins to accrue awards at dollar one of income. That might seem like a bit of a cakewalk. Remember, though, income increases are worth 10 times as much to the holder. Also, income contributes dollar for dollar to FCF, making this an instructive counterweight to value gains within TBR's "total return" format. By counter-weight, I mean: the TBR phantom stock plan isolates value creation by trading off investments, which reduce FCF, against income gains, which have a multiple impact upon value. The trade-off between these two factors means that new investments generally need to generate returns in excess of the cost of capital in order to increase incentive pay. That's where TBR takes the interplay among income, capital usage and the cost of capital and brings it home within an incentive plan.

A TBR computation is more complex than a basic form of EP. It requires thinking about capitalized earnings. But it does not necessarily drag you through the precise, perpetuity-valuation calculation of capitalized earnings we derived in Chapter 4. Rather, TBR's valuation conventions can be described in the usual value-as-a-multiple-of-income sense familiar to all in a price-earnings ratio format. Value is 10 times earnings, in our earlier example, so a buck of increased earnings means a 10-buck rise in value.

To understand TBR, you also have to get your head around FCF. Getting management to think about this subject matter in the context of value creation is a good idea. Education regarding value-based concepts like free cash flow normally is a good idea for companies going down the path of using value-based incentives to improve performance. In fact, this kind of executive education is a good idea at just about any company. Since it is something companies really should be doing anyway, the need to train should not be a strong objection to the use of metrics like TBR or, for that matter, EP. Instead, the situation should be seen as an opportunity to use incentive pay to support an important company process: financial training for a broad range of senior managers.

EP is a better bonus plan measure than TBR because it is periodic in format and simpler. TBR is used most often and most directly within phantom stock plans. In a phantom stock context, business units and private companies are trying to create well-functioning incentives and compete in an option-dominated executive labor marketplace. TBR is helpful here. Its value-gain plus cash-flow format stands up well next to the analogous bounties of stock-based pay.

Like the other metrics, TBR can be used to calibrate payouts based upon metrics like OI and ROIC. This is done commonly in bonus plans, performance unit plans and performance share plans. In performance share plans, this is a very good way to blend the line of sight of a value-based metric, especially at the business unit level, with the benefits of denominating senior management pay in corporate shares.

We'll see in Chapter 9 that TBR also can be used to set targets for business performance within incentive plans using other measures. Companies can use customized sets of goals for various business units, for example, while conforming them to a uniform TBR scale. TBR also is useful in the performance comparisons that sometimes enter into target setting as well as measurement within indexed plans. The total return format of TBR works some financial magic in these settings and some others because it allows the performance of very different businesses to be benchmarked in a consistent way. Low-growth companies with high FCF, for example, can be measured on a reconcilable scale with units having high income growth and capital needs. This approach remedies quite a number of the issues that throw off comparisons made in terms of other measures. My colleagues and I have applied this variant of TBR in various ways in scores of companies.

Shareholder Value Added (SVA)

SVA is equal to the valuation effects of improvements in income minus concurrent increases in capital. It basically is the same thing as net value added, or capitalized change in EP, except for its "annuity due" convention, which assumes that increases in income occur at the beginning of each year and are receivable then.[4]

In the SVA format, the $150 increase in income is worth $1,650, equal to the $1,500 present value of the income stream used in the TBR computation ($150 in Year 1 and every year thereafter) plus the current-year income of $150, receivable now and therefore not discounted. The change in capital is $1,200. SVA is equal to the value of the income, $1,650, minus the concurrent $1,200 increase in capital, or $450.

SVA seems a perfectly valid construct for use mainly in long-term incentive plans. EP is better for annual plans, for the reasons noted above. SVA would function well as a valuation formula in phantom stock plans, but I have not seen it put to that obvious use. For my own part, I prefer TBR in most phantom stock design situations because of the host of favorable dynamics noted here and in the next two chapters. Like other value-based metrics, SVA can be used as a calibration device for incentive plans stated in terms of other measures like OI and ROIC.

Cash Value Added (CVA)

Cash value added, in general form, is a cash version of EP. In CVA, the income construct is operating cash flow rather than income, and the capital metric is stated gross of accumulated depreciation.

In most CVA applications, the capital charge simply equals the company's cost of capital multiplied by gross capital. This causes the "recapture" problem noted in Chapter 7: the fact that cash flow metrics encourage investment in any asset with high cash flows irrespective of whether they are sufficient to fund both a reasonable return on the investment and a full recapture of its depreciating component. This can bias corporate investment and divestment policies in a range of harmful ways. My solution is to build a sinking fund factor into the CVA capital charge so it includes both return *on* capital and return *of* it.

This version of CVA is presented in the example. In it, the entire $1,200 investment is depreciating in nature so the return-and-recapture charge applies to its full amount. The capital charge is equal to $483 per year, an amount sufficient to provide a 10 percent per year return on the $1,200 investment and also fund its replacement (assuming zero inflation) at the end of Year 3. Year 1 operating income plus deprecation is $550, so CVA is $67 after subtracting the capital charge.

CVA accretes value differently than EP. Its economic depreciation format has the effect of leveling the capital charge and leveling CVA when income is fixed. The EP capital charge, in contrast, falls each year as the asset depreciates, making EP drift upward until the asset is replaced. CVA is more accurate in this regard, since the performance of the asset does not actually rise in real terms each year (and RVA is more accurate still, when inflation is a material concern). The upward drift of EP is said to cause something of a "harvest" bias, and EP does tend to rise during any of the short intervals when management can patch up fixed assets, keep them running and put off replacement outlays. That is more perception than reality because EP generally encourages economically optimal replacement policies when management has a long-term interest in it. Actually all these value-based metrics are said, unfairly, to cause a harvest bias simply because they create new, proper accountability for capital usage. But that is not a bias. It is the removal of one.

CVA is a good metric for annual or long-term incentive plans when the company has a strong focus on cash flow. Two independent power producers adopted cash versions of value-based plans, for example, one using CVA in a bonus plan and the other using a cash version of TBR in its phantom stock plan. The high priority on cash flow in such companies often is accompanied by low net income after high financing and deprecation costs.[5] Cash flow-based metrics also can be used in the broadcasting and real estate industries for this reason.

CVA actually does not encourage cash flow generation any more strongly than other metrics like EP or TBR; if it did, it would cause an anti-investment bias. Rather, CVA's format simply *signals* the cash flow part of the message, just as TBR signals an economic balance between growth and yield. Again, choices among the major value-based metrics mainly are format and communication choices, rather than choices based upon one metric having true analytical superiority over another.

Cash Flow Return on Investment (CFROI)

This metric, developed by a consulting firm called HOLT Value Associates, does strive for analytical superiority. Unlike the other metrics, it adjusts for inflation in an explicit way and so it does generate economically more meaningful results in cases where inflation would otherwise distort them. General computational procedures are as follows:

- First, restate gross capital to a current-dollar, inflation-adjusted basis. CFROI advocates assert that operating cash flow is stated in current dollars, so capital must be in current dollars if the metric is to be used reliably for many comparisons. The restatement involves digging into the gross fixed asset account and dividing it into "vintages," or the past years in which the constituent assets were placed in service. Alternatively, it is possible to estimate the past pattern of asset placement based upon asset life and the accumulated depreciation ratio. Past outlays then are adjusted to current value using an inflation factor like the GDP deflator or the producer price index (PPI), resulting in current dollar gross investment, or CDGI. This is the current replacement cost of the dollars invested in the past in fixed assets (not the replacement cost of the assets themselves). To this, add the current balance sheet figures for other assets (assumed here to be close enough to a current-dollar basis of presentation). In the Year 1 example, the only asset is the $1,200 outlay, and an inflation adjustment would be a mere $24 at a 2 percent inflation rate, so CDGI is $1,224. Many companies have older assets or ones in highly inflationary markets. In such cases, these adjustments are material and can help to judge results on a more consistent basis.

- Determine the average life of depreciating assets. This typically is approximated by dividing the gross asset balance by the annual depreciation charge. In this case, the asset life is three years.

- Assemble an internal rate of return calculation, using CDGI as a current investment amount, current after-tax operating cash flow as the level annual income amount, asset life as the number of years, and the non-depreciating portion of the balance sheet as the residual value. The resulting internal rate of return (IRR) — that is, the discount rate that equates present value with CDGI — is CFROI. In this case it works out to be 18 percent.

This is a cash flow-based measure, so we need to ensure that we are handling recapture of investment in wasting assets. CFROI handles this implicitly within the IRR computation, assuring that asset depreciation is funded out of cash flow before any genuine return accrues.

CFROI is not a simple metric at a conceptual or computational level. Also, it does not stand alone as a value-based measure and needs a sibling metric, just as ROIC does, to get outcomes that comply with value rules. CFROI-based goals can be combined with cash flow within incentive plans in the same way that ROIC and OI were in Chapter 7. It has been counterbalanced with CDGI growth, in one example. CFROI, though, is too complex as a practical matter for use in most incentive plans.

If inflation and cash flow issues are serious ones, I'd suggest remedying them through the target-setting process or within plans driven by other metrics (e.g., through differing inflationary expectations impounded in nominal costs of capital in one country versus another). If an inflation-adjusted VBM standard truly is useful, I recommend RVA over CFROI.

Real Value Added (RVA)

I developed RVA based upon inflation-adjusted valuation work I had done with multinationals when I was a valuation consultant in the 1980s. In the context of incentive metrics, I wanted to get at the inflation adjustment and cash flow basis of the metric CFROI without having to deal with its complexity in quite so overt a way. Real value added is equal to operating cash flow minus an inflation-adjusted charge for the use of capital. All of the complicated bits of CFROI are handled within the RVA capital charge, simply called "rent." Like the factor used in the CVA computation, it accounts both for return on capital and recapture of depreciating assets. It also addresses inflation. The rent computation of RVA works just like the CVA capital charge, except that the rate of return used to determine it is adjusted for inflation as in this example:

Real cost of capital = (1 + 10% cost of capital) / (1+ 2% inflation rate) − 1 = 7.84%

The RVA capital charge is like a rent expense, and rent is a rhetorically productive term for the computation. Everyone knows what rent is and what causes it to rise or fall, and this helps explain the complexities in computing this inflation-adjusted charge. It actually is useful as well as a more general description of the concept of an opportunity cost for business capital. All of our metrics include a cost of capital concept just as the DCF model does, so it is worth sketching out the ideas behind the RVA rent charge:

- Rent is higher (in relation to gross cost) if the property or asset has appreciated in value since acquisition. Rents go up when property values rise, irrespective of the historical cost of the property on somebody's books. Developers chased the undesirables off a vacant lot in the Wrigleyville neighborhood of Chicago in 1984, putting up some nice townhouses. That improved the value of the vintage greystones nearby including the one where I rented an apartment. My rent went up.

- Rent is lower to the extent prospective inflation and related capital gains (rather than rent cash flow) provide a portion of expected return to owners. When I was in the valuation practice at what was then Price Waterhouse, I had a window office on the 77th floor of what was then the Amoco building in Chicago. From my perch, I could see vacant lots used as parking lots and driving ranges. Investors expected to get a return on those parcels, but not through their cash flows. They were in it for capital gains and content in the meantime with, well, low-rent uses.

- Rent is higher to the extent wear and tear is expected to occur. I rented a compound radial arm saw recently from the local Ace Hardware store. You may by now wish I had used it to edit this book, but instead I put up some crown molding. My daily rental rate on this asset was far higher, as a proportion of its cost, than renting vacant land would be. A piece of equipment wears out, but land, as a general matter, does not. Ace needs to get enough cash flow from that asset to replace it at the end of its life, not just to get a current cash return on the cost of its investment. Rents are higher not only for depreciable assets over non-depreciable ones, but are higher for depreciable assets with shorter lives.

- Rent is equal at equilibrium to the level required to provide a total return to investors (cash flow plus capital gain) equal to the cost of capital. My Saturday newspaper has dozens of car lease deals advertised in it. If any of those dealers tried to gouge too much out of the market, they'd be undercut quickly by competing dealers. Competition drives rates of investment return down over time toward the company's cost of capital. This dynamic has been pressing on the car market for a long time. During the Cubs games that I can watch from Minneapolis on WGN, for example, I see ads for a particular car dealer that sponsored the Cubs when I was a kid in upstate Illinois. By now, surely, competition has driven profits in the car market toward some equilibrium. The same thing has happened in many other markets, so actual leases and rents tend to track synthetic ones like the RVA capital charge.

- A competitive lease market makes buying versus leasing a nearly indifferent matter, so rent is a valid opportunity cost to charge for the use of an asset. I rent certain shop tools like that compound radial arm saw. I buy cars rather than lease, but I bear the bulk of the same capital cost in the form of depreciation and lost interest income on the cash tied up in the car.

The general trick of RVA is to address the inflation and gross asset issues, but to cover them entirely within the intuitive framework of a rent expense. Results are stated in the residual income format of EP rather than the percentage-return format of CFROI, so the metric has more valid use in incentive plans. However, it makes sense only in cases in which inflation is a serious issue — e.g., a multinational wanting to state local currency performance on a consistent basis — and cases in which inflation is not seen as covered adequately by the nominal cost of capital or by target-setting procedures.

The rent analogies are useful in covering the general idea of a capital charge, but inflation really should not be a prominent part of a general, current discussion about value-based metrics. Why? Because Milton Friedman, back in 1970, made the revolutionary statement that inflation is always and everywhere a monetary phenomenon. Central banks in the U.S. and elsewhere have followed his advice for over two decades, and now most citizens of industrialized nations live without fear of inflation's disruptive, impoverishing effects. Ideas have consequences.

Now, in our discussion, inflation has no more weight than other technical issues. It is part of the discussion simply because CFROI happens to be an inflation-adjusted metric and was one of the major combatants in the metric wars of the 1990s.

VBM metrics might seem like one of those cornfield mazes. In fact, they might seem a bit like crop circles — hard to discern, apparently originating in outer space, and inviting suspicions of a hoax. Here, in summary, are the tested, successful paths out of the maze:

- EP is a solid metric for performance-based plans in companies intending to make a substantial commitment to VBM precepts and a clear break with traditional measures. CVA is more complex, but useful in cases placing a premium upon its cash flow format.

- TBR is great for phantom stock plans. It offers a stock option format with VBM functionality and can be used in important target-setting contexts.

- All the metrics can be used to calibrate award schedules for other types of plans. The most direct and obvious approaches are those based upon income and ROIC, calibrated using TBR.

- The CFROI framework is useful in analytical and planning applications, but the metric's complexity and return-only format make it useless in a pay context. Anything CFROI offers can be gained using other constructs in target setting, nominal cost of capital determination or, in the unusual case in which an inflation adjusted metric should be used in an incentive plan, through the metric RVA.

Common Values

We've talked about six metrics and one value-based calibration technique. Now we'll reconcile each to the DCF model. First, let's eliminate two of the seven. The "matrix" calibration method simply mimics one or another of the metrics so it does not need to be reconciled as a separate metric. CFROI is a return-based measure set as a percentage so, like ROIC, it needs to be combined properly with some measure reflecting enterprise scale (the present value shown with CFROI is the present value of the cash flows upon which it is based).

The other five metrics produce the same valuation results as a DCF model. This is demonstrated in Tables 8-1 and 8-2:

- Table 8-1 shows how EP, CVA and RVA indicate that the net present value of a given business decision is equal to that indicated by the DCF model. A business decision with a finite life is used for this purpose because these are metrics of periodic performance rather than valuation formulas. An equivalent present value is shown for CFROI simply to demonstrate that it is composed of the same original cost and operating cash flow elements as the other metrics.

- TBR and SVA, on the other hand, are valuation formulas. They're meant to estimate how current financial performance translates into enterprise valuation and return. In Table 8-2, we reconcile their valuation implications with those made by the DCF model. Results are presented in terms of net value added, as well, for reference. TBR and SVA reconcile to the DCF valuation as follows:

  - The metric TBR captures all forecast-term FCFs as well as any value gain arising from increases in income. The present value of these two items, when combined with the beginning income level and the contribution it makes to the DCF residual value, add up to the same set of cash flows being valued in the DCF model.

Year	0	1	2	3
Forecast of Results of Investment Outlay:				
Capital	$1,200	$800	$400	-
Operating Cash Flow		600	630	$662
Depreciation		400	400	400
Operating Income After Tax at 25% Tax Rate		150	173	196
Free Cash Flow	($1,200)	$550	$573	$596
Discounted Cash Flow Valuation:				
Present Value of FCF 10% Cost of Capital	($1,200)	$500	$473	$448
Net Present Value	$221			
Economic Profit (Economic Value Added):				
Operating Income After Tax		$150	$173	$196
Capital Charge		120	80	40
Economic Profit (EP)		30	93	156
Present Value of EP 10%	$221	$27	$76	$117
Cash Value Added:				
Operating Income After Tax		$150	$173	$196
Depreciation		400	400	400
Operating Cash Flow After Tax		550	573	596
Capital Charge (2.49 Capital Charge Factor)		483	483	483
Cash Value Added		67	90	114
Present Value of CVA 10%	$221	$61	$74	$85
Real Value Added:				
Operating Income After Tax		$150	$173	$196
Depreciation		400	400	400
Operating Cash Flow After Tax		550	573	596
Inflation Adjusted Cost of Capital 7.84% (2% Expected Inflation)				
Capital Charge (2.58 Capital Charge Factor)		474	483	493
Real Value Added		76	89	103
Present Value of RVA 10%	$221	$69	$74	$78
Cash Flow Return on Investment:				
Capital	$1,200	$800	$400	-
Accumulated Depreciation		400	800	$1,200
Inflation Adjustment		24	48	73
Current Dollar Gross Investment	$1,200	$1,224	$1,248	$1,273
Asset Life		3	3	3
Operating Cash Flow 10%	$221	$550	$573	$596
CFROI		18%	19%	20%

TABLE 8-2: PRESENT VALUE EQUIVALENCY OF DISCOUNTED CASH FLOW (DCF), SHAREHOLDER VALUE ADDED (SVA) AND TOTAL BUSINESS RETURN (TBR)

Year	0	1	2	3	Residual
Forecast of Business Results:					
Operating Income After Tax (OI)	$600	$750	$900	$1,050	$1,050
Capital	5,000	6,200	6,500	6,800	
Free Cash Flow		($450)	$600	$750	$10,500
Discounted Cash Flow Valuation:					
Present Value (PV) of FCF 10% Cost of Capital		($409)	$496	$563	$7,889
Enterprise Value	$8,539				
Shareholder Value Added (SVA):					
Operating Income After Tax (OI)		$600	$750	$900	$1,050
Capitalized Change In Income		1,650	1,650	1,650	
Change in Capital		1,200	300	300	
Shareholder Value Added		450	1,350	1,350	$3,150
Present Value of SVA 10%		$409	$1,116	$1,014	
Value of Initial OI Level	$6,000				
Enterprise Value	$8,539				
Total Business Return (TBR):					Total
Operating Income After Tax	$600	$750	$900	$1,050	
Value Gain		1,500	1,500	1,500	$4,500
Free Cash Flow		(450)	600	750	900
TBR, Annual		1,050	2,100	2,250	5,400
Three-Year TBR with FCFs Compounded		($545)	$660	$750	5,366
Present Value of TBR, Residual	$4,508				$4,031
Enterprise Value 10%	$8,539				
Net Value Added (Capitalized Change in Economic Profit):					
Operating Income After Tax	$600	$750	$900	$1,050	
Capitalized Change In Income		1,500	1,500	1,500	
Change in Capital		1,200	300	300	
Net Value Added, Prospective, on New Outlays		300	1,200	1,200	$2,700
Present Value 10%		273	992	902	
Present Value of Annual Base OI Level	$6,000	$136	$124	$113	
Enterprise Value	$8,539				
Reconciliation of Metrics:					Total
Change in Economic Profit		$30	$120	$120	$270
Capitalized		10%	10%	10%	
Equals: Net Value Added		300	1,200	1,200	2,700
Plus: Annual Increase in Base Income Level		150	150	150	450
Equals: Shareholder Value Added		450	1,350	1,350	3,150
Plus: Initial Income Level		600	750	900	2,250
Equals Total Business Return, Annual		$1,050	$2,100	$2,250	$5,400

- SVA, in contrast, does not give credit for all of the forecast-term income and its effects upon FCF. Rather, SVA focuses upon valuation effects of increases in income only. To reconcile SVA value with DCF value, you must add the capitalized value that the beginning income level contributes to DCF value.

What If You Held a War and Nobody Came?

The DCF reconciliation is a bit more complex than a cursory scan of the metrics, but the extra work is worth doing. The messages you may have heard in the marketplace for the last decade or more have emphasized that value-based measurement approaches differ greatly among themselves and accomplish things that traditional measures cannot. But the more rigorous process brings us to a different conclusion: in terms of our basic mission — linking results and value — these metrics are all the same. If they really were capturing economically distinct messages, they'd have different implications for value. They'd have different views on important matters like whether a particular business decision creates value or what a particular company is worth. They don't.

They'd also have different views on whether a particular level of performance warrants being paid. But the metrics, by themselves, don't say much about this. Many plans using economic profit pay out top-of-range awards when the metric is negative, for example, so the result of the metric computation apparently doesn't clinch the matter. Whether a particular performance level warrants being paid mainly is a matter of what target was established for company performance. SVA for Year 1 was $450 in our example, while economic profit came in at $30, but either could result in targeted levels of payout if it was used as the target performance level. Gains on a TBR phantom stock grant are not settled definitively by TBR performance. The grant size and structure link various performance levels with participant gains.

And, of course, you can get the same results using traditional measures, as we did using the OI/ROIC matrix. In Chapter 9, we'll do it using target-setting methods, again within incentive plans featuring no VBM yardstick. For now, let's just note that metrics and target setting are separate matters. No financial metric by itself has anything conclusive to say about what level of performance merits reward.

What About All the Stuff that Comes with the Metric?

Systems for value-based management often extend far beyond our investigation of the basic forms of the particular metric used. Where incentives are concerned, they're typically accompanied by systems used to set goals, by some advice on the design of those plans and by an elaborate set of adjustments for possible use within them.

They're said to be of a piece, but they're not. These other matters are not really features of a particular metric. Rather, they are choices to be made mostly independent of the particular metric being used.

Traditional bonus and performance plans are the primary ways that value-based measures are used in plan design. Some are used as phantom stock valuation formulas, but that does not distinguish one from another. The TBR formula used by Carlson Companies in its phantom stock plan, for example, is sometimes expressed to participants as the capitalized change in EP plus FCF plus the increase in capital. That's a complicated way of putting it, but Carlson Companies has its reasons, namely a desire to place separate emphasis upon EP, FCF and the importance of investing for growth.

The metric economic value added often is associated with a bonus bank incentive plan format. We expressed hesitancies about bonus banks in Chapter 5, but for now we just observe that, if a company wanted to use a banking format, it could do so using any metric under the sun. So, VBM metrics can be used in traditional plans and other metrics can be used in stereotypically value-based plans; metrics are one thing and plan design is another.

Metrics tend to be promoted alongside an apparatus of adjustments. For example, there's the practice of spreading out R&D costs over time when computing economic value added. CFROI is concerned greatly with inflation adjustments and cash flow. But capitalizing R&D is not an economic value-added adjustment in any precise sense. Rather, it is a generic procedure that many companies and analysts use to judge performance, deliver rewards or price the enterprise. And EP can be adjusted to reflect cash flow and inflation. Metrics should be seen as à la carte choices that don't come *with* anything at all.

Metric Adjustments — Compulsories Only

Companies using both traditional and value-based measurement approaches are obliged to adjust actual financial performance from time to time to deal with certain events like acquisitions, divestitures or large, non-recurring variations in income. Companies using value-based metrics like EP or TBR usually adopt some guidelines for plan adjustments when adopting incentives. For the majority of plans using traditional metrics, we find a rather mixed range of market practices:

- Some companies define the common measures net income, EPS, and ROE from a continuing operations perspective, thereby sidestepping much below-the-line effect.

- One-time or temporary effects upon income commonly are spread out over time or simply removed from measured performance.

- Many such events are contemplated during the company's incentive target-setting process (normally based upon budget), so actual performance does not necessarily require adjustment. Budgeted income for a particular year might be higher or lower than it otherwise would have been, due, say, to an acquisition made in an earlier year or planned in the current one.

- Events clearly outside of management's control often are removed at least partly from incentive plans, but companies do this most often through the budget process (basically by taking into account business conditions) and through the metrics (generally by up-weighting more controllable measures of results).

- When adjustments occur, they often are made in reaction to events that not only are seen as out of management's control or otherwise outside the scope of the performance/reward "contract" of the incentive plan, but also as surprises.

How best to deal with special events depends upon the metrics and target-setting methods used within the incentive plan. It also is affected importantly by the general set of practices and presumptions underlying incentive plan administration, including how the general notion of accountability is applied within such plans. That's probably why treatments vary so much from one plan to the next. Here, we'll sketch out a model treatment for making adjustments within incentives under these assumptions:

- The plan uses a value-based measurement approach and therefore places reasonable weight upon income, capital usage and the cost of capital.

- The matters requiring adjustment were not anticipated during the target-setting process.

- Incentive plans are meant to impose full accountability upon management for any events affecting business results, whether the current participant group caused them or not.

When these things are true, it is pretty simple to devise a general set of rules for dealing with most contingencies and still be assured that they don't short-circuit the intended incentive effects of the plan. The compulsory adjustment features needed in a value-based incentive plan are the same ones commonly addressed when administering more traditional plans:

- How to deal with large outlays like acquisitions, capital expenditures, and costly initiatives in areas like marketing and R&D

- How to deal with reorganization costs, divestitures and other material effects seen as nonrecurring.

In these cases, the goal is to maintain a continuous stake in business results and full accountability for them, normally by spreading out their effects over two to three years.

Acquisitions are the best place to start when talking about incentive plan adjustments, because methods in these cases cover most of the issues involved. Often, acquisitions are expected to take several years before they pay off at normal levels — before their financial performance reaches a level high enough to warrant having made the acquisition in the first place. The general solution is to spread the deal costs over time, commonly over a period of two to three years. If the company wishes to have strict adherence to DCF results, it may add an interest charge to these capital deferrals, one usually assessed as the cost of capital. A Spanish food company, for example, elected to treat capital expenditures in this way, because it wanted greater precision and was prepared to bear somewhat greater complexity in plan communication and administration.

However, that choice was unusual. Instead, costs typically are phased in without interest, with the understanding that this method imparts a modest pro-investment bias. The pace of the phase-in may be as simple as a straight-line pattern. It also may be set in such a way as to allow gains for executives to accrue at an agreed pace when deal performance is on track with expectations. In those cases, the agreed phase-in could be as specific as this example: 10 percent of capital in Year 1, 35 percent in Year 2 and the balance in Year 3. Some businesses expect to generate losses for a year or two after acquisition for various reasons, typically stemming from the pursuit of deal synergies or from investments upgrading capabilities of the target. Since these costs are one-time (or temporary) and investment-related, they may be eligible for capitalization and phase-in as well.

The best time to set the phase-in schedule for pay purposes is right at the time of the deal. This way, management is obliged to come up with a deal projection and use that same projection for incentive plan purposes. They can't use one, optimistic set of projections for deal purposes and diminishing ones later when negotiating incentive goals. The key matter in all such determinations is accountability:

- All outlays should be subtracted from performance over time.

- Management should be held accountable for getting returns on the deal outlay and for the timetable they set, since these were what the board relied upon when approving the deal.

In certain "strategic" acquisitions, companies permanently relieve their incentive goals from all or a portion of the cost of such deals, viewing the possible returns as too distant and uncertain to be included within the normal term of incentives. In "bolt on" acquisitions, corporate management buys a company and then assigns it to one of its business units, which is expected to run it successfully, even though it may not have had much input into deal selection or pricing. This is another case in which goals often are lightened.

The overall dynamic of decision-making at many companies would be improved if they accounted for all capital used, including in these two instances of common exception. For example, if business units are held accountable for bolt-ons, they might resist more strongly when corporate is about to make a bad deal. Most corporate acquisitions fail, so it is reasonable to suggest actions that change the underlying decision-making dynamics. Business unit management, since they possess much operating expertise, should be asked to step up in this way.

If strategic acquisitions are made with an expectation of longer-run returns, they should be assigned longer phase-in schedules rather than having their costs stricken out of the system. The critical governance dynamic is this: the incentive plan treatment of big deals should be used to encourage the truest projections to emerge at the time of the deal. This encourages the highest quality business decisions to be made when stakes are highest. The traditional approach to incentives and acquisitions involves incomplete metrics on the one hand and dissolving accountability on the other. When success matters most, it is a failure.

Major capital expenditures like new plant construction often are phased in like acquisitions. However, their timetables for returns often are more favorable, since premium acquisition prices are not involved. Simply excluding construction in progress from the capital computation is one method — outlays do not enter into capital until the new asset is placed in service.

Many incentive plans discourage divestitures because their metrics are heavily weighted toward income. Others encourage divestitures of those units that can be sold at a book gain since such gains can be taken into income for incentive purposes. Value-based incentive plans work much differently. Their general workings, as well as their divestiture adjustments, are of use in seeing how these transactions should be treated for purposes of executive reward. These plans convey a claim upon longer-term value creation, so they create the same economic trade-offs facing owners, encouraging a business sale when its economic benefits exceed the value and returns the asset would generate over time if retained.

In such plans, divestitures get the opposite treatment of acquisitions. The gain or loss on sale in these cases is removed from income and treated in the capital or free cash flow computation only. Take a company with beginning capital of $400. If a unit with a book value of $40 is sold for proceeds of $100, assets rise by $60 ($100 in new cash net of a $40 reduction in business assets). This difference is a book gain that shows up in equity as well (ignoring taxes), so capital ends up at $460. Next, we assume the $100 in proceeds are used to pay dividends, repurchase shares or to pay down debt, so capital falls to $360. Or we assume the money is characterized as "non-operating cash" for purposes of the plan and therefore not included in capital. (If proceeds are redeployed into other operating assets, they will not reduce capital, but that is a separate matter.) In this example, $40, net, goes out of the company for capital measurement purposes, and capital falls to $360. The drop in capital adds $40 to free cash flow. The gain adds $60 to income, so the total free cash flow impact simply equals the sale proceeds at $100. So deal proceeds increase free cash flow within the incentive plan.

Income lost as a result of the sale reduces the plan's income construct. A drop in income has multiple effects upon valuation. If proceeds of $100 exceed the unit's valuation, it's a sale candidate, and vice versa. In a long-term incentive plan, this dynamic usually works well enough by itself. Participants are encouraged to weigh the near-term effects of sale proceeds against the value the business unit would have contributed over time, just as shareholders would wish. In situations in which short-term sale bias is seen as a risk, divestiture proceeds may be phased in.

Since major initiatives in areas like marketing or product development often are like capital expenditures, made in pursuit of long-run returns, these can be spread out and charged against income over time rather than all at once. They also may be removed from the income computation and charged against capital or FCF, so long as they represent major, one-time, separable outlays and not just a ramp-up in ongoing expense levels. This latter treatment is rather lenient. Spreading out such costs and charging them into income normally is a sufficient solution.

R&D expenses are the clearest candidates for regular adjustment, pivotal as they are to long-term business results in many industries. Taking these costs out of the income statement and phasing them in over two or three years is the simplest approach. This mutes any gains to be had by cutting back on R&D in an attempt to hype short-term earnings. The better approach here, as in many other cases, is the one addressing the incentive structure more generally; lengthening the effective time frame of the incentive structure renders pointless many short-term tactics. If executives hold a sustained interest in capitalized business results, the company need not regularly capitalize short-term influences on those results.

Non-capitalized leases are a common, material adjustment to business results in the EP framework. Companies can rent facilities or equipment. This reduces income statement impacts relative to longer-term leasing or cash purchase, in amounts that can be very large in companies with big facility investments like retailers.[6] In those cases, the question is this: Are you going to police this particular category of decision-making, the lease-versus-buy calls made by a small part of the management cadre, using an adjustment that makes metrics cloudy for all participants? In most cases, the possibility of distortion from this quarter is best handled episodically, if it becomes a problem, under the normal administration powers of an incentive plan. In this example and others, the most important thing is that management understands the ground rules. Asset rental is not left open to manipulation in that case. Nor are other forms of off-balance-sheet financing and a myriad of other potential distortions. Adjusting for everything, all the time, is no more effective as a deterrent than keeping Mayberry's Barney Fife locked and loaded.

Restructuring charges are major income hits incurred with the expectancy of benefits over several years. In these instances, the arguments for one-time treatment as FCF have validity. However, some companies do "restructurings" every year or two. In those cases, the charges may have at least a partly recurring nature. If so, they ought not to be seen as one-time events. Spreading them out over a couple of years makes sense in most cases.

Major, temporary volatility in income is another possible object of adjustment. Some long-term incentive plans use current income levels as a basis for attaching a rough valuation to the company, a valuation that can be described as the enterprise value evidenced by current operating results. That is explicitly the case when plans use capitalized metrics like TBR or SVA. It is implicitly true in some other plans like ones in which operating income and ROIC goals are set up based upon how they affect enterprise value and returns. Lastly, continuous earning capacity is an implicit assumption underlying most incentive pay for senior management. If a plan at a typical company pays out targeted awards at $10 in income, or its equivalent in EPS or ROE, this almost always is premised on the idea that $10 is at least a sustainable earnings level and, more often, a level upon which future years can improve.

If the income level being used to value the company is not expected to persist, then it should be adjusted to a more representative level. Think of it this way: the stock market does not regard obviously one-time, temporary fluctuations in income as something causing multiple changes in valuation, and incentive plans based on operating results should not, either. Companies need to review income levels each year to see whether they are obviously unrepresentative of the future, being affected by clear, material one-time effects. If so, they may warrant adjustment in the current cycle or future ones. The general treatment would be to include such events in the capital (or free cash flow) element of measured results and not in the periodic income part. This kind of adjustment usually is not needed in a long-term incentive plan unless there is a purely non-recurring fluctuation in income of at least 25 percent. Otherwise, the basic plan mechanism (overlapping grants, "ratcheting" targets, subtraction of incentive plan cost accruals to arrive at income) smooths out such effects reasonably well over time.

Risk-Based Capital Requirements and Return on Economic Capital

Regulators have compelled U.S. banks to adopt methods for estimating risk-based capital requirements and some other financial institutions are using them as well. These metrics are starting to be used in incentive plans. As noted in Chapter 5, risk is a subject affecting the design of incentives and how they work in a wide range of ways. Methods for risk-based capital allocation merit a look from companies in many industries, since formal tools of risk analysis and management are likely to become more prominent generally. Here is the process some financial services industry clients have followed in adopting such standards:

- Risk-based capital levels are specified for each business unit. These levels generally are equal to the capital needed to offset practically all losses (e.g., up to between the 99th and 99.9th percentiles) arising from all sources of risk. These capital requirements often exceed loss reserves and book equity, resulting in a larger level of notional risk-based capital, or "economic capital," by business.

- Business performance often is measured by a metric like return on economic capital (ROEC). That's equal to net income (typically restated as if the business actually did have a lot more equity capital) divided by economic capital.

- Consolidated levels of economic capital are set by adding up the risk of various business units and taking into account portfolio diversification effects when they are combined to produce consolidated results. ROEC benchmarks generally are equal to a low-risk cost of equity or to ROE norms for heavily capitalized peers.

The use of ROEC-type metrics in pay plans is not very far evolved. What can be said is that their income and capital elements are amenable to use in ROE/income matrices and in value-based metrics like residual income or total business return.

Be careful, however, to avoid any double hit for risk. This means making sure that the risks addressed when expanding the denominator of the ROEC calculation (normally reducing ROEC) are not double-counted in the benchmarks against which ROEC performance is compared. "Levering" or "un-levering" a beta coefficient is an example of one way in which an equity return benchmark can be placed on a consistent basis with a company's measure.

I do not suggest working up a risk-based capital adjustment apparatus purely for purposes of an incentive plan. Instead, companies should piggyback the design upon financial indicators that the company otherwise would be producing and communicating during the normal course of business. I also suggest harmonizing the relevant messages about risk assessment and business decision-making so the incentive rollout and risk-based capital management initiative are consistent.

A company may not be able to use its whole risk adjustment apparatus for incentive purposes. Many risk assessments are subjective and forward-looking, particularly at the business unit level. Basing measurement on those constructs would be a bit like basing pay on subjective, internally-generated measures of enterprise value — it might be sound in theory, but on a practical level, it would generate a lot of arguments about the assumptions every year. Generally, well-specified historical risk indicators will be more practicable to administer in a pay context. And they can be updated each year so they do capture changes in risk, but with a one-year lag. There are some forward-looking risk indicators (like implied volatility on traded options) that may be practical to consult for risk-adjustment purposes. In many financial services companies, existing procedures for marking to market already implicitly consider forward-looking market yields and therefore apply a kind of prospective risk assessment and pricing by asset.

One issue to address is the extent to which investors can diversify the risks of their investment in the company, resulting in lower perceived risk and perhaps in financial results adjusted more lightly for risk. When companies from all industries adjust their results for risk, they usually do so by comparing results to a risk-adjusted benchmark for return. Metrics like EP and TBR do this comparison explicitly and so does relative TSR. Many plans do it implicitly by benchmarking return-based measures like ROE and ROIC against some target or norm. When companies set their costs of capital, beta coefficient is the risk indicator most often used. As noted in Chapter 4, the beta coefficient prices risk only to the extent it co-varies with risks in a diversified portfolio (and therefore is "undiversifiable" or "systematic" risk). Risk-based capital allocation methods, in contrast, usually assess risk as the full variation in business results and not just that part that coincides with the market (they do account for covariance and related diversification effects among business units, but not necessarily against a market portfolio).

How Not to Choose Among Value-Based Metrics

Proponents of value-based metrics often argue that one metric is better than another if it achieves better correlation with value creation. I recommend that the choice of metrics be based upon *ex ante* correlation with value creation at your specific company. That is, it should be based upon the approaches that are most likely, in your specific setting, to encourage business decisions that create most value.

VBM proponents often support their metrics based upon statistical data: *ex post* correlation of metrics with value creation across broad samples of companies. But that assertion suggests that one of the metrics somehow has achieved a much better tracking of market value than the others. However, these metrics are very much the same, each reflecting value through the same three basic drivers.

Most high quality studies of these matters accord little statistical explanatory power to value-based metrics beyond the level held by income, capital and the cost of capital. That means operating income and ROIC will predict value just as well as value-based metrics. The various metric adjustments may work to align measures better, empirically, with value creation. Spreading out R&D costs is a genuine example. But these adjustments could be applied within any metric, so they can hardly be used to attribute greater empirical power to one metric over another.

I've always been a bit skeptical of studies claiming high predictive power for particular metrics. In some such cases, statistics are used in the way that the proverbial drunkard uses a lamppost — for support and not for illumination. Consider the example shown at the bottom of the page. The first panel in the figure describes a 10-company universe in which value is based entirely upon income. Converting operating income into ROIC or EP, in contrast, actually weakens the connection with market value by introducing a variable — capital, in this example — that has no connection with market value. Nonetheless, ROIC is made to look like an omniscient metric in the second panel; it correlates fully with value simply because capital appears in the denominator of both ROIC metric and the market value/capital being used to validate it. The third panel does the same favor for EP. (See Figure 8-2.)

Each measure has a 100 percent correlation with value. But that does not mean they are good predictors. It just means they are piggybacking on the

	FIGURE 8-2: **METRIC FALLACIES**						
	Economic Reality			**ROIC Correlation**		**EP Correlation**	
	Income	**Value**	**Capital**	**ROIC**	**Value/ Capital**	**EP @ 10%**	**EP/ Capital**
Company 1	$2	$20	$100	2%	20%	$–8	–8%
Company 2	4	40	100	4%	40%	–6	–6%
Company 3	6	60	100	6%	60%	–4	–4%
Company 4	8	80	100	8%	80%	–2	–2%
Company 5	10	100	100	10%	100%	0	0%
Company 6	12	120	100	12%	120%	2	2%
Company 7	14	140	100	14%	140%	4	4%
Company 8	16	160	100	16%	160%	6	6%
Company 9	18	180	100	18%	180%	8	8%
Company 10	20	200	100	20%	200%	10	10%

power of income to explain value. This is about as powerful as saying, "If you give me your watch, I'll tell you exactly what time it is. I'm that good." This denominator issue gets even bigger when, as often is the case with value-based measures, capital is a heavily adjusted construct. Statistical results sometimes are inflated as well by the presence of statistical outliers within the sample.

Scope and Purpose for Value-Based Metrics

There has been a real debate in the past about the use of value-based metrics within companies. Proponents have claimed that value-based metrics need to be implemented into every business process within a company, in a metric-centered kind of re-engineering. They claim that implementing a metric like EP upgrades a company's financial processes. Some believe the metric needs to be featured in all of the company's incentive plans, irrespective of organizational level. I do not agree with any of that.

My experience is that companies actually "using" value-based methods are doing so because they've included them in some sensible way within senior management's pay plans. Companies that apply them in other areas — in project evaluation, for example — tend to use them as one among many tools. In most applications, value-based metrics do not really amount to an improvement to financial tools used by most companies. The metrics are DCF-based, after all, and most companies use DCF or equivalent tools already. For the same reason, value-based metrics don't add much to a securities analyst's toolbox, either.

When a company implements value-based metrics for pay purposes, it does not have to run out and change all the company's other financial processes. What it is doing, instead, is to conform the pay plans to the DCF procedures already in use. In the end, it is the link to senior management pay plans that decides whether a company really uses a particular value-based metric.

Beyond the realm of senior management incentives, these metrics are used most effectively in broader-based pay plans and in business literacy initiatives. Companies have undertaken many very insightful and effective approaches in these matters, often assisted by my colleagues. We can attribute the many successes in that area to the compelling and detailed value drivers often identified in the process, as well as the creativity and impact of the rollout. These things are the keys, not the choice of one overarching metric or another. In more broadly-based initiatives, the focus of performance improvements often is on income anyway, not capital or its cost, since that is where most employees can contribute. That does not prevent companies from using value-based metrics effectively in broad-based pay and communication efforts. Rather, it simply encourages them to focus most strongly upon the income element of whatever metric is used and upon those value drivers that participants can influence most strongly.

The place where VBM metrics bring their strongest differential impact, where their rubber really hits the road, is within a senior management incentive plan. At that level in the company, people can affect not only income over the long term, but also capital usage and, to an extent, business risk. Value-based metrics, and value rules more generally, are designed to talk to these people as their primary audience. The next three chapters continue to expose how to do that, laying out methods for devising incentive targets and ranges and for designing cash and stock-based incentive plans.

Endnotes

1   The capital charge is levied against the beginning capital balance in this example because that creates certain computational consistencies with other metrics. Basing the charge on average capital balances (e.g., monthly, quarterly) actually is more common.

2   This is done by improving the target-setting and range-setting procedures used in annual incentive plans (Chapter 9) and by creating more compelling long-term incentive plans (Chapters 10 and 11).

3   Eric Olsen of Boston Consulting Group coined the general term "TBR."

4   SVA was developed by the consulting firm ALCAR.

5   Keep in mind that, in high leverage companies, it is necessary to size the incentive plans properly in relation to the small amount of shareholder resources involved.

6   The adjustment in such a case is to compute the present value of the lease expenses, include it in capital and amortize these costs into income. Rent policy can distort financial results. My general recommendation is to use unadjusted results unless the issue is material and cannot be addressed properly otherwise. As the discussion of "rent" in the RVA section of this chapter noted, I regard rental expense as a fairly complete representation of the cost of asset use over time.

9

Ownership, Not Gamesmanship: Setting Targets and Ranges for Performance-Based Plans

few years ago, gadfly Jim Hightower made this remark about George W. Bush's successes in business and Texas politics: "He was born on third base and thought he hit a triple." The comment attributed the president's accomplishments entirely to his family's wealth of financial and political capital. But the real story is mixed, as it often is in business. George W. Bush's successes were partly due to big advantages he held all along and, just as is the case with other politicians, there was some luck. At the same time, his accomplishments also reflected real merit and performance, and were indicators of how he could perform in a bigger role in the future.

Hightower's quip encapsulates a lot of issues that apply to the standards used in judging business success. Conferred advantage, luck and true performance have similar markings, and corporate performance standards often confuse them. Companies mean to base incentive pay upon true performance, but they're actually paying a lot for all three factors.

Fortunately, value rules make it a lot easier to judge success of management teams. These rules can help make the process less political and focus it more directly upon real success. Value rules can be used to disentangle performance from the other forces that drive a particular outcome.

If you want to judge business success and the fairness of its reward, you have to take sensible account of the capital being used. It would indeed be a mistake to attribute President Bush's past successes purely to individual merit. He drew heavily upon family capital, including the valuable Bush brand name. Many companies make a similar mistake, delivering accolades and rewards based upon incomplete evidence such as revenue and profit growth. In fact, high revenue and profit growth may have been bought at too high a price in capital usage, leading eventually to failure, not economic success.

Bush's political success owes strongly to his own traits and actions irrespective of which base he was born on. But a rival who places too much weight on the value of the capital he started out with will never give him any credit. Companies sometimes make this mistake when constructing targets and metrics. They need to consider how much capital an executive team is using, but when they try to do so, they sometimes fall victim to distortions. In business as in politics, accounts can be biased.

Where you place in life's various contests depends upon your own performance, but it also is affected by where you start out, how the score is being kept and the competition. Everyone in a peer group does not have the same chance of attaining its 50th or 90th percentile. If the president is benchmarked against a cross section of his age group in terms of political success, he looks pretty good without even getting to the governor's office, simply because he once received a large minority of votes in a congressional race. But as a scion of the Bush family, this would not by itself have been an impressive showing. Being elected governor, on the other hand, is no mean feat regardless of one's money and family name. In business, too, one has to be careful about the traps of cross-sectional inference when judging results. Kmart's results, for example, don't provide much useful information when judging Wal-Mart. Problems are rife in this area and will be more so as companies begin to rely more heavily upon peer-based standards within their pay structures.

Political performance, like business performance, often is judged against expectations. The president has benefited at various times from being underestimated. At other times, the bar of expectations has been raised to the point of flawlessness. Managing expectations is a game that can be played expertly and to great advantage by the top talents in both business and politics. Investors want people with these negotiation skills in the big jobs in companies, working on their behalf in a tough, competitive business world. They just need to be sure those skills aren't being used against them when setting performance expectations. And they need to be sure the bar is not set so high that it ensures failure.

Luck can be a factor in political success and in business. On the corporate side, most companies don't really want to pay a lot for luck. But they do. There are ways to concentrate pay on the more controllable parts of business success. Using these, a conscious decision can be made about how much is fair to pay for luck and to what extent people need to make their own luck. You might just pay them for actual results during their careers working for your company, for example, after which they can try their luck in politics if they wish.

The subject of pay standards is like politics — it often is avoided in polite conversation. The topic brings up differences that are difficult to reconcile using the fixed, polar arguments of the parties. Companies' incentive pay structures avoid the subject almost all of the time. First, most of the tough conversations are outsourced to the stock market, concealing any specific demands for performance within the market's mechanism of expectations and valuation. The balance of standard setting is based upon the annual budget process and so is tacked on, in a sense, to the agenda of a meeting already underway. Metrics, award leverage and ranges often are dictated by market norms rather than by any distinctly stated conviction. All in all, the really tough subjects are bypassed within corporations just as they are in politics, without ever taking a firm stance.

Political courage, on the other hand, is about being open, honest and unbiased. Good standard-setting approaches are the same. The best are those that speak in the unvarnished language of value rules. They often commit the Washington, D.C., definition of a gaffe — inadvertently telling the truth.

Target-Setting Norms

To this point, many serious issues in incentive structure have been examined and the rules for a new framework have been set. A big step has been taken by filling in that framework with metrics. Specific metrics have been identified, along with the right ways to combine them. Lastly, value rules have been used as a procedure for evaluating any new metrics that may arise. With the addition of targets and ranges for pay and performance, the key parts of performance-based incentive plans will have been assembled.

Companies use budgets or other internal, negotiated standards most often to set performance targets in their annual incentive plans. Fully 60 percent of respondents to Towers Perrin's annual incentive survey cited budgets as one source of annual incentive goals. Nearly half, or 49 percent, noted that management and the board determine goals, and 48 percent cited growth or year-over-year improvement (as a temporal rather than timeless standard) as the basis for their targets. Responses total more than 100 percent because many companies cite several benchmarks when describing their processes. Companies also cite a growing focus on externally based standards and criteria like shareholder expectations, peer group performance, and the cost of capital. Still, these are cited much less often: 27 percent, 18 percent and 7 percent, respectively.

This means that the majority of plans still are subject to the standing criticism: that management can get paid more to manage expectations than to manage the business. Performance targets normally reflect an internal negotiation and, at some companies, they are sandbagged routinely. Aggressiveness is penalized from an incentive standpoint because aggressive goals simply raise the bar for a given pay opportunity. The process often is seen as unfair. Important resources — capital and management time — may be misspent. These outcomes are the opposite of what the process is meant to accomplish: strong performance standards, high-quality resource allocation and overall fairness. As it was put in 2001 in the *Harvard Business Review*, "The corporate budgeting process is a joke, and everyone knows it." Another Review commentator advocated doing away with the budget process entirely.[1]

Take Account of Investors, Create Clear Line of Sight

We saw in Chapter 4 that investor expectations, not internal budgets, determine whether a particular performance level causes a company's share price to rise or fall. If a company wants to set targets that align senior management's rewards with their contribution to investor return — and it should — it will have to take account of these external standards and expectations.

Does this seem like a wacky new idea? It isn't. The bulk of senior management's incentive pay already is delivered this way. What has just been described is the target-setting and reward mechanism underlying stock-based pay. By now, much trouble has been taken to discredit companies' heavy reliance upon stock options. One of the things that stock-based incentives do well, however, is to reflect shareholder expectations.

As seen earlier, the market value of a company's shares equals the present value of expected future performance. Option grants normally are made with a strike price equal to the current stock price. Getting a gain on the grant usually means meeting or beating the expectations contained in the strike price. Of course, the specific performance scenario held by the market may change after the grant, and so may other valuation criteria like the longer-run economic prospects and the price of risk. Nonetheless, periodic option grants can be seen, in gross terms, as an incentive system that is re-calibrated periodically to prevailing shareholder expectations through new grants at the current market value. The problems, of course, are that these expectations may be a mystery to option holders, the subsequent movement in share prices may be as well, and the option holders may not have much influence over most of the matters involved.

Nevertheless, stock-based incentive pay is the main way senior management gets paid, and long-term investor expectations are at the core of that mechanism. That by itself is a very good thing. At the same time, operating incentive plans (with clear, proper goals) achieve much better line of sight and efficacy for the various levels of senior management at issue. Are these two conditions mutually exclusive, leaving a "null set" of solutions? Not at all. These two guidelines have a large area of intersection, and all of the incentive design methods in this book are right in the middle of it. When you use them, you will be taking incentive dollars out of vanilla grants of restricted stock and stock options and making better, greater use of performance-based plans. You'll retain the compulsory features of stock-based incentive pay — the links with investor expectations, valuation criteria and gains — but deliver them in clearer and more compelling formats.

To do this, you'll need to pay more attention to the criteria and demands of the market rather than relying strictly upon the inside game of company budgets. This is not a "six-of-one, half-dozen of the other" choice. Budgets and shareholder expectations are not the same thing. Budgets feed market expectations when management shares some of their figures with Wall Street. But management may not share their best guesses, and analysts may not find management's figures credible. Actual budgets used in various parts of the business may not roll up to the figures that have been shared with analysts. And, even if they do, that is a far cry from having a system of goals actually driven by shareholder expectations. An overall earnings per share (EPS) target, for example, even if it equals the market consensus, says nothing about the quality of those earnings from a valuation perspective. Companies often hit their overall budgets but don't get the hoped-for reaction from the stock market. It is economic performance against investor expectations that decides whether business results will create value, not EPS performance against budgets.

Sandbagging (arguing individual incentive performance targets down to easily achieved levels) is a problem acknowledged by many and isolated by empirical research. It surely is a serious problem at some companies, but probably not endemic at most. If it were, pay surveys would show bonus payouts consistently above target. The numbers do sometimes exceed target, but that tends to occur in years that were really great for corporate profit, when performance did exceed expectations broadly.

When sandbagging is a big part of the system and a big concern for executives, the company has a bigger problem than unfairness. The company's planning processes (including the annual budget) serve as an important governance tool, one meant to do an efficient job of allocating resources. Companies that do this badly, and national economies that do, for that matter, tend to under-perform.

Gamesmanship vs. Ownership

How might sandbagging actually play out? Suppose our intrepid Homer and fellow members of his group's management have one of the better businesses within the overall company. They can deliver strong operating income growth with healthy returns on the new money they invest. And, if it were their company, they'd run it to do precisely that.

But they don't own the company. The financial interest they hold in the business unit consists only of this year's bonus and some vague hopes about future ones. Homer's financial claim on the unit's long-term results is limited, discontinuous, diluted and uncertain. It is nothing like ownership.

The only way his team gets paid for the group's performance is by beating the annual incentive targets for their group, a rather mild source of upside because it is only 50 percent of the bonus and none of long-term incentive pay. Plan goals get moved around every year as priorities and conditions change, so team members expect to get paid only for results they deliver this year.

But, ownership or not, this plan is the only performance incentive they have. So, what should they do if they care about getting paid? Try to get lower growth targets each year, hit them relatively easily and get payouts well above target. This might call attention to the game and result in higher targets the next year. Next year's targets are uncertain for a lot of reasons, though, so it is best to go for the sure thing and sandbag now. What shouldn't they do? Reveal how good they think things are. They'll just end up with higher goals and probably the same pay. What would a real owner do? None of this posturing at all.

It is a pretty easy game and one that is played often. Why haven't companies shut it down? They either don't think it is much of a problem or they don't think they can solve it. They think basing pay on budget-based goals is the easiest approach. Actually, pay-driven posturing and the adversarial climate it creates can render the process tortuous, torturous and even tortious. Companies want to get focus and accountability around budgets and business plans. They think linking them to incentive pay is a means of doing so. Instead, pay may bias and subvert these important processes.

There are many things a company can do to create a high-performance management culture. Some will succeed without any help from the particulars of their incentive plans. But most companies expect their expensive, high-profile pay programs to provide some assistance in encouraging the highest results. When senior managers have financial interests resembling ownership, it is pointless for them to do anything other than deliver performance in full. Otherwise, they're cheating themselves.

Companies often share concerns about their procedures but continue to struggle rather than change them. That is due to the most common mistaken belief about budget-based targets: that there are no practical alternatives. But there are.

Setting Targets Based Upon Shareholder Expectations

It has been noted that stock prices reflect expectations for future performance of a company and its business units — information that can be particularly helpful in target setting. To get this information, a company needs to consider some basic principles of business valuation. Figure 9-1 sketches out the essentials of the business valuation process we introduced in Chapter 4. Figure 9-2 depicts the general idea of estimating shareholder expectations.

There is a set of performance expectations that underlies the pricing of a company's shares. These goals can be estimated by running the valuation process in reverse; by fitting the company's share price to a set of performance expectations. If the company achieves them, and other valuation parameters are fixed, it will generate total investor return equal to the cost of capital. Centering award potential here is an alternative to using the budget as the incentive

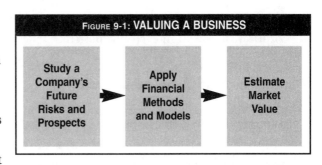

FIGURE 9-1: VALUING A BUSINESS

Study a Company's Future Risks and Prospects → Apply Financial Methods and Models → Estimate Market Value

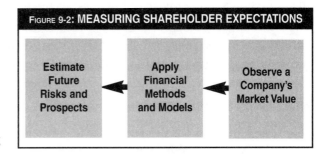

FIGURE 9-2: MEASURING SHAREHOLDER EXPECTATIONS

Estimate Future Risks and Prospects ← Apply Financial Methods and Models ← Observe a Company's Market Value

target. It provides an external and shareholder-oriented alternative to a process of internal negotiation.[2] Towers Perrin assisted Vectren Corporation in setting fair targets for its incentive plan without using internal budgets, in a process profiled in *CFO Magazine*. The targets were based upon expectations held by Vectren shareholders, ones driving the company's stock price.

This approach can be used not only to set performance targets, but the full range of performance eligible for reward under the incentive plan. As noted earlier, the largest part of incentive pay (stock option grants) already operates within the mechanism of expectations, linking expected results with predicted option gains. Those option grants would pay zero returns at a particular level of performance and higher gains at higher levels. The target-setting process based on discounted cash flow (DCF) can be used to determine which performance level is associated with a zero-level return to investors, for example, and what level drives a return equal to double the cost of capital. The DCF-based simulation model used in Chapter 2 is an example of how to estimate stock price reactions in scenarios like those, when performance varies from target. Results are used to set an overall payout range for performance.

In a full implementation of expectations-based target setting, a company is:

- Taking the connection between business results and investor return, specifically the one held in the market valuations of a company and used already to deliver most of its incentive gains

- Removing the market noise and concentrating instead upon the "signal" — the link between operating results and performance

- Isolating the linkage between expected performance and value not only at the corporate level but in each business unit

- Using this system of performance/valuation links within goal-based incentive plans used throughout the company.

To apply this kind of information to business unit target setting, the overall value of the company must be apportioned among its operating units. This is accomplished using valuation guidance from peer company stock prices for each major business unit. The overall exercise reconciles performance expectations for the business units — and their valuations — to those of the overall company. Similar peer-based valuation inferences allow private companies to set their incentive targets based upon appropriate market expectations.

Returning to Homer, let's look at how this process is applied. Here's what we know going into any such exercise:

- His parent company has a market value that is based on a certain set of expectations regarding performance of Homer's business unit and others. Reasonable valuations of these expectations should reconcile with the overall market value.

- Homer has publicly-traded competitors, too, whose stock prices contain relevant information about industry prospects and risks.

- Securities analysts follow the stock of Homer's parent company and those of his competitors. They publish a lot of commentary useful to judging valuations in the industry, and more can be found in the business press and through discussions with management.

Let's look at an example of how that information can be used to develop a reasonable set of targets for Homer's group. This method takes a little work, but it is easier than all the pay-driven posturing and negotiation involved in Homer's budget each year.

The debt and equity of Homer's parent company has a value totaling $7.5 billion; that's its "enterprise value." To figure out the value of Homer's business unit, we need to apportion that $7.5 billion among all the company's business units in such a way that it foots to the total of $7.5 billion. We do this by examining prevailing valuation multiples for publicly traded companies that are peers of Homer's group and for other business units within the company. Commonly consulted yardsticks include the ratio of enterprise market value to revenue, EBITDA, operating income and the ratio of the market value of equity to earnings (the price/earnings ratio, or P/E ratio). If a basic comparison of Homer's group's prospects with those of peers suggests that his has a generally higher income growth profile, lower risk or lower capital requirements, we would value it in the upper end of the range of peer multiples, and vice versa.

The average company in Homer's industry is trading at 15 times earnings. In this case, let's assume our relative assessment of Homer's group against a range of peer yardsticks leads us to value Homer's group at this average multiple. The unit posted $125 million in net income last year, and this seems to have been a representative earnings year, so the multiple can be applied without having to normalize last year's results. A market value of $1.875 billion (or 15 times earnings) is attached to Homer's group. Other business units are valued using similar procedures.

Note this procedure has not required an independent, absolute valuation analysis. Instead, it starts with a given valuation for the parent company and simply assigns us the task of apportioning it roughly among business units. And it does not yet require us to set out absolute expectations for performance. Instead, it requires a relative assessment of business size and positioning. Homer's group might be bigger, be in a faster-growing sector, have more highly distributable earnings or involve less business risk than other units. Any of these drivers, all else equal, would mean allocating more of the consolidated value to Homer's business. It is a relative process, one that triangulates the value of Homer's business against peer valuation norms as well as its parent company's stock price.

The absolute process comes next. We've just allocated the $7.5 billion valuation of Homer's parent company among its business units. Homer's group attracted $1.875 billion of that valuation. That's the starting point for defining a specific set of performance expectations. We do that by assembling a discounted cash flow valuation analysis of Homer's group. (See Figure 9-3.)

We've already reviewed some information helpful to judging business conditions and prospects: analyst commentary, management's remarks, historical and any forecast financial statements. Next:

- We determine the cost of capital for Homer's business unit using methods described in Chapter 4 (assume 9 percent).

- For now, we sidestep the process of setting income growth targets for Years 1 through 5 (that is what we solve for, later, at the conclusion of the analysis).

- We set up assumptions to govern the income forecast for Years 6 through 10, basing them upon a general pattern of decelerating growth in income and value creation. This convention is driven by how competition is known to affect business returns over time. In this instance, income growth is assumed to decay toward long-run norms at 15 percent per year, from whatever rate is attained in Years 1 through 5.

- We set capital requirements each year for five years based upon the assumption they will resemble past capital levels in relation to income (consistent with about 17 percent return on invested capital [ROIC] in this case). During Years

6 through 10, this ROIC performance is assumed to decay toward the cost of capital of 9 percent.

- We use typical methods to value Homer's group at the end of a customary 10-year forecast period. We assume its income will grow 1 percent per year in perpetuity, a rate meant to reflect long-run inflationary expectations[3] (the level of inflation impounded in the 9 percent nominal cost of capital).

At this point, every aspect of a basic DCF valuation scenario has been set out except for the growth rate in income for the next few years. We solve for the growth rate in income over Years 1 through 5 that, when combined with the other assumptions, results in a present value for Homer's group equal to $1.8745 billion. That rate is eight percent, meaning that eight percent annual growth in operating income over the next five years is implied by the valuation at 15 times earnings.

The result is based upon many assumptions, so a prudent step is to go back and re-square the results with the evidence. One example of a basic reconciliation step is to examine the sales levels involved in the performance scenario. The forecast sales growth rate should be consistent with industry evidence and

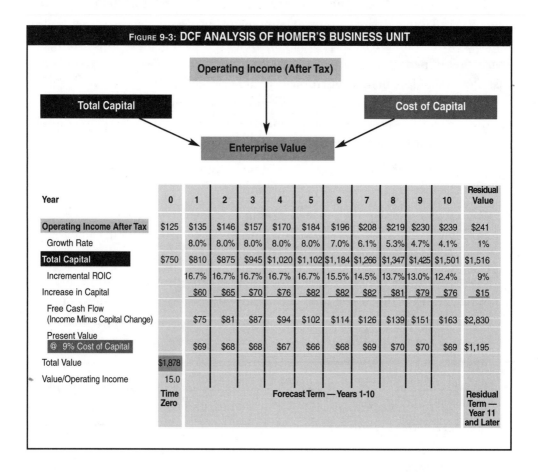

FIGURE 9-3: DCF ANALYSIS OF HOMER'S BUSINESS UNIT

Operating Income (After Tax)

Total Capital

Cost of Capital

Enterprise Value

Year	0	1	2	3	4	5	6	7	8	9	10	Residual Value
Operating Income After Tax	$125	$135	$146	$157	$170	$184	$196	$208	$219	$230	$239	$241
Growth Rate		8.0%	8.0%	8.0%	8.0%	8.0%	7.0%	6.1%	5.3%	4.7%	4.1%	1%
Total Capital	$750	$810	$875	$945	$1,020	$1,102	$1,184	$1,266	$1,347	$1,425	$1,501	$1,516
Incremental ROIC		16.7%	16.7%	16.7%	16.7%	16.7%	15.5%	14.5%	13.7%	13.0%	12.4%	9%
Increase in Capital		$60	$65	$70	$76	$82	$82	$82	$81	$79	$76	$15
Free Cash Flow (Income Minus Capital Change)		$75	$81	$87	$94	$102	$114	$126	$139	$151	$163	$2,830
Present Value @ 9% Cost of Capital		$69	$68	$68	$67	$66	$68	$69	$70	$70	$69	$1,195
Total Value	$1,878											
Value/Operating Income	15.0											
	Time Zero					Forecast Term — Years 1-10						Residual Term — Year 11 and Later

commentary. Also, the forecast should be reconcilable in terms of the ratio of operating income to sales (operating margin) and the ratio of sales to net assets (capital turnover). The DCF scenario can't involve a big expansion in margins, for example, unless this prospect is supported by evidence like strong pricing trends or economies linked with growth. And it can't involve greatly increased capital turnover unless supported by things like high initial inventory levels or low initial capacity utilization. There are only three financial quantities involved in a basic forecast: sales, operating income and capital usage. However, simply by examining the ratios among them — incremental ROIC, margins and so on, we create many opportunities to check the forecast against external norms.

Results also may be squared with those of other business units within Homer's company and to the company's overall stock price. The sum of the business unit DCFs, adjusted for corporate costs, should equal the overall company's stock price. At this point, the business unit valuations will have been reconciled to the parent stock price using each of the two most common methods used to value closely held businesses — the market comparison approach (using peer valuation multiples to apportion value among the business units) and the DCF approach (establishing a specific performance scenario for each unit).[4] The forecast for each business unit, as well as the overall system, is driven directly by the expectations and valuation criteria held by the external market. This process leads to performance goals that are supported by market evidence coming from several external sources. The results are made to fit into a box called market value.

For Homer's business unit, it asserts that 4 percent to 6 percent income growth over the next few years, combined with other reasonable parameters, just doesn't get to the valuation. Growth of 10 percent to 12 percent, in combination with other clear business attributes, would quickly lead to a higher valuation than those commanded in this industry. Our finding of eight percent means that the company should be using operating income growth targets of seven to nine percent per year over the next few years (fixing capital and risk levels at target).

If the incentive plan is based purely on operating income, then the analysis provides a direct basis for future target setting. If it uses other measures, then the income and capital levels involved in the forecast need to be translated into those other measures. Projected ROIC can be figured for each year by dividing forecast operating income by capital. Net income can be estimated by projecting future debt policy and subtracting interest expense. Subtracting projected debt from capital, we have forecast equity levels for use in projecting ROE. Income, capital, interest and debt levels tell us how much cash flow is available to equity-holders each year. If we subtract dividends from this at a supportable rate, the balance can be used to determine new share issuances or repurchases. That gives the forecast of outstanding shares that enables us to figure EPS. Pulling in a sales forecast gives us not only sales but capital turnover and margins, and so on.

What if, in our review of Homer's business unit, we learned that it was recovering from a cyclical downturn and that results in its industry were about to rebound greatly? In that case, it would make sense to attach much more of the growth forecast to its first year or two. Many other circumstances might indicate that growth is placed more fairly in the three- to five-year time frame. The very general shape of future performance expectations tends to become apparent quickly enough in a review of business conditions and prospects. Specific goals, on the other hand, are much harder to set out with confidence, just as they are in traditional budgeting.

The expectations-based target-setting procedure improves this process by forcing it into the market value box. Company value, market valuation parameters and specific information about business prospects must be reconciled. The traditional process, in contrast, is not only internally focused, but comparatively anchorless.

What if corporate management insists upon using growth rates of 10 percent or more rather than the 8 percent guideline indicated for Homer's business unit? This appears to result in structurally uncompetitive incentive opportunities in Homer's group. That's a bad idea when you consider that this is the only piece of pay connected with the group's performance. It also works against the company's pursuit of fairness vis-à-vis the external marketplace. Normally, setting uncompetitively high targets is a bad way to save money. If company leaders want to demand above-market performance from the various teams comprising the senior management group, they ought to provide above-market pay at target.

What if Homer and his group of executives argue that the target should be 4 percent or 5 percent growth per year and that they're in the best position to judge this? Normally, setting uncompetitively low targets is a plausible way to make money, but not when companies set targets using value rules, as we'll see next.

Bulls Make Money. Bears Make Money. Pigs Get Slaughtered.

Business valuation is a useful subject when setting targets. Value rules not only help to produce reasonable targets, but also can improve the dynamics of the target-setting process. Consider the effects upon various types of executives.

My experience is, those who are bullish on their business typically do not complain about an objective system with high line of sight, concentrated upside and flexible and fair targets. To them, it is a way to get paid for what they deliver. They may note the complexity of a new system, but they appreciate that target setting and metrics will be at least a bit complex if they are to capture important dynamics of performance. And they're all about performance — they're bulls.

Those with a bearish business outlook often appreciate the new system, as well. With the prevailing pro-growth bias removed, they see they can get paid for what they do — not growth, typically, but higher free cash flow (FCF) generation. The traditional system, in contrast, creates many opportunities to *not get paid* for FCF performance.

Both bulls and bears can make money under value rules. Businesses with all types of outlooks can generate solid returns in the form of FCF, value gain or both. They can share enough of their results to make it competitively worthwhile for senior managers. They don't have to be bulls to get paid, nor bears. They just have to be right, properly investing in good business prospects or, if they don't have many, returning capital to investors.

The pigs are the ones who end up disappointed. Critters like these want to take a big bite out of the business irrespective of their own contribution. When they see a new system with transparent opportunity and accountability, they see the trough being a bit harder to get to with their usual tactics. They don't want to consider performance and rewards principles that work for owners. They don't want to see clearer accountability. They certainly don't want to talk about the amount of investor resources they're eating up in the form of incentive pay and how that benchmarks to market norms. Instead, they'll use whatever rhetoric and tactics they can to make the new system go away. How do you tell a bull or a bear from a pig? Listen for the squealing.

I've been in tough conversations with these folks a few times. They like to argue for low performance targets, meaning they just want pay higher than what normally is warranted in the marketplace for their level of results. The industry vernacular changes a bit from one to the next, but the story is the same. They insist they really can't be expected to generate income meeting peer or investor standards. They need more money for their business, beyond what they're using now to generate low yields. They avoid firm promises, playing up the unknowns that affect any business.

If Homer and his team want to argue for lower goals, they normally have to resort to one or more of these arguments. In value-focused companies, these are losing arguments. Why? If their business has a modest income outlook accompanied by big capital needs and uncertainties, they've hit the trifecta of value destruction. Their forecast is on the unfavorable end of all three of the main scales of valuation: low income, high capital usage and a high cost of capital. What if, for example, Homer's company agreed to the goals in the earlier plan but insisted that, to make them achievable, they would need to go out and make acquisitions with costs totaling $500 million in the first couple of years? If they are right, then their company is worth less than previously thought. These outlays would reduce the value of the company by nearly $500 million in present value terms, or by about one-fourth. The implications of their demands — the downward revaluation of the business unit — calls into question their performance to date and the extent to which their business merits investments and can fund incentive pay. If business is not worth much today, then the past services of its management may not have been, either. The tactics needed to sandbag end up discrediting the sandbagger.

In a system based upon shareholder expectations, target setting and valuation are two sides of the same coin. They, too, are forced into a box called market value. Overall, a system based at once upon valuation and shareholder expectations encourages everyone involved to tell the truth and to do their best.

What if Homer and his fellow "sandbaggers" actually are telling the truth and their business genuinely has a poor outlook and valuation? That is a shame, but it does not rule out competitive incentive pay. Pay levels simply need to be scaled to competitive market norms, as they would in any other business, and held in proper proportion to value creation. At this point, to define a fair incentive goal, it is a good idea to start talking in percentage terms. If a particular business unit is worth $1 billion, then a high performance level in annual value creation — 20 percent total return — is worth $200 million. At half the enterprise value, it is worth $100 million, and so on. Every point in the likely amplitude of business results is worth one-half that of the bigger concern.

Imagine that a competitively sized bonus award for senior management amounts to $10 million in a scenario involving $200 million in value creation. In this case, $5 million ought to be fair for a company half as valuable, representing the same percentage of value, income and return.[5] The less-valuable business still can earn $10 million in a typical value-based incentive plan. It simply has to generate the same $200 million in investor return the larger one did.

Don't Sweat the Small Stuff

It is said that in academia the battles are so vicious because the stakes are so small. Executives are different. Executives are motivated more by cash than by concept. They won't spend a lot of time arguing over the latter unless there's a lot of the former at stake. That's why they bought so many copies of the book, *Don't Sweat the Small Stuff*. For this reason, it is wise to focus on the details of executive pay. We're sweating the big stuff right now, and let's keep at it.

The usual stakes on annual target setting for bonuses are too high. They raise too many hackles. Each year's bonus opportunity is set in a new budget negotiation, perhaps involving new priorities, standards and metrics for success. Executives can reasonably be expected to discount future bonus opportunities in favor of the more concrete rewards possible in the current year. The system imparts a clear bias toward the near term. Option and stock-based "long-term incentive" grants offer such poor line of sight that they do little or nothing to offset this bias. This places too much pressure on short-term target setting. Management needs to get it all in this year because, in the time horizon of the typical incentive structure, there is no next year.

Most non-traditional plans aren't any better. Some systems place a big weight on nonfinancial value drivers, leading indicators and other forms of nonfinancial or individual goals. In these cases, there is a strong tendency to immunize participants from the realities of current financial performance and certainly from any part of it said to be uncontrollable. And as we've seen, value-based metrics like economic value added often are accompanied by many financial adjustments meant to nail down annual results with precision. Non-traditional plans tend to over-design and over-adjust the metrics and goals, reversing every accounting issue, immunizing every blip in results and spreading out costs of every initiative that lasts more than a few months. They try too hard to get the current year's goals lined up exactly right. This increases, if anything, the annual arguments about standard setting.

And, whatever approach you use, all this work only gets you to the beginning of the year. Speak now, the system says, but don't hold your peace. If things don't work out, jump into the contest for relief at the end of the year, because that is a good game, too.

The short-term nature of incentives troubles more than the target-setting process. It discourages long-run thinking. Business opportunities offering long-run value creation and longer-term incentives — higher future bonuses, basically — are spurned routinely in favor of anything offering bigger payouts this year. Maximizing value requires senior management to have a long view. The typical bonus plan encourages management to live for today, managing near-term expectations and results into a modest, narrow range.

Homer is typical. How would he respond to this system? Many important decisions that Homer may face are ones with multi-year implications. Take an acquisition with average business risk and a simple profile of investment return:

- Year 1 investment of $50 million, zero profit

- Year 2 operating profit after taxes of $5 million

- Year 3 operating profit after taxes of $20 million.

Value based upon Year 3 profit is around $220 million (based upon a 9 percent cost of capital and therefore a valuation multiple around 11). At a glance, one can see this deal creates value. Will Homer get paid to do it? At this point, we don't know. After all, Homer's current incentive structure doesn't pay much attention to capital or its cost, so spending $50 million in Year 1 with no return won't reduce his pay appreciably. And any income gain at all is gravy.

Next year and the year after, the acquisition's results may help him meet his profit targets. But that is a big "may." What might happen instead is that, during budget negotiations in any of the next few years, profit targets get raised to the point where they leave Homer and group management with little benefit from the deal.

In that case, this good acquisition actually may end up providing Homer with nothing but uncertainty. The bonus plan itself could change, too. Homer and anyone else can see clearly that this business decision is a good one. But there is a patch of dense fog between Homer and any pay for this deal. His financial stake in the outcome is not like that of an owner, so chances are strong that he will not act like one.

Most pay structures just don't convey a very firm claim on the multi-year results of business decisions. Lots of companies are saying, "trust me," in effect, when this type of decision is concerned. And some are giving ample reason not to trust them by continually revising plans, priorities and targets, thereby making the ground rules unstable at best.

This approach is in great conflict with the general notion of incentives for the people in management. The most important things management does — the biggest decisions, the factors most determinant for long-run success — tend to involve large, uncertain commitments of company resources. One big strategy change, acquisition, new product, plant construction or reengineering initiative can make or break Homer's group's results for years. Success or failure on these types of things — all of which play out over a period of years — can dwarf the effects of a lot of good, tactical work in the short term.

Homer's company's shareholders want company executives to take on potentially profitable initiatives and to do a good job assessing their risks and effects over the next several years. Homer's bonus plan, in contrast, is standing on his shoulder and whispering, "Why take the risk? You can make about as much money over time avoiding risk and keeping expectations low. Didn't anyone ever tell you not to rock the boat?"

Overall, the incentive structure encourages management to sweat the small stuff. Solutions to this issue involve incentive structure more broadly. Here are some solutions involving not only targets but plan design and metrics:

- Make broader use of long-term incentive arrangements, such as performance plans and phantom stock plans, concentrating them on business unit results in particular. This creates a more concrete claim upon long-term results for most people who are in a position to affect them. Many companies have a medium-term operating incentive plan now, but they tend to be for a limited participant group and to focus on overall corporate performance.

- Calibrate targets and metrics in these plans to focus more closely upon value creation. Long-term cash plans at companies that have them often suffer from the same measurement issues that bonus plans do.

- Make sensible, basic adjustments to performance so that effects of big-ticket decisions (e.g., a merger, major capital expenditures and other large investment initiatives) are phased into results over a reasonable amount of time and in a way that everyone involved understands.[6]

Target-setting solutions are helpful, as well. We've just seen that we can base goals upon the measured expectations of shareholders, as evidenced by the market value of the company. This system, used consistently for years and taking into account capital usage (e.g., by including "base" income expectations and a return on any new capital), creates an ownership claim. Value-based metrics like total business return (TBR) also allow better benchmarking of performance against peer companies or among business units, enabling a more consistent regimen of performance assessment and targeting.

The general theme of each of these solutions is to stabilize opportunity within the annual plan and make it less of a negotiated matter. This extends the effective time frame that executives apply to business planning by solidifying the financial claim they hold on future results. If Homer has a fairly firm idea of what his bonus opportunities will look like over the next few years, he is more likely to believe that current commitments and risks are worth taking because he'll be paid fairly for the eventual results of his actions.

Stabilizing the plan also takes the pressure off getting the targets exactly right each year, because a particular result pays out the same whether attained this year or next. That makes for a better process: a "win-win." This is a very simple but powerful tactic. Companies should set durable, adaptable standards for performance and rewards, ones that unify the interests of all the parties at all times and under all conditions.

Setting Targets Based Upon Total Business Return

Another example of this approach is to calibrate plans in relation to fixed annual standards for TBR, which, recall, is equal to the capitalized change in income plus free cash flow. TBR-based standards are flexible. They allow targeted pay levels to be earned based upon the many combinations of business performance that can bring about a particular level of return. That means they don't force us to hang our hats on a point estimate of a single goal like income growth, for example, or upon a particular combination of income and ROIC. And where ownership is concerned, they create it for management without diluting it inappropriately for owners. TBR measures performance based upon gains in value and upon FCF generation, so it creates an ownership interest consisting of the elements of investor return contained in the DCF model:

- TBR's valuation concept is based upon the increase in income. This means any set of goals that lines up with TBR will ratchet required income levels from one year to the next, paying management to grow income at whatever feasible rate creates most value over time.

- TBR creates a first-dollar claim on all free cash flow every year, so goals set up in its image will do so, too. That means participants share in all income each year and co-invest in all capital outlays.

One client set targets for each of 10 business units based upon a uniform standard of 15 percent TBR as a percent of beginning value. This standard was translated into the goals used in each plan. That is, as in the case of expectations-based target-setting, the levels of income and capital implied by the TBR targets were used to set up equivalent goals stated in other metrics (e.g., ROIC, EPS and cash flow). In a simple example, three business units can each earn the same, targeted incentive award based upon very different profiles for performance:

- Homer's business has operating income growth of 8 percent per year, leading to valuation gains of 8 percent per year. It has free cash flow equal to about 7 percent of beginning value. TBR is 15 percent.

- Another group grows twice as fast at 16 percent but has modestly negative free cash flow at 1 percent of value. TBR is equal to 15 percent in this case as well.

- A last example is a classic cash cow, providing zero operating income growth, but requiring so little reinvestment that free cash flows equal 15 percent of value.

This approach treats the units in roughly fair and consistent terms, attaching reasonable weight to income growth and free cash flow. And metrics can differ greatly from one business unit to another. One unit might use revenue growth, operating margins and ROIC, for example, while another might use economic profit. The TBR method places the underlying connection between value creation and rewards on a consistent scale. So plans are at once fiscally uniform, supportive of value creation, and specific to business unit circumstance.

Beginning capital, for purposes of TBR-based standard setting, is generally equal to the greater of capital or capitalized income. Companies with low performance in terms of ROIC are assigned higher growth targets through the device of using their capital levels as a beginning value for purposes of the plan (rather than basing value upon a multiple of current earnings, as in the other cases). This has some specific implications. Income is used as an indication of the company's value and of the opportunity cost of the capital invested in it, except when income is too low in relation to capital to serve this valuation purpose. When income is low, capital itself is used as the default valuation of the business. This approach assumes the historical costs of net assets, because they consist of amounts advanced in the past by investors, represent a benchmark against which yields should be earned.

When a business unit's capital has been increased in a merger or acquisition, this method assumes that it should earn par returns against the amount of the transaction outlay. In these situations, the pace of such demands is set by the phase-in of the acquisition price into capital. In another unit with older assets and no step-ups in its history, capital may be a very low number that cannot be used for this purpose. This issue throws off comparisons of ROIC or economic value added since those metrics depend so heavily upon the beginning ROIC level. It also skews some of the more capital-driven of the target-setting systems used in connection with the latter metric. This is less of a problem in the TBR system. In the low-capital company's case, the more relevant figure — current income level — is used as the basis for valuation. And the TBR metric itself, as well as any plans based upon it, pays no attention at all to beginning capital and its issues. This is a simple concept, but it remedies many of the issues that beset systems for standard setting.

Figure 9-4 summarizes the issues we have been examining, indicating how they might be addressed within a traditional standard-setting approach. If the traditional system tried to take account of risk, for example, it would be obligated to sort business units into various risk classes (three categories are assumed). It would have to make similar assessments to deal with other matters like the general role of capital usage in value creation and the weight to be placed upon

FIGURE 9-4: TBR AND TARGET SETTING — FACTORS POTENTIALLY DRIVING TARGETS				
Factor	**Effect on Budgeting**	**Number of Separate Assessments Needed**		
		Low	**Medium**	**High**
Risk	Higher risk may increase goals	1	2	3
Capital needs (FCF)	Higher capital needs may increase goals	4	5	6
Actual performance	Praise, gratitude, empathy, scorn or indifference	7	8	9
Investment horizon for new money	Big outlays and deals get fuzzy, negotiated treatment over time	10	11	12
Differing financial metrics	May bollix any chance of consistency	13	14	15
Whether recently acquired	Potentially unrealistic goals, metrics or both (goodwill in or out)	16	17	18
Shareholder criteria/expectations	Indirect, inconsistent or absent	19	20	21
Composition of return: growth vs. yield	Requires separate benchmarking. Relative emphases unrelated to value. Cash yield often ignored.	22	23	24

actual historical performance in setting future targets. Figure 9-5 shows how these matters are addressed within a TBR-based targeting system.

The traditional system does not take proper account of these important drivers of expected financial performance. The TBR framework handles them in a consistent and implicit way. Risk differences matter greatly when judging business performance, and the TBR system addresses this criterion explicitly through its use of a risk-adjusted cost of capital. All else equal, the TBR approach places higher income demands upon riskier business units. The TBR system also takes clear account of capital needs, subtracting them in full when measuring FCF and balancing it against increases in value.

TBR is a resilient framework. However, companies with persistently higher growth prospects may be able to generate outsized returns under the TBR system because, for so many of these companies, neither current capitalized earnings

FIGURE 9-5: TBR AND TARGET SETTING — TREATMENT OF DRIVING FACTORS			
Factor	**Effect on Budgeting**	**TBR Treatment**	**Separate Assessments Needed**
Risk	Higher risk may increase goals	Adjust WACC (2 or 3 classes)	
Capital needs (FCF)	Higher capital needs may increase goals	Explicit focus on new money in goals (e.g., ROIC, EP, TBR)	
Actual performance	Praise, gratitude, empathy, scorn or indifference	Only affects opportunity cost (Capital or capitalized OI)	
Investment horizon for new money	Big outlays and deals get fuzzy, negotiated treatment over time.	Captured in typical OI and capital rules.	
Differing financial metrics	May bollix any chance of consistency	Given consistent, proportional treatment in TBR terms. Assumptions may be required in translation.	0
Whether recently acquired	Potentially unrealistic goals, metrics or both (goodwill in or out)	TBR only cares about new money (but balance may affect opportunity cost)	
Shareholder criteria/expectations	Indirect, inconsistent or absent	Roll up to consolidated expectations. Drivers are WACC, capital and OI.	
Composition of return: growth vs. yield	Requires separate benchmarking. Relative emphases unrelated to value. Cash yield often ignored.	Captures each in proportion to impact upon return and value.	

nor capital adequately capture the opportunity cost of capital invested in the business. In such instances, business units may need to be separated into a few classes based upon growth prospects. (See Figure 9-6.)

This categorization may take some work. But it is a lot easier to slot business units roughly into one of two or three growth classes than it is to run a full budget-based negotiation to set growth targets for each. TBR-based results, though, won't be as precise. But the system aligns payouts well with economic performance over time, and that should appeal to both participants and owners. Like other external or mechanical approaches to target setting, the TBR method is meant to supplant other, more subjective influences on incentive targets. (See Figure 9-7.)

FIGURE 9-6: TBR AND TARGET SETTING — ADDRESSING GROWTH'S EFFECTS		
Factor	**TBR Treatment**	**Separate Assessments Needed**
Near-term growth variation	Fairly addressed through ratcheting effect on goals. Ramp-up in a new business may be covered by use of capital as "value."	0
Compositional differences in return: growth vs. yield	Captured in TBR formula	0
Persistently different growth expectations. Likely, wide variation in valuation multiples	Categorize business units into two or three general classes based upon longer-term growth prospects (easier than doing separate valuations or negotiations). Roll up to consolidated goal.	2 or 3

FIGURE 9-7: TBR AND TARGET SETTING — FACTORS NOT DRIVING TARGETS		
Factor	**TBR Treatment**	**Separate Assessments Needed**
Negotiating skill		
Perceived performance		
Command of buzzwords	None	0
Time spent at HQ		
Wine-related knowledge		
Golf handicap		

Dodging the Issue

TBR also can be used to sidestep these contentious details of target setting. Award sizes can be benchmarked based upon the expected values of awards and the economic sharing rates they imply. Homer's management team might simply receive 1 percent of their business unit's results in TBR terms, per annual grant, if that figure reconciled with market-competitive long-term incentive values for their jobs and with relevant market figures for dilution. TBR has a capitalized format, so it automatically connects targeted operating results with their implications for valuation and economic dilution. This allows results to be benchmarked directly against the economic sharing rates inherent in stock-based incentive grants. This is another way in which productive features of stock-based plans can be used within an operating incentive plan format offering higher line of sight. In particular, the annual share usage in an option plan is like a gain-sharing plan based on valuation gains, a "target-less" one. This can be converted into a clear, value-based formula like total TBR, then pushed down to the business unit level in any of a range of plan formats.

When long-term incentives are restructured in this way, they increase line of sight of the overall system without making the specifics of target setting into a greater point of contention. As a practical matter, companies conducting such pay restructurings simply are taking the value of option grants they'd have otherwise made and issuing similarly valued TBR plan grants, as long as those aren't too costly in relation to income and cash flow.

The TBR grants do involve some assessment of likely performance just as target setting does. Otherwise, they couldn't be valued and granted properly. However, all they require is that the company line up pay outcomes across a broad range of acceptable performance scenarios. That's easier than zeroing in on any one of them as the target and therefore a specific point of dispute. Vanilla stock option grants don't require companies to argue about performance targets. Other, more effective forms of incentive pay don't necessarily require that, either.

There are other methods under which flexible, economically fair results can be pursued. Though each of these examples is uncommon, they illustrate interesting principles:

- Choice-based targeting systems can be a useful general method. In one version, participants can choose among award schedules in which higher basic performance at targeted pay levels is accompanied by a higher upside. A "buy-in" phantom stock plan deal is another example of this approach (though it sometimes risks securities law complications and motivational issues). Another technique, known as a "Soviet" incentive scheme, actually stems from methods used to set factory production quotas in the old U.S.S.R. and to address the sandbagging endemic in that nation's planned economy. It is based upon a matrix that rewards setting high targets and coming in close to them, with payout proportions favoring the confident people who can deliver.

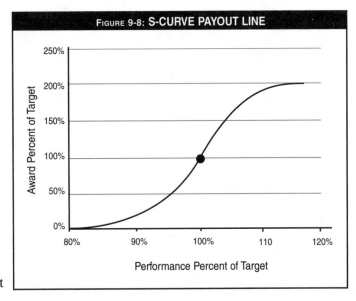

FIGURE 9-8: S-CURVE PAYOUT LINE

- The shape of the award schedule itself (the payout curve) has important effects. It determines the range of results eligible for reward and, therefore, whether it sometimes pays to defer or accelerate costs or opportunities. It also can drive the urgency associated with any actions affecting business results. Devised well, it can help to create a continuous stake in results and overcome some of the temptations to manipulate them. A lower slope at the extremes, in the S-curve example below, reduces any temptation to move results into the current year or the next. (See Figure 9-8.) With lower slopes at the edges, ranges can be expanded to cover a wider range of outcomes, keeping hope alive in the range's extremes without putting too many incentive dollars at play there. A higher slope in the middle of the range heightens urgency through the interval over which performance gains are most likely to play out. This increases pay at the highest rate when forecasts are most accurate.

- Setting income targets based on beginning capital levels is another example of a target-setting algorithm. Under one version of this approach, goals for income growth might equal a standard, modest percentage of prior year income plus a fair return on any increase in capital during the preceding year. In place, this procedure works similarly to an incentive plan based on the beginning-capital version of the economic profit metric.[7]

Range and Domain: Setting Intervals for Performance and Pay

Most operating incentive plans involve finite performance ranges. Homer's bonus plan example used the common parameters of 80 percent to 120 percent of target for performance. Below 80 percent, no bonus is paid; above 120 percent, awards are capped. Most companies, when devising these parameters, want awards payable within the performance range around seven or eight times in a 10-year span. This means an overall in-range probability of about 75 percent in any given year. Applying common, symmetrical performance ranges, this means a 25 percent overall chance of being out of range — 12.5 percent on the downside, below threshold, and 12.5 percent above the range maximum.

Our studies of the general variability of business results around budgets or trends suggest that companies are setting their ranges properly to meet this criterion. Given the typical variability around trend for operating income, for example — a standard error of 15 percent to 20 percent around a given target — a company would expect its operating income to fall within the typical 80 percent to 120 percent performance range seven or eight times out of 10. There are reasons to debate whether caps should be used and where they should be set, and we'll cover that shortly. In the meantime, though, observe that the market practice does line up well with company intentions regarding the frequency of out-of-range performance levels.

However, performance ranges can be problematic. Some companies, pursuing fairness or perhaps expediency, apply the same performance/payout schedules in many different business units. Sixty-five percent of respondents to Towers Perrin's annual incentive survey reported setting threshold and maximum performance levels at fixed percentages of target. The actual range of possible business results, in contrast, can vary greatly from one business to another. In these cases, the one-size-fits all approach can have effects that are at once uncompetitive, irrelevant, or extremely compelling depending upon which part of the company one works in. A substantial minority of surveyed companies did indicate they consider factors like probability of achievement or the statistical sensitivity of results when setting performance ranges. Since most don't, the potential problems appear widespread.

Let's see how it works for Homer. His plan has a payout range of zero to 200 percent (200 percent is the most common maximum payout). Fifty percent actually is the most common threshold award, but we used 0 percent — the next most common approach — for simplicity. Homer's payout moves 100 percentage points in relation to target for 20 percentage points of movement in performance, so the plan's leverage can be described as 5:1. The group-level piece of Homer's plan is based entirely upon operating income.

That is Homer's deal. What can we say about the appropriateness of his ranges? Assume it is late in the year and targets are being set for next year, so Homer has some idea of what next year's bonus targets and plan will look like. He's figuring that his operating income goal next year will be equal to 8 percent growth from whatever this year's level turns out to be. Let's look at some examples to illustrate how ranges might affect his decisions:

Let's say Homer's group is having a bad year and performance is coming in below threshold, just below 80 percent of the $200 million target, or $160 million. If they really pull out all the stops, they might be able to make a little money this year. Now, suppose instead that they take a "big bath," accelerating some discretionary spending into this year, deferring certain sales transactions by a few weeks and accruing some reserves — perhaps warranties or the bad debt allowance — a bit more aggressively than they might have. This buys down their incentive target for next year, hypes next year's results and ends up paying much more. Say they move $10 million in operating loss into the fourth quarter of this year with these maneuvers, effectively banking the same $10 million in profit for realization over the course of next year. This 5 percent or 6 percent movement is well within the normal variation in operating results for Homer's group, and a manipulation of business results in this amount often is within the span of control.

Profits fall to $150 million this year, costing members of the group nothing on the operating income side of their bonus plan because they were already below threshold. Next year's profit target is 8 percent higher than actual operating income, so it will be set at $162 million rather than at the $172.8 million that would have prevailed. And performance, which might have come in at the $172.8 level, will now be $10 million higher at $182.7 million instead. Homer's performance ends up at 112.8 percent of target rather than at 100 percent. Five-to-one leverage means the operating income part of the bonus pays out at 164 percent of target rather than 100 percent. From an owner's perspective, there is no difference between the two scenarios because two-year income is the same. But management incentive pay is much higher in the second one.

Next, consider the case in which Homer's plan has a 50-percent award threshold, so he and his team can increase their bonus from 0 percent to 50 percent of target simply by hitting the $160 million performance level. In that case, he ought to do anything he can to bring in a little more profit this year. Cutting way back on discretionary expenses is a popular strategy here, although many such cutbacks — advertising and R&D come to mind — risk diminishing the longer run earning power and valuation of Homer's group. The award schedule pays them to do it nonetheless.

Let's put Homer into another type of award schedule that is a composite of several client situations. Each company liked to set high performance demands, imposing great penalties when goals weren't met. Threshold performance levels for income are set very high at 95 percent of target. The income growth targets themselves are quite hard to hit, being set at 12 percent or 15 percent rather than the 8 percent level we regarded as fair. Otherwise, the schedule is the same as before for Homer.

This demanding regimen creates a screamingly high leverage ratio of 20:1 as performance moves from threshold to target; 100 points of award in relation to target are earned over a performance interval of five percentage points. The more typical leverage level of 5:1 prevails above target. Operating income goals are hard to hit, so chances are, Homer's group will be well below target next year, with zero awards as a real possibility. Under these circumstances, Homer is better off shifting any income above target into next year. Operating income that exceeds target this year by $10 million, or 5 percent of the $200 million income target, increases awards by 25 percent of target. The same $10 million shifted into next year could help him move from threshold to target, passing through the entire 20:1 leverage zone and earning a 100 percent of target award rather than the zero that might otherwise have been paid. In this case, shifting $10 million into the next year quadruples the impact upon pay without any improvement in results over the two-year period. Participants once called a plan like this an "every other year" bonus. Goals had been set very high to emphasize high expectations, but the plan made the timing of income more important than its amount.

Now suppose that Homer's plan is instead based upon sales and operating income, with a joint threshold on each goal, so that failure to hit threshold on either goal wipes out the whole budget. Depending upon the way the year is shaping up, participants could end up with a very strong encouragement to gouge customers, make unprofitable sales, or shift revenue or expense from one year to the next.

If plans use limited ranges at all, then at least some of these scenarios are feasible. Adjusting ranges at least roughly for variability is a typical design solution. Companies with particularly volatile or unpredictable results do tend to have wider award ranges within bonus plans. To be more systematic, companies can use either of the methods noted earlier: DCF-set scenarios or TBR ranges. They also can look directly at the variability in the financial results of their own businesses by looking at their history or that of peers. If a particular company has results that have varied widely around budgets and trends, holding all else equal, that company should have a wider performance range. (See Figure 9-9.)

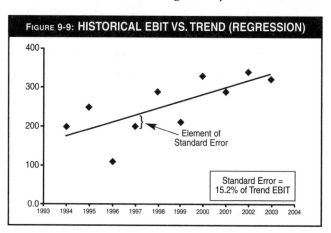

FIGURE 9-9: HISTORICAL EBIT VS. TREND (REGRESSION)

Element of Standard Error

Standard Error = 15.2% of Trend EBIT

As shown in the figure, these data are helpful when assessing the future predictability of results and, therefore, in setting ranges. A company with a regression standard error of 16 percent, for example, would have ranges set at +/- 20 percent if it wanted to have a 10-percent chance of either an above-range performance level or one below threshold.[8] The general procedure to apply these within a set of bonus plans requires:

- *Measuring the variability of business unit results around past budgets or, as an approximation, around a regression trend line of past performance.* Using these results, the company's business units are sorted into two to four categories of variability. Peer

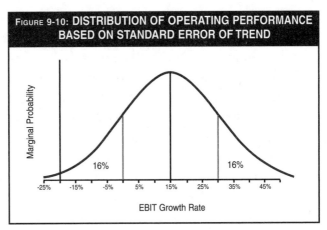

FIGURE 9-10: DISTRIBUTION OF OPERATING PERFORMANCE BASED ON STANDARD ERROR OF TREND

company analysis and other sources of benchmark data on business uncertainty may be useful to consult as well.

- *Using these risk data to construct performance ranges.* (See Figure 9-10.) For the more uncertain businesses, a relatively wide range from threshold to maximum performance — like 70 percent to 130 percent of target — may be reasonable. Very stable, predictable businesses may warrant a range of 90 percent to 110 percent of target to move from threshold to maximum payouts, and so may relatively predictable metrics like revenue. An intermediate risk group may employ the typical 80 percent to 120 percent range.

Under this approach, statistical inferences are used to set ranges that all have roughly the same chances of hitting threshold, target and maximum award levels. The company's ranges end up being very consistently derived and, at the same time, are tailored to the characteristics of the particular business.

The stakes on the bonus range-setting process are greatest in large, complex companies because they have so many business units. That also is where the chances of costly error are greatest because the ability of corporate staff to monitor such important matters is more dispersed. In those cases in particular, it is worthwhile to be thorough and systematic when setting ranges.

Prerogatives of Rank

To judge performance and set targets, companies often rank businesses against peers or other business units. In these cases, basic issues with traditional metrics may confound such performance comparisons. Business units might have identical economic performance, for example, but they could look very different in terms of ROIC, depending upon their histories and the accounting treatment. One unit may have 50th percentile ROIC and the other one 90th.

The fact is, not every company has the same chance of hitting a particular percentile for financial performance like the 50th or 90th. Rather, characteristics of the metrics themselves may place a company ahead of or behind the pack. Business conditions at a company might make it strong on FCF, but weak in any race for income growth. The methods discussed in this chapter — targets effectively driven by TBR or by its market version, total investor return — are helpful in stating performance on a consistent basis.

Total shareholder return (TSR) actually is the easiest common metric to benchmark against peer standards. A company's expected level of TSR generally is equal to its cost of equity capital, and its expected rate of stock price growth is equal to the cost of capital minus its expected dividend yield. A typical company's chance of hitting the 50th TSR percentile of its peer group is 50 percent, assuming the levels of business risk and financial leverage driving its cost of equity capital resemble those of peers.

There are other issues with peer ranking, concerning not the expected level of results, but its variance. These issues affect the methods used to set ranges. In the approach used earlier, the method of looking at time series variation around a company's past results (rather than cross-sectional variation among peers) was adopted because of lack of comparability across companies. Figure 9-11 illustrates the issue. In this extreme example, operating income growth is completely predictable at each company.

		Year			
Company	**1**	**2**	**3**	**4**	**5**
1	2%	6%	10%	14%	18%
2	2%	6%	10%	14%	18%
3	2%	6%	10%	14%	18%
4	2%	6%	10%	14%	18%
5	2%	6%	10%	14%	18%
6	2%	6%	10%	14%	18%
7	2%	6%	10%	14%	18%
8	2%	6%	10%	14%	18%
9	2%	6%	10%	14%	18%
10	2%	6%	10%	14%	18%

FIGURE 9-11: **CROSS-SECTIONAL VARIANCE EFFECTS**

Conclusions:
Average of Cross-Sectional Standard Deviations   6.3%
Average of Individual Standard Deviations   0.0%

Cross-sectional data suggest a different result since they pick up differences in growth from one company to another. It makes business performance for a particular company look more variable than it is. The general risk is that cross-sectional data can lead to an inappropriately wide performance interval. As we'll see shortly, this leads to very low award leverage.

As companies make more sensible use of operating incentives in the post-option era, they certainly will be drawn to employ more peer-based inferences and metrics, ranking their business units among themselves, against peers and over time. In these matters, they will need to pay close attention to the statistical quirks and target-setting issues present in this area.

Games without Frontiers:
Placing Limits on Performance Ranges

We noted earlier that most bonus plans and performance plans involve limited payout ranges, with 200 percent of the target award being typical as the upper limit of payout and zero or 50 percent being common thresholds. Phantom plans,[9] in contrast, tend to offer upside limited only by the valuation of the business unit or the private companies in which they are used. Some bonus plans and performance-based long-term incentive plans are unlimited as well. More often, though, companies put payout limitations in place to control the functioning of the plan, rejecting unlimited payouts due to perceived fiscal risk.

But unlimited plans do not have a monopoly on fiscal risk. Performance plans are imprudent when they use flawed measures, goals or ranges, sometimes allowing large payouts when performance actually is destroying value. Phantom stock plans, on the other hand, and other plans with unlimited upside, can be designed with many safeguards and a very strong connection with value creation, over time and over a broad range of outcomes.

Finite ranges by themselves just don't protect the company from unreasonable payouts. Actually, as the examples earlier were intended to demonstrate, finite incentive ranges are one of the areas in which incentive design choices can lead to business trouble. Payouts can be out of hand even when they are well within range. This can occur for a number of reasons:

- Payouts can be too dilutive at target, and performance levels and goals can be too easy to attain.

- Metrics and award schedules can allow payouts for bad business decisions.

- Granting structures (e.g., end-to-end performance cycles rather than overlapping ones) can encourage hyping short-term pay with unsustainable results.

- Narrow ranges can encourage management of income or simply discourage high performance.

As noted, finite ranges may encourage manipulation of the timing of revenues and costs, fitting wide-ranging business results over time into the narrower interval that is eligible for reward. There are better safeguards than narrow ranges. Proper metrics, targets and ranges are the key safeguard. A range of fiscal controls is set out in the next chapter, as part of the exposition of TBR-based phantom stock plans offering unlimited upside. When companies have properly designed plans, they can expand their upside and make them more compelling without straying into a fiscal danger zone.

Weightings, Award Leverage, Influence and Testing the Plan

Performance/award ranges have an impact upon plan leverage. The median leverage of annual incentive plans is around 3.5:1, but actual leverage can vary from 1:1 to as much as 20:1 for the various performance metrics and intervals involved.[10]

High leverage may be used to create a strong incentive to improve results. It may also fit businesses in which the likely range of business results, along with management's ability to improve them, is unusually narrow. Wider ranges and concomitantly low leverage may fit in cases where results are less predictable or performance gains are easier to effect.

Weightings matter, too. Incentive plans may employ metrics that track results at the corporate level, the division level, at intermediate echelons like group or sector, and below the division level in units like profit centers and ventures. Each of these organizational levels can have different degrees of importance, or weight, in the overall delivery of awards.

Leverage is another form of goal weighting. Small changes in business unit results might have large incentive payout effects, while corporate payouts may vary much less. In that case, business unit results are featured more heavily than their mere weighting would suggest. In this regard, leverage is a stealth variable in incentive design. Within the overall incentive structure, the leverage placed upon business unit results (or upon any goal) can be more important than the weighting of the goals themselves.

Leverage is the slope of the payout line. We saw earlier that 100 percentage points of gain earned over 20 percentage points of performance improvement achieves 5-to-1 leverage. In computing leverage, the "rise" in income is as important as the "run" of performance by which it is divided. So the setting of performance ranges re-enters the discussion when it turns to the subject of leverage. For example, in many businesses, earnings are much more volatile than revenue. Yet, some plans attach the same performance range to both sales and profit goals. A wide interval, attached to a relatively predictable goal like revenue, lessens the effective leverage attached to that goal.

The most important type of goal weighting, however, is individual influence. If awards under a performance plan are weighted equally upon corporate and business goals, then the plan will appear on its face to place equal importance on them. However, the fact that business unit executives have more influence upon business unit results increases their effective weight. In fact, a typical business unit bonus plan for executives may be divided into two parts: a functioning incentive plan based upon business unit results and a general, corporate results-sharing arrangement unrelated to their own efforts.

With all of these design factors moving around, it can be difficult to divine what performance a company is paying for, how strongly and under what circumstances. The level of expense involved in executive incentives, on the other hand, demands some cost/benefit analysis of incentive policy. And that can't be done without closely examining the inner workings of the plans. For this reason, as well as others cited earlier, a testing and simulation step should be included in the incentive design process. This step should address the precise workings of the company's plans, the connection between business results and the stock price, and a wide range of possible business decisions and results.

Testing and simulation techniques provide a way in which all of the design choices involved in incentive structure combine to pay off for various business results. Unfortunately, these important terms in companies' plans often consist of an accumulation of past, one-off design choices made in response to issues pressing upon the company's incentive plans at the time. The result of these decisions, taken together, can be rife with unintended consequences.

Comprehensive testing can focus on the efficacy of the overall structure and isolate the impact of changing one or a few aspects of it. When applying simulation methods in Chapter 2, we saw that pay structures — even simple ones — have a number of moving parts that make it hard to see the true range of potential results. The complexity of just about any pay system means that incentive design is a very good area in which to apply scenario modeling and simulation methods. These techniques expose issues otherwise concealed within the incentive structure, helping to ensure it is effective and worth the expense it entails.

Endnotes

1   Ibid, Jensen, November 2001, cited in Chapter 3. Second item appeared in February 2003.

2   For an early application of investor expectation measurement to the matter of incentive target-setting, see Stephen F. O'Byrne, "EVA and Market Value," *Journal of Applied Corporate Finance*, Vol. 9, No. 1 (Summer 1996).

3   The residual value is equal to final-year FCF, increased by 1 percent, then divided by the cost of capital reduced by 1 percent; that is the present value of a perpetuity growing at a 1 percent per year rate. One to 2 percent is a reasonable assumption in the United States.

4   These valuation methods are described in Chapter 10.

5   Assuming a 1:1 ratio of pay cost to company size, which is not precisely accurate, but close enough to make the points presented here.

6   Covered in Chapter 8.

7   Source of Soviet incentive matrix idea: Mark Ubelhart. Source of "beginning capital" EP method: Scott Olsen.

8   The examples used thus far have assumed that the variance of operating income around trend or budget is normally distributed. Our study of this actually finds the distribution to be somewhat leptokurtic, but we've used the normal distribution nonetheless as a reasonable and convenient approximation. Had we used the actual distributions, the bulk of our conclusions about incentive efficacy and the weakness of traditional methods would have been strengthened because there would have been more, larger out-of-range observations.

9   These are non-qualified incentive plans in which participants earn cash payments based on the value of the company. They are covered in Chapter 10.

10 Source: Towers Perrin annual incentive plan design study.

Business Units
and Private Companies,
Phantom Stock and
Performance Plans

Most medium- and large-size companies aren't run entirely from a head office. They have at least three or four business units, and many have dozens or even hundreds of groups, divisions, profit centers and joint ventures. For these organizations, a single business unit rarely accounts for enough of the results of the parent company to drive them.

Nonetheless, business unit executives get incentive pay based mainly upon corporate rather than business unit results. This pay takes two forms:

- Stock options, which deliver gains based upon stock price gains of the overall company

- Annual bonuses, which, in most instances, reflect the financial performance achieved by the business unit and by the overall company.

As illustrated in earlier chapters, this typical incentive structure has some serious flaws. Stock options offer poor line of sight as incentives for most of the people receiving them. The issue is much worse at the business-unit level because so many factors intervene between business unit results and corporate stock option gains:

- Results of a typical business unit are overwhelmed by results of other business units at consolidation time

- Corporate actions have big effects, too, raising worries about pay effects of overpriced acquisitions, failed reorganizations and high levels of expense

- Stock market volatility consistently clouds the linkage between business results and share prices.

In the far-flung organizations that comprise the bulk of the business world, management decisions taken at the business-unit level are critical to success. Yet, this is where incentives are the least effective.

For many business unit executives, an industry competitor's stock has a stronger connection to the value of their own business unit than does that of their own diversified parent company. Think about it. You could better correlate the pay of business units in your organization with their market values by making option grants on other companies. Seem absurd? You're already doing something like it. The option gains your business executives earn have more to do with what happens at other companies (the other units within your company) than with their own company's results.

And don't think that annual bonus pay will create an ownership mindset, either. Bonus plans often entail flawed metrics, counterproductive target setting, schizophrenic award ranges, short-term bias, risk aversion and, sometimes, risk indifference. The one thing that bonus plans do offer to corporate executives is relatively high line of sight. Considering the other issues, though, high line of sight is not always an advantage. Some of the avenues to bonus rewards involve the destruction of value, so it is not necessarily wise to illuminate them with cash.

The bonus situation at the business-unit level is worse. Bonus plans at the business-unit level have all of the problems noted above, and they don't even create a very strong stake in good performance. For a typical business-unit executive, half of bonus potential is driven explicitly by corporate results.[1] The whole bonus often is jeopardized by circuit breakers on the overall plan — ones that depend upon corporate financial performance. So, the typical bonus is less than 50 percent concerned with business-unit performance.

Companies believe that by dividing results between business unit and corporate results, they have created a kind of equality of interests — one that will win support for corporate initiatives and encourage enterprise-wide resource sharing and teamwork. The company may achieve these things, but it won't have the bonus plan to thank. If your business unit is one-tenth of the corporation, one dollar fielded for the business unit is worth 10 times as much as one for the corporation. In this game, the home team wins every time.

When companies devise their corporate/business-unit goal weightings, they fail to take account of this imbalance. Overall, as noted in Chapter 2, company costs for management incentives are based 80 percent to 90 percent upon corporate results. But even in a major group, business unit executives' own results typically drive 20 percent or less of overall incentive pay, with remarkably little effect upon option gains in particular.

If you want your company to have functioning performance incentives, the threshold criterion is line of sight; if an executive does something that increases business value, will he or she be rewarded by the incentive plan? Even in a company with the typical, "simple" incentive structure of bonuses and option grants, it is very difficult for business unit executives to ascertain whether their actions will affect pay and to what extent.[2] The structure of incentive pay for business unit executives in most companies does not encourage them to maximize long-run results or value. Rather, it encourages them to manage results into a modest, predictable range in the near term.

The reality is that a typical company's "business unit incentives" are neither business-unit constructs nor incentives in the cause-and-effect sense implied by the term. If you think incentives are important, you have to see this as a very serious problem. The bulk of the value of most enterprises is found within their operating units. So are most of their executive decision-makers and, arguably, most of the business decisions that might create value. This is the organizational level where incentive plans ought to be making their most important contributions to business performance. They aren't, and that's a widespread, ongoing problem in business organizations.

Why Haven't Companies Already Fixed This Problem?

In Chapter 2, we inspected the foundation of the typical executive incentive structure and found cracks like these:

- Design choices are driven by pursuit of conformity over efficacy.

- Plans use budget-based targets, standard ranges and traditional metrics because, in essence, companies don't think they have a choice.

- Accounting rules made stock options the surplus cheese of the executive labor market.

These problems were remedied in earlier chapters, and can be remedied in business units as well. First, we need to address the barriers to change.

Companies worry that business unit interdependencies will be harmed by separate-company pay. This concern often is present, even though operations of a typical business unit or group tend to be fairly separable from those of other units and from the corporation as a whole. Indeed, significant business units almost always warrant separate financial statements tracking their income and capital. And companies feel confident enough in their present standards and metrics to provide some bonus pay based upon results of their business units, looking most often at operating income against budget as the basis for distributing rewards. Companies often voice concerns about the controversial or distorting effects of things like allocated costs and transfer prices. Business unit incentives encourage companies to have more accurate transfer pricing and cost allocation procedures, and that *reduces* distortions by improving the accuracy of performance measurement.

Attaching a reasonable cost to capital and to corporate staff support, for example, should encourage business units not to waste either of these resources.

Companies also fear adverse effects on teamwork and on support for corporate initiatives. However, business unit participants have so little impact on corporate results that corporate-level incentives can't be said to encourage those things now. Whether or not a company is getting corporation-wide teamwork probably does not have much to do with how much variable pay happens to be driven by corporate results.

Despite these concerns, companies almost always put some weighting on business unit results within bonus plans. And when they do, they make the unit bonus plan the only element of incentive pay offering any line of sight. If business unit incentives were going to turn a typical enterprise into a set of warring fiefs as a result, they'd have done so a long time ago. And perhaps they did, but the effects must not have been that harmful on balance because companies have not backed off their use of business-unit bonus pay. The typical company should not fear the Pandora's box of business unit incentives. It has been wide open for a long time, apparently with manageable consequences.

Executive turnover sometimes can create difficulties when managers move from one business to another. But most business units have a stable management team. Turnover normally is under 10 percent per year. (Terminations normally run from 3 percent to 5 percent.[3]) Corporate pyramids, demographics and growth rates make it unlikely that a particular executive will be promoted in any given year, so career tracks don't make the typical business unit into a revolving door. And the career rule is hardly "up or out." Team members are expected to contribute in their roles for a period of at least a few years. It is unusual for an executive-level job to be occupied by a tourist. Overall, business unit executives are like corporate executives — they're expected to make a medium- to long-term commitment and to see it through. It is perfectly appropriate to design incentives around this premise in most cases. If someone does make a job transfer within a multi-unit company, they may retain a trailing grant under a business-unit incentive plan or the grant may be cashed out. The situation is administratively stickier than the case of an executive who holds only stock option grants and a corporate-driven bonus as incentives, but the added complexity is worth the trouble in most instances. Making executives retain an interest in a business unit they are transferring from may encourage better hand-offs, more viable successors and a stronger focus on the long run even when someone is short-time. The same argument applies to the retirement provisions in incentive grants for corporate-level executives.

Companies sometimes hesitate to match authority with accountability in business unit pay plans. Instead, they meld business unit executives into enterprise-wide sharing schemes like options and corporate bonuses. Many of these units were established businesses that were acquired by their current owners and continue to have mostly separate names, products and operations. Almost all have material levels of autonomy. They're apparently separable from the mother ship; business units are bought and sold every day.

And they're often pretty big, too. Lots of business units have sales in the hundreds of millions or billions, large enough to be good-sized public companies in their own right. One client, a division within a subgroup of one of the world's largest manufacturers, has profits in the range of Monsanto or Clorox. Business units usually have a full set of executives in staff and operating posts. There may be material support from corporate staff, but corporate staffs often get outside help as well, so that hardly makes the typical business unit a satellite. And one must note that business units often see the role of corporate headquarters as one that is, well, perhaps not pivotal to the unit's success.

Some units have separate boards of directors, outside sources of debt financing, equity partners and even public shareholders. They usually have a material degree of:

- Autonomy in investment decision-making
- Influence in those decisions that do go through the corporate review process
- Impact on charting their futures within the strategic planning process.

And, like corporate executives, business-unit managers are in the decision business. They're charged with creating value over the long term for the corporate shareholders. In short, typical business unit managers are, in most instances, perfectly qualified candidates for the types of incentives recommended in this book, ones involving high line of sight and an adherence to value-based principles.

In a few situations, a decisive money stake in business-unit financial results could be harmful — ones where interdependencies are genuinely high, for example, or the level of autonomy is very low. In these cases, a more limited set of value-driving goals may serve as a better basis for judging management's success than the overall financial results emphasized by most phantom stock and performance plans. In the usual case, however, there is a clear gap between the pay structure that a typical business unit's circumstances warrant and what the executives actually get. What serves investor interests best, in most cases, is to create within business-unit management a decisive financial interest in business success, one oriented toward value creation and toward the longer term.

Current incentive designs that seek to take into account business-unit results do so badly. Often, business units are placed in a one-size-fits-all incentive scheme irrespective of their prospects, risks, capital requirements and other driving characteristics. This leaves little opportunity to emphasize the distinct priorities of the individual business unit. And why does everyone have the same plan? The quick answer is fiscal uniformity and administrative ease. But each is an illusion, and each is profoundly counterproductive. In fact, plans designed with these objectives often cause enormous fiscal disparity and administrative difficulty.

Business-unit managers are the ones best qualified to run their businesses. They're best able to assess its long-run prospects and take educated risks, while exploiting their close knowledge of relevant markets and operations. They usually know more about their businesses than corporate management does. And, within the customary latitude of business unit governance, they're in a position to do more about it. Corporate managers should exploit this informational asymmetry. Without ceding any power, they easily could encourage business-unit managers to do some things they are not paid to do now:

- Clearly identify their best business prospects.

- Demand the right resources, no more or less.

- Chase only profitable growth and distribute cash when appropriate.

- Balance risks and the long-term like an owner would.

- Chase business opportunities with continuous and undiluted zeal.

Are these things happening at your company now? If incentives were linked to their own business-unit operations, divisional managers could find ways to unleash the entrepreneurial drive so often ignored or thwarted in the present regimen of rewards. If corporate managers put in the right incentives at the business-unit level, they'd make their own jobs easier and encourage better overall performance in the consolidated enterprise.

Private Companies

The situation of private companies is a lot like that of business units when it comes to devising long-term incentives. Many private companies hesitate to use actual shares as incentive currency due to a range of legal and funding concerns. At the same time, they often find that public companies are business competitors and rivals in the market for executive talent. They need to compete with the large stock and option grants public companies make. When they do so, their design choices overlap strongly with those of business units.

Even when not concerned so acutely about competitive norms, they are interested in long-term incentive plans because they can help improve business results. A pay package with a given value is better designed, from an owner's viewpoint, if it has some long-term incentives in it. As shown in earlier chapters, this is just a far better way to pay top managers than devising pay packages out of salaries, bonuses and benefits.

Private company situations and solutions actually warrant a look from the public company sector. In private companies, owners are not the anonymous, fractionalized, hypothetical characters in the corporate governance tableau. On the contrary, they're often found right down the hall. And when you're spending too much of their money or otherwise disappointing them, they'll often come right up to you and tell you what they think about it. *That* is shareholder activism. Perhaps you noticed that private companies didn't spend a lot of time embroiled in the stakeholder debate of the 1990s. They knew all along who the stakeholders were and what management was supposed to be doing for them. As a general matter, private companies do not encourage navel-gazing on company time.

When it comes time to devise incentives, private companies often are quite comfortable with clarity and accountability, but not hugely concerned about matters like the accounting treatment of stock options. As a result, some private companies are on the leading edge of incentive design.

There are a number of ways companies can better encourage the critically important executives found in business units. Solutions include phantom stock plans, performance plans and performance share plans that place heavy weight upon business unit results. These techniques are effective in private companies as well. Solutions also include, of course, the interventions in the areas of metrics and target-setting discussed in Chapters 6 through 9.

Phantom Stock and Subsidiary Equity

Phantom stock plans provide a useful starting point for a discussion of business unit and private company incentives. The range of phantom stock plans used in the market embodies the best and worst of incentive design. If designed well and used in the right setting, phantom stock can create a compelling economic stake in long-run value creation. This can increase greatly the efficacy of management incentives and contribute to success, all in a fiscally prudent and predictable way. If designed badly or misapplied, a phantom stock plan can be confusing, ineffective and internally controversial. Even worse, badly designed phantom plans can encourage business decisions that destroy shareholder value and subject the company to inappropriate levels of expense.

Phantom stock also is quite useful in illuminating key aspects of incentive plan design that affect other kinds of plans, including:

- The general structure of overlapping grants and long-run payouts used in other types of long-term incentives at the business unit and corporate levels

- The potential impact of metrics upon decision-making

- Approaches to setting goals and the role of expected performance in judging success and delivering pay

- The strength of the connection of long-term rewards to actual results, with implications for line of sight and for plan funding.

The discussion of business unit long-term incentives focuses upon phantom stock plans, but the findings are applicable to subsidiary equity plans as well.

TBR Phantom Stock Plan Example

The initial example of a phantom stock plan uses a particular form of the performance/valuation measure called total business return (TBR).[4] This example introduces key terms and features of phantom stock plans and sets up a "straw man" example against which to compare several alternatives cited later. TBR-based phantom stock also is, in its own right, a widely applicable and resilient approach that fully meets the criteria established in Chapters 3 and 4 for effective incentive design:

- **Basic plan mechanism.** A grant entitles the participant to the TBR generated by a block of stock. TBR is the increase in the value of the business over a period of time plus the cash flows generated by its operations. This two-part measurement approach is like measuring capital gains and dividends (total shareholder return) on a stock investment. A $100,000 TBR phantom stock grant entitles the participant to the return generated by a $100,000 block of stock, in much the same way that a $100,000 option grant delivers the gains on $100,000 in shares. In this case, however, the grant is based upon the value of the manager's own division rather than on actual corporate shares.

- **Valuation and TBR computations.** For purposes of the plan, the business unit is valued at 10 times income, defined as after-tax operating profit. That is, the business is valued using one of the simplest possible approaches: a fixed multiple of income. The TBR plan determines the company's value by making an estimate of how current, actual financial results — if they were to continue for a long time — would translate into a current valuation for the enterprise.[5]

Figure 10-1 is a basic example of the plan mechanism. In the example, the business increases its income by $25 million, raising the value of the business tenfold, or by $250 million. It also generates $200 million in free cash flows, so its total business return is $450 million. TBR is 45 percent of beginning value, so the gain on a $100,000 grant is $45,000.

Thus, participants share in value creation in a format using simple measures and a simple valuation approach. This is a straightforward structure and one that offers:

- **Flexibility and consistency.** This form of TBR can take businesses with many different levels of risk, growth and capital needs and evaluate their results on a roughly consistent footing. This feature helps in benchmarking pay and performance and addresses many issues that confound traditional performance metrics.[6]

- **Alignment with value-creating business decisions.** Since business investments normally increase the level of capital used by a business unit, investment outlays by themselves reduce free cash flow. Returns on those investments should increase income over time, causing a tenfold increase in valuation. Therefore, $10 of new investment must generate at least one dollar of income — a 10 percent return, equal to the cost of capital — to break even in TBR terms.[7]

- **Long-term orientation.** The way to maximize gains under the plan is to maximize TBR over the long run. By making annual, overlapping grants with maturity dates staggered into the future, these plans do not reward the short-term price bumps that can put standard options temporarily in the money. One-time

FIGURE 10-1: PHANTOM STOCK GRANT — THREE-YEAR EXAMPLE

Performance Scenario

Year	0	1	2	3
Operating Income After Tax (OI)	$100	$105	$120	$125
Capital	$1,000	$1,050	$1,100	$1,150

Grant Term = 3 Years

TBR Computation

Total OI	$350
Δ Capital	$150
FCF	$200

Plus

Δ OI	$25
÷ WACC	10%
Value Gain	$250

Equals

TBR = $450

Award Computation

TBR	$450
Beginning Value ($100/10%)	÷ $1,000
TBR%	45%

Phantom Stock Grant Size	$100,000
TBR %	X 45%
Award Earned	$45,000

increases in income or reductions of expense are valuable. Every dollar counts toward TBR just as it would for a business owner. However, sustainable increases in income increase TBR by a factor of 10. Permanent increases in expense have a tenfold downside impact. In this respect, the plan encourages both business growth and cost control, with long-term effects being most important.

TBR Phantom Stock Grant Term, Frequency and Vesting

Here are the key terms and features that can be applied to many kinds of phantom stock and other long-term incentive plans:

Grant term. Grants under plans of this type normally have a three- to five-year term, which is adequate in a prospective sense to directly encourage management's role in value creation. Longer grants — particularly in a formula-based plan like this TBR example — may allow plan liabilities to hit inappropriate levels.

Grant frequency. The plan should last much longer than five years in most settings, but it does so through the device of annual grants with vesting and maturity dates that extend progressively into the future. End-to-end grants — rather than overlapping, annual ones with staggered vesting and maturity dates — normally are a bad idea. A situation in which all of an individual's TBR grants vest at one date is a hazardous one — it may encourage management to hype income in that one year using the many tactics normally available for such an effort. Annual TBR grants, on the other hand, mean that *management has a clear financial claim on results in every year of the near, medium and long term.*

Vesting. Like other kinds of long-term incentives, these grants vest on a cliff or pro rata basis, most often over three- to five-year terms. As with stock options, vesting typically is synonymous with exercisability, but not always. One company issues grants that vest on a cliff basis three years following grant, then become exercisable 33 percent per year at the end of years three through five of a six-year grant term. This approach provides competitive vesting terms, as well as a high level of control and liquidity, while limiting the risks of exercise *en masse.* As with other long-term incentives, unvested grants normally are forfeited upon voluntary or involuntary termination. Death, disability and retirement are circumstances in which grant vesting or payment may be accelerated.

Change in control. Stock-based incentive grants normally provide accelerated vesting in the event of a change in control at the corporate level as well as implicit credit for stock price gains on the deal. Though TBR phantom stock grants are analogous in structure to stock options, practice is mixed in regard to whether participants are entitled to either benefit. The TBR formula itself describes a default treatment. If a business unit with a TBR phantom stock grant is sold, the proceeds are treated as a reduction of capital. Income falls to zero and so does the capitalized value of earnings, so a net TBR gain occurs to the extent the sale price exceeds value. Participants generally are better off if the sale price is favorable in relation to the economic results that would otherwise have come in and rewarded them over the next few years. That's the same trade-off facing shareholders.

The particulars of change-in-control terms in a TBR plan are matters decided by circumstance, inclination and pragmatic concerns. Choices center on:

- Whether the plan should provide TBR gains from a change in control in a particular business unit or private company or, on the other hand, regard proceeds in excess of capitalized earnings value as being, at least in part, a windfall

- Whether to formalize the change-in-control benefits as part of the program design or to deal with them on a discretionary, episodic basis.

Strictly from an incentive viewpoint, it is a good idea to set out change-in-control terms clearly. If the company is unlikely to be sold, but management is concerned about that possibility, then contractual change-in-control protections are a valuable kind of insurance that can be underwritten cheaply. If sale is likely, however, then these provisions clearly encourage management to sell at the best price. At the same time, they should prevent unearned gains that can occur when market value at the sale price replaces the comparatively modest formula valuation used in the plan. Basing change-in-control payments 50/50 on sale price and formula value is a reasonable compromise in many cases.

TBR Phantom Stock Grant Structure and Leverage

TBR phantom stock plans are designed to compete with the equity-based incentive plans used by public companies, especially stock option grants. Phantom stock grants also can be structured like whole shares of stock so participants receive accrued returns at exercise or maturity and the beginning value per share.

Like restricted stock, full-value phantom shares have a greater per share value than stock options at grant, which enables a company to grant fewer shares and still offer competitive grant value. These grants are used more often when retention concerns are particularly important. Appreciation-only grants — in which awards are based entirely upon TBR performance and not upon the beginning value — are used in cases when performance and award leverage dominate the discussion. Discounted grants are possible, too, along with grants that act like premium options, and pay out only when returns exceed some hurdle rate.

Figure 10-2 shows hypothetical payoffs on various grant structures that were examined by a wholly owned realty subsidiary of a diversified company during the design of its incentives. The chart shows equally valued grants of full value phantom stock (exercise price at zero) and discounted phantom stock (exercise price at 50 percent of beginning value), as well as grants with exercise prices at current value and at a 25 percent premium to current value. The full-value phantom stock grant was valued at 90 percent of face value, while the premium, discounted, and standard grants were valued at 15 percent, 60 percent and 30 percent, respectively.

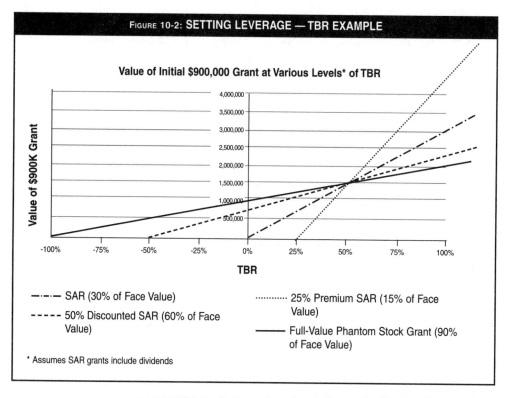

FIGURE 10-2: SETTING LEVERAGE — TBR EXAMPLE

Value of Initial $900,000 Grant at Various Levels* of TBR

— ·— SAR (30% of Face Value)

- - - - 50% Discounted SAR (60% of Face Value)

············ 25% Premium SAR (15% of Face Value)

——— Full-Value Phantom Stock Grant (90% of Face Value)

* Assumes SAR grants include dividends

The discounted and full value grants involve gains (and forfeitable grant value) at many different performance levels. The at-the-money and premium grants, in contrast, are more concerned with leverage and home-run potential. As the chart demonstrates, the exercise price on a phantom stock grant is a variable affecting plan leverage, retention power and dilution. Companies should examine these trade-offs when structuring phantom stock grants just as when structuring grants of real stock and options.

Dilution Guidelines and Competitive Award Levels

A general guideline for use in assessing dilution related to business unit incentives is to keep the face value of annual TBR grants in a range of between 0.5 percent and 2 percent of company value per year. This is based upon typical grant structure, and upon market benchmarking for long-term incentive grants and participant group sizes, with the assumption that business unit long-term incentive grants are the only form of long-term incentive grant made to business unit executives. Companies should keep in mind that other incentive plans — ones at the group or corporate level — may pose financial claims on the results of a given division and thereby enlarge the footprint of incentive costs on business results.

Companies should regard these grant guidelines as an upper limit and not a grant pool. They should set individual award levels based upon their own market objectives, competitive norms and the expected value of the specific financial claims they are creating within the incentive plan.

As a general guideline, a typical five-year grant of TBR-based phantom stock is worth about 40 percent of face value, which is about the same as what typical option grant values are worth as a percentage of face value.[8] This TBR grant lasts only five years, so holding all else equal, it should be worth less than a 10-year option grant. Offsetting this is the fact that vanilla TBR grants accrue gains from the first dollar of income gain (or free cash flow), while option gains hinge on the market's generally higher expectations for meeting performance. Full-value TBR phantom stock grants tend to be worth around 100 percent of face value.

A company's market value may be far higher than the value indicated by a formula like the one used in this version of TBR. However, this does not mean that phantom stock plan gains under a market-valuation approach will be higher than those under a TBR plan. For a typical company, a TBR phantom stock plan would be expected to generate grant gains at an annual rate of 10 percent to 15 percent per year. Market-based plans would be expected to generate gains at a more modest rate equal to the cost of capital, but against a larger grant size (e.g., 1 percent of a higher valuation). Either approach delivers customary and reasonable levels of gain for good performance as long as grants are competitively sized in present value terms.

Stock-based incentive grants, when compared to TBR grants, offer easier administration in certain regards. Stock gains are struck only at the corporate level and overall granting levels, and impacts are easily measured and benchmarked.[9] The greater incentive power of well-designed phantom stock, where fitting, outweighs its higher administrative complexity. At the same time, companies need to be diligent in these matters to avoid unintended levels of dilution. A number of methods to deal with dilution, volatility, distorting events and other matters are set forth later on. One technique these safeguards rely upon is the practice of annual granting.

Valuation Approaches for the Phantom Stock Plan

One of the key requirements of a phantom stock plan is to determine the company's value from time to time. The TBR formula described earlier is just one example of a valuation approach for a phantom stock plan. Many businesses with phantom stock plans simply have their shares valued by an outside expert in order to determine share valuation and gains. They're unlisted companies, for the most part — business units and closely held companies — so they can't get a market quote on their shares.

This approach is used even more often when the plan uses actual shares rather than phantom stock. The market-value approach allows companies to have equity-based incentives that work in a way most similar to the option and stock grants used by public companies, aligning gains more closely with actual market value than a formula-based plan would do. Liquidity is not as great as with public company options or stock, since shares typically are valued at annual intervals (sale constraints do limit liquidity in the public company sector). Some companies incorporate quarterly and even daily valuation into their plans by pegging their share prices to those of publicly traded peers.

When companies go down the market valuation path, they should use an independent valuation expert. This avoids the administrative difficulty and potential conflicts that an internal market valuation process might engender. This approach also can add significant administrative costs. However, having shares valued makes sense in a range of settings. The market-value approach often is chosen when the company is obliged to have shares valued periodically anyway for investor reporting, buy/sell agreements, or to enable use of non-quoted stock in a qualified retirement plan. It also can make sense in private companies that expect to go public within a few years. In these cases, the company may be growing so rapidly or have such volatile or uncertain prospects that a formula-based approach is not seen as useful.

In many other settings, however, market value simply is regarded as a more complete and accurate way of judging management's contribution to value creation and therefore a better basis for delivering incentive gains. Of course, that is the *de facto* stance of so many public companies that use options and other kinds of stock-based incentives as the centerpiece of their incentive structure.

Where formula-based valuations are concerned, most companies administer these on their own with limited input from outside advisors. Formula-based plans require adjustment from time to time. However, these are limited in scope and tend to focus upon the treatment of specified events, ideally within guidelines established at the time of plan design. Market valuation, on the other hand, is compelled to address a broad range of matters affecting future business prospects and risks. This requires many subjective adjustments so it is best assigned to an outside expert.

Market Valuation Techniques

Two methods used most often in market valuation of closely held businesses are market comparison approaches and discounted cash flow valuation.

Market comparison approaches. Under this method, stock prices of comparable public companies are used as evidence of the value of a private company. Recent sales of similar companies — whether in private market transactions or public company takeovers — are reviewed as well. Capitalization multiples are then compiled, ones relating various measures of business performance and scale to company valuation. Here are some examples:

- Market value of capital to sales, gross margins, capital, operating income or cash flow, or EBITDA (earnings before depreciation, interest and taxes)

- Market value of equity to net income, equity cash flow, or book value of equity.

A multiple for the subject company is determined based upon how it compares to companies in the peer group in terms of the quality of its performance and other factors driving its future economic earning power. This may result in a valuation at, above, or below the median of the peer group multiples.

Discounted cash flow valuation.[10] Under this method, a detailed forecast is developed for the company's financial results, typically for a period of five to 10 years. Cash flows distributable from operations — free cash flow that can be paid out of the company after satisfying its reinvestment needs — are computed for each forecast year and then discounted to present value at a discount rate that takes into account the company's degree of business risk. The "residual" value of the company — that part of its value that is based upon cash flows expected in years beyond the forecast term — is estimated as well and discounted to present value. The overall value of the enterprise is equal to the present value of free cash flows during the forecast term, plus the present value of the residual.

Results of different market valuation methods normally are studied together in a process of reconciliation. This makes sure the basic drivers of value in the industry and the company's own performance and prospects are reflected properly in the overall value. If the compensation program requires a determination of share price, this is computed by:

- Subtracting debt and preferred stock value from enterprise value, leaving the value of common equity

- Assuming there is a single class of common stock dividing the overall value of common equity by the number of outstanding common shares.

Discounts for Lack of Marketability and Control

The valuation may be adjusted further in a private company situation. In particular, the share price may be reduced by a liquidity discount, or discount for lack of marketability. These average about 35 percent of the share price.[11] A minority discount also may be needed to reverse out any control premium implied by the discounted cash flow valuation scenario or by market data on any control transactions of comparable companies. Some marketability discount applies at the time of a private placement, for example, since shares at that time do not enjoy the full liquidity of publicly traded ones. Any such discount would be small, however, since private placements tend to be undertaken in cases in which a liquidity event like an initial price offering (IPO), resale or redemption is expected within a few years. The valuations used to determine IPO prices, on the other hand, tend to be stated on an "as if public" basis, so no such discount applies.

As a practical matter, however, much analysis of share price and investment returns that is done in pre-IPO and private placement situations takes no explicit account of discounts for lack of marketability or minority interest status. Rather, analysis tends to focus upon eventual share price valuation in a future IPO or sale and upon cash flows during the holding period, backing into levels of estimated return based upon the price to be paid now. Practical issues with marketability and control — as well as their risks — presumably are addressed within the structuring of these financing transactions as well as in the investment returns expected from them.

Our experience since the late 1990s is that many pre-IPO companies in technology sectors — larger ventures — determined their share prices using market appraisals while in the pre-IPO phase. Their unusually high use of incentive stock options — tax-qualified stock options under U.S. law — encouraged them to do a good job of documenting the market value used for option exercise prices at the time of grant. Also, the SEC looked closely at market valuation matters in partial public offerings of technology subsidiaries in an effort to gain an accurate portrayal of their separate-company performance. Some such companies pursued market appraisals to document the company's value at the time of an option grant to prove that the options were issued at exercise prices equal to market value, hoping to avoid P&L charges for heavily discounted stock options.[12]

Valuation Accuracy vs. Incentive Efficacy

Specific trade-offs affect the decision of whether to use market valuation or a formula-based method to value shares within a business unit equity plan. The valuation method — the connection between management actions, business results and rewards — is, after all, the engine of the phantom stock plan.

Market valuation is the most accurate approach, better in terms of valuation accuracy and timeliness than the alternatives that compose the balance of this section. However, market valuation also is the approach with the highest adminis- trative cost due to the appraisal fees involved. It also tends to involve the lowest degree of line of sight — the least tangible perceived connection between what incentive plan participants can do, how it might affect market valuation and what they might get paid. Gains under many stock-based plans are unconnected to business unit management's actions for two main reasons:

- Business units often don't have much influence on overall results.

- Stock prices move around for many reasons unrelated to consolidated performance, particularly during the one- to five-year time frame that matters so greatly within an incentive plan.

Using a business unit equity plan — whether based upon phantom or actual equity — addresses the first of these issues by focusing upon performance and value creation at the business unit level. However, if market value is used as the basis for reward, the second issue may remain troublesome. The plan will reflect not only the results produced by the business unit, but also the vagaries of market valuation. Valuation formulas, by contrast, link rewards directly with actual business results, not with the unrelated portion of market stock price movement. The TBR plan, specifically, is driven by the portion of value creation that management can affect (income and capital) without a lot of susceptibility to market factors (e.g., shifts in the cost of capital or in market expectations for future performance).

Companies wishing to impose clearer and more compelling linkages between actions, success and pay often pursue one or another of the alternatives to market valuation. These companies offer fully competitive long-term incentives, often very similar in basic structure and award potential to the stock options used so heavily in the public company sector. At the same time, they achieve other design goals like providing clear line of sight in their incentive plans, linking pay strongly with actual results over the long run and funding plan payouts with actual income and cash flow.

Reconciling Market Value and Formula Value

When well constructed, valuation formulas align with market value over time. The difference between market value and a typical formula valuation is greatest when company valuation diverges greatly from a modest multiple of current earnings. If the company expects exceptionally high growth, then current earnings are very low in relation to the future earnings levels reflected by the high multiple. A low multiple usually means earnings are regarded as unsustainable or especially risky. Free cash flow enters into the equation as well. Companies with highly distributable earnings tend to be valued, all else equal, at higher multiples.

These valuation gaps subside over time as the company's actual performance plays out. When multiples are particularly high, for example, they often reflect hopes for income growth expected over the next few years.[13] The formula-based plan, in such a case, will show a rapid rise in value as income actually grows. It tracks value and returns over time in proportions similar to those indicated by market appraisal. In these high-growth cases, care must be taken that the run-up in earnings does not distort the formula valuation or cause inappropriate payouts.

Here are a couple of simple ways to address these issues:

- A start-up subsidiary expected high levels of growth in earnings and cash flow, ones likely to cause the company's cash-flow-based valuation to rise greatly over time. The company simply made lower grants than they otherwise would have, ones still competitive in present value terms.

- A travel and marketing services company expected a big rebound in earnings from the levels prevailing just before adoption of a TBR plan. The beginning capital level was used as a representation of value at the outset rather than capitalizing an earnings level seen as a low outlier.

The big differences between the market-based and formula approaches lie in the timing of value creation and in the standard of proof applied. The formula approach accretes value into the current period based only upon actual performance. The market appraisal, in contrast, also takes into account expected changes in future performance. The latter approach connects pay with timely and accurate market values, while the former connects it with value-creating financial performance only as it is earned. The formula-based plan effectively says to management, "Show me the money." This is a reasonable demand in view of senior management's decision-making role and the medium- to long-term time frame of many of their actions.

Formulas, Funding and Fiscal Fears

The distinction between market and formula valuation is important to plan funding as well. Market valuation can increase phantom stock gains well beyond a level warranted by current financial results. That means plan costs may become intolerably high in relation to company earnings or may even exceed the company's current ability to pay. And, if financial results eventually disappoint, market-based plans may have paid out big gains based upon anticipated performance that did not happen.

Public companies face these same concerns with option and stock plans, since the costs are borne by owners in the form of cash used to repurchase shares, dilution or both. But for nonpublic companies or business units, gains normally must be paid in cash, so funding can be a more acute concern. Formula valuations tend to tie plan expense accruals and payouts more closely to company earnings and cash flows, lessening the importance of the funding issue.

This linkage to actual results is not foolproof. Financial results can be volatile, hard to interpret and subject to manipulation in the short term. It is risky to have a lot of money riding on any one year's results, for example, and well-designed plans don't. Terms like these can ensure plan gains and costs align closely with value creation over time:

- Making multi-year grants — typically between three and five years in overall length — so pay is based upon sustained performance. Limiting grants to five or six years is prudent to prevent liabilities from compounding beyond anticipated levels and to prevent large batches of exercisable grants from overhanging the results of any one future year.

- Using annual granting and multi-year vesting, so that exercise or maturity dates are spread over several years

- Using the ending value each year as the basis for cash-out and as the exercise price for future grants. This has a ratcheting effect on goals, requiring that gains in earnings be sustained to deliver high payouts on many grants over time.

- Administering grants with close attention to annual share usage. As noted earlier, grants amounting to between 0.5 percent to 2 percent of value annually tend to keep plan liabilities in reasonable proportion to owner gains while providing competitive grants to management participants.

- Subtracting plan accruals before calculating earnings and valuation. This procedure smooths out fluctuations in income, valuation and plan gains, particularly when grant overhang is high. In such cases, large increases in income and value could cause plan accruals to spike to a very high percentage of current income.

So, the important choice between market versus formula valuation is not simply a question of the cost of annual appraisals. Rather, the choice also may depend upon factors like applicability of valuation formulas, timing of when value creation is recognized, funding and cost concerns, as well as the overall effect upon line of sight and plan design efficacy.

Market-Indexed and Performance-Based Valuation Formulas

Some companies use indexing as a way of producing a daily or weekly share valuation in a private company. For one window manufacturer, for example, shares undergo a full valuation annually using a traditional appraisal process. Values are updated daily based upon movement in an index of companies engaged in the same industry sector, with new financial data on the company and its peers used to reset valuations on a quarterly basis.

Indexing can be used as a valuation method by itself. Market-indexed valuation provides a kind of compromise between formula valuation and market valuation. In one simple example, the company is valued at a multiple of income determined by an industry peer group. This method gives management directly observable credit for improving results (income) while also reflecting market valuations of similar companies.

More complex formulas may be devised to address specific business circumstances. A privately held catalog retailer valued itself based upon a market-determined multiple of earnings or revenue, whichever was higher. This enabled the company to bear downturns in profitability related to marketing campaigns geared toward longer run business growth.

The incentive context in which indexing is applied most often is in incentive plans in which awards are earned (or vested or accelerated) based upon relative total shareholder return (TSR). These plans normally are used by public companies that can measure their TSR from a stock market perspective. (Comments on this method appear in Chapter 11.)

Since these methods normally involve multiples based upon explicit performance measures like revenue, EBITDA or income, they provide some explicit instructions on how to create value. For example, increasing income typically increases value. This is a positive attribute in terms of line of sight. Still, this area requires great care. The indexing algorithms, if badly designed, can create many situations where management is paid for poor performance (a bit like some EBITDA issues noted later). Also note that indexers bear market-value-based repurchase liabilities while still private. These costs may or may not be fundable from their operating results.

Valuation multiples used in incentive plans can be made to vary not only based upon market movements, but upon company performance. Figure 10-3 is an example used in a captive finance subsidiary of an automotive manufacturer. This company's phantom shares are valued as a multiple of earnings, but the multiple varies based upon net income and return on equity. The multiples were established by:

- Performing statistical analysis of peer company valuation multiples, isolating the incremental impact of return on equity (ROE) and earnings growth upon price-earnings (P/E) ratios. This analysis provided the target multiple, helped set target performance levels and guided the general range of valuation multiples to be used.

- Constructing a discounted cash flow model that syncs up with the range of multiples indicated by the regression analysis. The exact P/E multiples used to populate the matrix were generated by running scenarios within the DCF model.

This general approach can be applied to many industries and metrics. An example in the independent power industry featured valuation multiples earned based upon operating cash flow and gross capital usage. As in the case of the captive financier, valuation multiples were generated using discounted cash flow scenarios, ones that set the company's value at each performance scenario (that

Figure 10-3: TBR AND INCENTIVE DESIGN — PHANTOM STOCK BASED UPON P/E RATIO

Step 1: Determine Value of Business at Various Performance Levels

Net Income Growth	ROE 10%	ROE 15%	ROE 20%
10%	2.1	3.0	2.1
20%	3.3	4.8	5.4
25%	4.1	6.2	7.0

Step 2: Use Results to Calibrate P/E Matrix

Net Income Growth	ROE 10%	ROE 15%	ROE 20%
10%	8	10	11
20%	10	15	17
25%	11	17	19

is, at each cell in the valuation matrix). The high-growth, low-capital scenarios involved larger free cash flows and bigger gains in income and, therefore, higher valuations.

At the same time, these methods require that high performance be sustained over a period of years and that related valuation gains be proved, in effect, before being fully rewarded under the plan. The valuation scenarios satisfied both these requirements because:

- They allowed for multiple expansion, assuming that a company with high earnings growth would be able to continue that growth into the future.[14]

- They used those higher expectations as conditions for payouts on later grants. For the formula valuation to rise continually at above-market levels, the company would have to continually surpass performance expectations.

In each of the foregoing examples, business valuations could expand greatly based upon actual results. So each of these plans delivered potentially strong award leverage and payouts. Compared to the fixed-multiple approach used in most TBR plans, these methods are a bit more like market valuation, allowing for the possibility that a high-performing business could attract a high valuation multiple, one well ahead of its current performance level.

The upside and its fiscal risks are moderated by higher performance expectations and the ratcheting goals they create. Under this plan and other well-designed ones, payouts are not persistently high unless management consistently beats reasonable performance expectations. Those are the circumstances under which companies create extraordinary amounts of value for owners. Those are the only circumstances warranting extraordinarily high incentive awards for management.

A pure market valuation-based plan, on the other hand, or one simply using a high, fixed valuation multiple may pay out systematically for growth expectations that are never attained. Companies sometimes wish to create wide play in valuations and gains as a way to create greater plan leverage and motivational power. In such cases, performance-based adjustments can be a more prudent path than a market-indexed plan since the latter essentially writes a blank check based upon the market's vagaries.

Combining Performance Valuation and Indexed Valuation

Like other kinds of valuation formulas, the market-indexed variety can be adjusted to emphasize key messages about business priorities. The following example, used in a wholly-owned Internet service provider (ISP), shows the extent to which formulas can be tailored to deal with unusual situations, even ones including extremes in terms of valuation levels, volatility and unpredictability. (See Figure 10-4.)

In this case, comparative EBITDA margins drive the revenue multiple used. The indexed valuation approach was chosen because this newly acquired company wanted employees to continue to participate in ISP market valuations. At the same time, the company and its new parent wanted to use a valuation formula to connect pay directly with key goals. The two-stage valuation format is indexed fully with market movement while emphasizing measures like revenue, EBITDA and free cash flow.

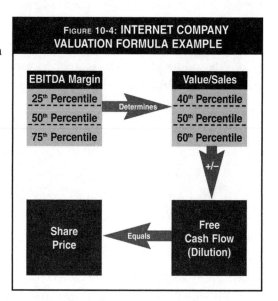

FIGURE 10-4: INTERNET COMPANY VALUATION FORMULA EXAMPLE

The format also was meant to index the stock market's criteria for business results and success. The format is an example of a flexible target-setting method that effectively placed the company in a race for revenue and EBITDA, with its peers as competitors.

The formula was designed to track subtler market signals as well. EBITDA was expected to become more important in the stock market's valuation of such companies. Revenue multiples were expected to fall and EBITDA levels were expected to rise. The formula was designed to track this trade-off, assigning higher importance to EBITDA as it emerged as a stronger driver of market value. The messages the plan conveyed to management were those conveyed in gross terms by industry stock valuation criteria.

This valuation formula was intended to last, and it has generated proportionally reasonable results through the course of wild, mainly downward market movements. All the while, it has clearly reflected the company's key financial priorities. For purposes of this discussion, it is useful since it illustrates the extent to which market and motivational dynamics can be articulated in a plan's valuation formula. This approach illustrates two important points about market-indexed formulas:

- The formula looked to dot.com market norms to determine the company's value, irrespective of whether those market valuations made economic sense and largely without regard to the company's ability to pay. This is an extreme example of a company bearing market risks, but the parent company understood these risks fully. It had made a strong commitment to allowing employees in this newly acquired business to continue to participate in the ISP equity market. If peer stock prices had risen greatly and the company incurred large repurchase commitments, it might have initiated a partial public offering to hedge these liabilities. In any event, it stood ready to settle the grants in cash.

- The mechanism of peer performance comparisons and indexing can be complex in itself, particularly when the peer data involve irregular information, range discontinuities and general volatility. These factors were dealt with in this ISP plan by standardizing peer data. The standard deviation of peer EBITDA margins and revenue multiples was calculated, solving for the company's relative performance and attaching a multiple to it as if each of those ranges of data were normally distributed. This method produced more continuous and regular scales while still fully reflecting the play in peer data. This method is applicable in many peer-indexed approaches to performance measurement.

EBITDA as a Valuation Yardstick

EBITDA is used commonly in some industries as a valuation yardstick. It should be used with care within incentive plans because it is an incomplete measure. It does not take account of the financial claims that taxes and asset replacement can pose on owner income, so it does not provide enough information to judge whether a particular business decision creates value or not. EBITDA-based goals may encourage the company to make investments with low, value-destroying economic yields.

EBITDA was used in the ISP incentive valuation formula described above and was paired with revenue, which is an even less complete indication of performance. In that example, the valuation format was constructed to provide a continuing, market-based stake, to set out the company's main financial goals, and to reflect drivers in the rewards scheme in proportions indicated roughly by the stock market over time. The company in that example was not using the valuation formula as direct guidance to investment decision-making. Rather, that company was well aware of the deficiencies of the EBITDA metric. It knew it must rely upon thorough procedures in financial analysis to keep big-ticket decisions aligned with value creation, because this particular type of plan design would not be adequate in this regard.

The issue is an important one at some other companies. They use TBR-based phantom stock plans in which shares are valued based upon a multiple of EBITDA, often unaware of the fiscal risks that this approach can involve and the extent to which it may harm the quality of business decisions. Here is the basic problem:

- If a company is valued at eight times EBITDA, for example, then an investment which reduces free cash flow by $1 million would have to produce EBITDA of $125,000 to break even in TBR terms. So the formula in that case would impose a threshold EBITDA yield on new investment of 12.5 percent per year.

- EBITDA is computed before taxes and before any provision for recapture of investment in wasting assets (e.g., before depreciation charges). To increase value, a company needs to get returns on investment at least equal to its cost of capital. A 12.5 percent return, once adjusted for taxes and for recapture of most kinds of depreciating assets, is not high enough to create value and may actually be negative.

Such plans directly reward management for many kinds of value-destroying decisions, particularly in the short term before short-lived assets reach their replacement dates. Lower EBITDA multiples reduce these risks, but many of them remain a concern even with multiples as low as four or five.

Equity-Based Incentive Plans Based Upon Book Value

Small-company phantom stock plans sometimes use book value as the basis for valuation. This also is the method used, in effect, in many professional services firms owned by partners or principals. Book-value plans typically reward the participant for increasing stockholders' equity accounts and accumulating earnings for shareholders. Here are a few observations about how these plans function:

- Like the TBR approach, this method is based upon actual financial results, accreting value only to the extent they have been achieved. However, book value gains do not take into account whether participants have increased the earning power of the business during the measurement period. Rather, they simply reward accumulation of earnings irrespective of whether earnings are rising or falling. Falling earnings tend to mean a falling valuation, so these plans carry the risk of paying out substantial rewards even if performance suggests destruction of value. They also may under-reward companies with value-creating earnings growth.

- Book-value plans don't necessarily attach a complete or consistent cost to the use of capital and may reward results that do not create value. Since book earnings drive book value plans, they reflect the hodgepodge of issues involved when computing equity-based metrics like net income, EPS or ROE. They may omit any cost for the use of equity capital, miss the impact of financial leverage on that cost, or both.

Like plans using other highly flawed financial metrics, book value plans offer the advantage of being admirably simple and familiar.

Anti-Dilution Features

Phantom and subsidiary equity plans usually have anti-dilution clauses protecting plan participants and sponsors from some serious risks:

- They protect against the possibility that the business's owners will pay out a lot of money in dividends or otherwise withdraw capital, reducing earning power and value.
- Correspondingly, they prevent capital infusions from inadvertently enriching participants.

Such clauses can take a range of forms. The free cash flow (FCF) computation involved in TBR is one example. It tracks the investor money going into and out of a business. A $100 million capital infusion by itself simply reduces TBR by $100 million, so management is affected by dilution in proportion to that felt by owners. Capital transactions can also affect share value through share issuance or redemption, real or phantom. Another solution is simply to subtract net capital infusions from any value gain, as in the "net gain" format used in incentive plans of some corporate start-ups.

Adjusting Valuation Results

Each valuation approach relies heavily upon current earning power, risk, earnings growth and capital requirements as well as other financial drivers of business value. Whether value is determined by appraisal or formula, care must be taken to see that the earnings base being capitalized into value is representative of continuing earning power, not distorted by temporary blips or downturns. In indexed plans, the same needs to be true of the multiple arising from the peer group. This tends to be less of an issue since peer-group multiples are less volatile than company income. Peer multiples often are computed as a peer group's average, median or inter-quartile mean.

Further smoothing in the market-indexed plan design, as well as many others, may be accomplished through devices like:

- Capitalizing trailing average earnings of the company and its peers

- Establishing alternative minimum or maximum valuations based on net assets, equity or sales, etc.

- Establishing a maximum range of price movement per measurement period ("collaring").

These adjustments tend to spread out the timing of price movements, making them depend more fully on sustained financial results without limiting the valuation ultimately attained. Current earnings or cash flows can be adjusted directly if they contain a large temporary or one-time element.

In these cases, the "total return" format of many formulas provides guidance on how to adjust. Acquisition outlays, or one-time losses, for example, tend to run through the FCF computation only — all at once or over two or three years — so that management's performance in TBR terms reflects these hits only once in total. In contrast, general variation in income has a capitalized, multiple impact upon valuation, since it tends to affect not only the current year, but also expectations going forward. The plan's general architecture (e.g., overlapping multi-year grants, iterative subtraction of plan accruals from income) does a lot to regularize gains over time. In testing of the typical TBR plan, for example, the plan's overall structure can allow up to a 25 percent completely temporary variation in income without material distortion in measurement or rewards over time.

Financial results may need adjustment to deal with unusual company circumstances. An independent power producer (IPP) provides an example of this. As an IPP, the company held various percentage interests in many power plant investments. In this situation, typical approaches to consolidation could have distorted measurements of capital, pulling all the debt of a 51 percent-owned investee onto the books, while eliminating all the debt of a 49 percent-owned venture. We devised an approach called "proportional consolidation" for this company's incentive plan, one in which its capital levels reflected its exact percentage share both of investee holdings and obligations.

The captive finance company's incentive plan provided another example of how a company's circumstances may require an adjustment. The measures used in the plan — net income and return on equity — are affected by variations in financial leverage. This factor was a potential source of volatility and bias within the plan, so results were restated pro forma to reflect a targeted, fixed capital structure. A similar plan used in a district power business, on the other hand, was not adjusted since management insisted that debt levels were fixed by certain financing constraints. Shortly after implementation, management figured out a way to overcome those constraints, greatly increasing the plan's gains as a result. The parent company promptly canceled the plan. In that case, everyone involved would have been better off if the plan had been adjusted in some reasonable way for capital structure as recommended.

Performance Plans

Performance plans are the other type of long-term incentive plan used in business units and private companies. These plans come in two main varieties:

- *Performance unit plans.* These provide cash awards based upon attaining long-term performance goals. Basically like bonus plans in structure, they tend to be based entirely on financial performance in relation to pre-set goals, to have award ranges limited on the upside, and to depend mainly upon corporate-level performance. When we cite performance plans and performance shares as business-unit incentives, we are referring to plans that are based at least partly upon business unit results. The term performance "unit" refers to the fact that some such plans have been denominated in "units" whose value might vary based upon financial performance or other factors.

- *Performance share plans.* These allow participants to earn shares of the parent company based upon attainment of pre-set goals. This basically is a performance unit plan denominated in shares rather than cash. They provide a fairly straightforward means of encouraging long-run success for business units. At the same time, by using stock, they maintain a firm link to parent company success. If subsidiary shares are available for use in an incentive plan, then these may be delivered in a performance-share format as well. Performance share plans are addressed in Chapter 11.

Performance plans have much in common with phantom stock. Their general architecture involves many features of phantom equity or subsidiary equity plans like overlapping grants, staggered vesting and maturity dates and, when designed well, proper connections between financial performance and executive rewards. We don't need to embark upon a fresh discussion of performance plan design at this point. Rather, the steps in performance plan design already have been covered in this book's earlier discussions of:

- Metric selection, target setting and range setting

- Term and vesting of long-term incentive grants.

Phantom Stock vs. Performance Plans

Performance plans can emphasize value creation in the same terms as a phantom plan that uses a valuation formula. The TBR-based phantom stock plan presented earlier can be converted into an equivalent performance plan, as one example. This approach would simply involve:

- Making performance plan grants each year, ones with a total term of three to five years and either ratable or cliff vesting.

- Setting up an award schedule involving a 1:1 connection between TBR and cash payout, with zero payment at zero TBR and a long interval on the upside.

This can be accomplished without using the metric TBR as a performance measure in the plan itself; a matrix format example of such a plan is coming up shortly. This approach does what TBR phantom stock and other value-based incentives can do. It creates a one-for-one linkage between value creation over time and pay, and it does so across a wide range of performance levels. It reflects the first-level financial drivers of value creation — income, capital and the cost of capital — in reasonable proportion. If a company simply captures these basic trade-offs and applies them to business unit pay, it will have a better functioning rewards structure than most from a shareholder value perspective.

Performance plan designs don't always capture this dynamic. In fact, typical performance plans are bedeviled by the same design issues that affect bonus plans. Their traditional metrics and negotiated targets create a range of situations in which management can be paid well for decisions that actually destroy value. This book's advice on metrics and target setting (Chapters 6 to 9) is entirely applicable to the design of performance share and performance unit plans.

Value-Based Incentives vs. Performance Plans

A great advantage of performance plans is that they use well-known metrics, which are presented in familiar, straightforward award schedules. They're fairly simple and don't require the company to roll out and communicate a new measurement approach or valuation scheme.

In many cases, the choices available for a business unit or private company's long-term incentives are reduced to two main approaches: a traditional performance plan paying in cash or corporate shares or a business-unit phantom stock plan. Companies sometimes believe they face a hard choice in this area:

- They can use simple, familiar plans that people understand, but that may not always align with value creation. In this case, companies are obliged to rely heavily on other governance tools — budgeting, strategic planning, investment and deal evaluation, performance evaluation, moral suasion — to be sure that business decisions consistently favor shareholder interests.[15]

- They can have value-based incentives, ones that align results well with value creation and can be deployed with confidence at the business unit level where line-of-sight effects are greatest. However, such plans are less familiar and more complex than traditional ones. They pose risks of low comprehension, mistrust and even some adverse effects on decision-making like the "harvest bias" that managers may mistakenly adopt when incentives are changed to reflect capital usage.

This is a false dilemma. Companies can offer value-based incentives and they can do so in easy-to-understand formats. One example of this method, the matrix-based incentive structure, is Figure 7-4. This incentive plan uses the common, familiar metrics of operating income and return on invested capital. It arrays performance and reward schedules in a matrix format, one used in many performance plans. Yet, it is fully a value-based plan since it delivers payouts driven by net valuation gains. Performance is rewarded in reasonable proportion to value created over time. Decisions that don't generate net gains in value do not increase pay.

Value Rules vs. Private Equity Incentive Structures

Companies financed by private equity are an interesting category of private company to consider. They often take positions in ordinary businesses and turn them into great performance for investors, so their incentive practices warrant some attention. The long-term incentive stakes created in a business financed by private equity, in contrast to more typical long-term incentive grants, tend to be:

- Tied to events — deal formation and exit — rather than to periodic granting
- Comparatively illiquid during their expected lives, with liquidity often tied to the targeted exit strategy
- One-time in nature, effectively accelerating long-term incentive stakes that might have been accumulated over time
- Partially purchased by management, with amounts affected by individual resources and risk tolerances
- At least where the buy-in portion is concerned, not subject to the customary employment-related vesting of long-term incentive grants
- Limited to a small group of top officers rather than a more broadly defined group of key management decision-makers and contributors
- Riskier, being affected strongly by the high levels of financial leverage normally involved in the deal.

This distinctive approach has contributed to high performance for private equity investees and high risk-adjusted returns to their investors. Private equity houses apparently are effective at acquisitions, for example, while most acquisitions made in general industry fail. If private equity houses were not better than general industry at taking a controlling interest in a company and managing it for returns, their portfolio performance would be persistently below the cost of capital. After all, the main way they get businesses is to compete for acquisition transactions. Their prospects at acquisition success should not be as good as that of companies in general industry, since they normally cannot pursue the synergies often desired by a trade buyer. They are succeeding, in a sense, with one hand tied behind their backs.

Excutives usually hold relatively big stakes in a private equity-owned company and often earn big gains, but that does not mean they are overpaid in a market sense. It is important to properly compare the partly bought, front-loaded and risky nature of management's "deal interests" with the more typical annual granting of long-term incentives by public companies. Equity stakes for individual executives should be annualized, reduced by the value of any interest bought, valued appropriately at the time of grant, and offset against the more parsimonious salary and bonus plans that sometimes prevail in these deals. After these adjustments are completed, equity interests normally are comparable between private equity and public sector companies. Private equity stakes may be higher, but not dramatically out of the normal range and usually not without business reasons.

Here's a quick reconciliation of private equity investee pay to market norms. Take a company that posts good economic performance over five years: a 10-percent return to all debt and equity investors, consisting of free cash flow for debt paydown and interest expense as well as increases in enterprise value. This company provides a benchmark private equity yield in the upper teens:

- A $1-billion investment, with total returns compounded annually at ten percent per year, reaches $1.61 billion at the end of five years.

- $700 million in debt, at a 6 percent after-tax debt cost, reaches a value of $940 million dollars when compounded annually to the same date (for computational convenience).

- The ending value for equity holders is $1.61 billion minus $940 million, or $670 million. That is a 17.5 percent annual return on the initial equity of $300 million.

If management owned 15 percent of the upside through stock, options or override interests, its gain would be 15 percent of $370 million, or about $55 million. That's more money than a few top officers normally make on their option grants in five years. But their salaries and bonuses tend to run at least a bit lighter than they would in the more typical corporate setting. And some of their gain, let's say a third in this case, owes to their buy-in. Their buy-in may be intertwined with other terms, but it can be separated for analytical purposes. So we have $37 million in gain on the "long-term incentive grant" part of the deal. The other $18 million of management's gain is a return on their $15 million investment and not "pay" at all. The remaining $37 million is either their gain on $30 million in options or its equivalent in the form of an override arrangement or other performance-based incentives.

What pay would one otherwise have? Run-of-the-mill returns would be equal to the typical cost of capital, now in the 7 percent to 9 percent range for many companies. At an 8 percent rate of return to investors, 20 percent debt and a 4 percent after-tax cost of debt, option gains run at around 9 percent per year. Officers with options on $30 million in shares in total would earn gains around $16 million over five years. The private equity management team has three to four times that gain, in this example. But their company-provided incentive opportunity is the same $30 million in options, so their greater gains are due to performance and leverage rather than more generous incentive grants.

Their equity stakes look pretty big at first glance. But a 20 percent stake in a company's results is not necessarily generous if it requires a large buy-in and if it involves a particularly performance-contingent stock option or override structure. When levels like 20 percent are quoted, they often are the incremental stake at the top of the performance scale rather than the overall, share-equivalent value held by management. A deal offering an 8 percent stake actually might be more generous, if it is an outright grant of full shares.

High performance in private equity investees can be attributed in part to closer governance by the owner group and to more effective incentives for senior management in such deals. Equity participation in such deals tends to be limited to a few top officers who are committed for the duration of the current deal and who often sign on for the next phase, whether it is operating as a public company, a subsidiary of a trade buyer or going after another buyout deal. Incentives for a broader group of senior managers, however, need not follow in every respect the one structured for top officers. Requiring buy-in from a broader group of managers certainly can be messy, for example. And the annual granting, maturity and vesting structure of typical long-term grants can be helpful in plan administration and efficacy. Putting in a well designed, long-term incentive plan for this broader group could result in a better incentive structure than most public and private-equity-funded companies. It would retain what appear to me to be the important elements of the private equity reward system — having a strong stake in business results and a clear stake in both cash flow and valuation gains — without imposing the illiquid and event-based nature of the top officer deal.

Some private equity investees have substantial capital needs. The classic mature-company LBO, in contrast, has highly distributable earnings and very low investment needs. Much of the performance gain in such businesses stems from committing the company to pay out much of its cash flow from operations for debt paydown and compelling it to take a very sharp pencil to any business investments. The presumption in many such cases is that the company is best run without a lot of new investment because it does not have very good opportunities to earn high returns on new money.

This is another example of the "harvest bias" cited earlier, and it is risky when applied to companies that do have prospects for profitable reinvestment and growth. One dollar of free cash flow is worth a dollar, but one dollar of permanent gain in after-tax operating income can be worth ten dollars or more in market value. That is not necessarily a problem with the typical LBO structure, however. It balances these factors well enough since gains to equity-holders can come from cash flow used to pay down debt or from gains in enterprise value due to higher earnings. The same is true for investees with higher growth prospects and higher capital needs. The basic structure of these deals creates clear credit for "total return" either through debt paydown or greater eventual gain. That's why the same structure — and the same investors — can handle the low-growth, classic mature LBO as well as higher growth investees.

The comparison of typical pay with private equity pay lends us this general guidance:

- Having a concentrated, leveraged stake in business results can focus management more strongly upon business success.

- Companies can create this kind of financial stake without increasing pay. By restructuring existing pay to concentrate on business unit results, companies can create a stake for senior management that is close to what they would receive in a buyout transaction (aside from the part they receive by buying into the deal).

- Private equity deals involve buy-in, but so can incentive plans. If participants wish to hold a greater stake, they can take elective actions like putting off exercises, deferring gain into accounts that appreciate on a phantom share basis, or taking bonus potential in phantom shares instead.

- The economics of such deals can be created without an actual buyout transaction and without heavy debt levels. They can be created in phantom form, and higher award leverage can stand in for the financial leverage connected with high debt levels.

- Private equity success does not depend upon milking the company for cash flow and under-investing in long-run earning power any more than public company success flows from an opposite set of biases. The structure of these deals provides credit for FCF and for valuation gains, a productive emphasis upon "total return" that can be designed into many types of plans.

Summary

For many companies, business units are where the rubber hits the road. That is where their company's value, opportunities, detailed business knowledge and key decision-makers are concentrated. If they are to get business results from the enormous amount of money they spend on executive incentives, they must overcome hesitancies about having serious incentive pay at the business unit level. This chapter has set forth the reasons why companies should go down this road and provided examples of how to do it prudently and effectively, along the way exposing a range of approaches that apply equally in the private-company realm.

Endnotes

1   Source: Towers Perrin annual incentive design study.

2   Computations of the corporate-driven part of incentive costs, statistical simulations and relevant discussion were presented in Chapter 2.

3   Based upon data used commonly, when valuing long-term incentive grants, to estimate the likelihood of vesting by management participants.

4   TBR's definition and structure were set forth in Chapter 8 along with those of other value-based metrics. TBR-based solutions to target-setting were described in Chapter 9.

5   This "capitalized operations value" or "warranted value" concept is described in Chapter 4. It is the residual valuation method used in the basic valuation model set forth in that chapter. The multiple of 10 used in this example corresponds to a cost of capital of 10 percent.

6   This is part of the flexibility of "total return" frameworks as demonstrated in Chapters 4 and 8.

7   Ten percent is the threshold in this example when the cost of capital is 10 percent. This simple version of TBR is an approximation of valuation effects, and of the economic threshold for value-creating investment decisions. Effects are not precise, as noted in Chapter 8, but function well on balance within the overall context of the plan.

8   That is based upon annual TBR of 12 percent, a 10 percent discount rate and a 3 percent annual likelihood of forfeiture.

9   Stock-based incentives do involve many legal and technical issues, but these do not go away when a company replaces part of its stock-based pay with operating incentives like TBR phantom stock plans. Dilution may fall under the stock-based plans, but the bulk of other issues remain active. Making more kinds of incentive grants, on top of stock-based grants, does make matters more complex.

10 Discussed in Chapter 4 in detail.

11 See *Business Valuation: The Analysis and Appraisal of Closely-Held Companies* by Pratt and Schweis.

12 I believe that the general idea of the valuation discounts noted earlier is appropriate when valuing pre-IPO shares, but I'm not expressing a view on their effectiveness in regard to SEC or tax matters.

13 The effect of medium-term expectations upon stock prices was covered extensively in Chapter 4.

14 The forecast assumed that high performance would degrade over time to industry norms, consistent with the DCF forecast conventions noted in Chapter 4.

15 To a large extent, public companies have opted out of the "operating incentive" format, relying instead on stock-based incentives that outsource the tasks of measurement and reward to the stock market.

Using Stock
to Build Effective Incentives

Most companies try hard to drive business performance using stock as an incentive vehicle. But they are going down the wrong road. They believe that stock-based pay — grants of stock options and stock — place the company's incentive structure squarely where it should be: at the intersection, if you will, of governance and valuation. This makes sense because within the corporate governance system, management serves as the agent of shareholders, and managers are supposed to steer the business to maximize its valuation for owners.

Companies presume, reasonably, that incentives ought to be used to encourage value creation for owners. Shareholder advocates and many others believe the best route is to concentrate management's financial interests in company stock so they are aligned with those of shareholders. Companies follow these directions closely, paying senior management largely in options and stock and requiring them to hold on to many of the shares they collect over time.

These turned out to be incomplete directions to the destination. Stock-centered incentive policies create only vague and distant incentive effects for most people in senior management. Stock-based pay, particularly in the form of option grants, does not contribute materially to company performance. Stock-based pay is no doubt helpful in some matters, such as helping to attract and retain talent. But it can be unhelpful in other areas, creating risk aversion or insensitivity to risk, driving high share dilution and weakening motivational effects at many points along the road.

Most people don't really govern the business in a way that affects the stock price or their gains. The directions they receive from their stock-based incentives are, in effect, "you can't get there from here." The few who can affect the stock price aren't necessarily getting clear directions from the stock market, either. On the contrary, they may find its gyrations about as lucid as some rambling street preacher. In the end, simply handing out big chunks of pay in the form of shares or options does not by itself create enough directive power to actively govern much of anything. What we actually find at the intersection of valuation and governance is value rules. Value rules reflect the basics of business valuation. And they take an active role in governance by connecting the dots from decisions to results to valuation.

They are designed based upon the company's structure and the real characteristics of its inhabitants. A typical organization's pay scheme seems to envision a centrally focused interior plan, a soaring structure against which most people are made to look small. Value rules draw mainly horizontal spans, rewarding a team for performance contributions made at a level they can see and affect. In the architectural metaphor, they emphasize the scale of the people rather than the hierarchy, elevating rather than diminishing their presence within it. That is a comparatively empowering approach to design. It acknowledges the power that senior management teams hold over their respective areas of the enterprise. It also focuses on the power that money may hold over senior management.

This chapter concerns how best to use stock in the structure of incentive pay. That is a big topic. The competitive marketplace contains hundreds of different variations on stock-based incentives, each with its own context and rationale. If we surveyed all that, we'd end up sifting through a lot of complexity. That's not the purpose of this book. We're not presenting all the approaches out there as if they have roughly equal validity. I don't believe they do. Some ideas on incentive design are generally valid, and some ideas, even some commonly held ones, are not. The charge here is to provide decisive and actionable advice in the important matter of executive incentives. To do that, the discussion needs to focus on the basics and do so systematically. Companies should think in very basic terms about what they are trying to accomplish with incentive pay within the various parts of the workforce where it applies. They need to see what stock really can do for them in the context of rewards and what it cannot. That will lead directly to the best choices and eliminate much of the cacophony of competing plan design ideas. In this area, as in others, if you drill down to the bedrock principles and base your structure upon them, you can build something that will stand.

What Is It Good For?

Where exactly do we locate stock-based pay on a road map to business performance? As I have noted, stock-based incentives don't function as a performance incentive, in a proper cause-and-effect sense, for most of senior management. However, stock can fulfill a range of important functions within the rewards system, not only for management, but the broader workforce. Stock can be effective within broader efforts to create a sense of affiliation and engagement. For example, it can be powerful to tell younger managers that the grants they are receiving are the same incentive device given to all of senior management, right up to the CEO. Advocates in the ownership movement convincingly assert that broad-based stock ownership — through employee stock ownership plans (ESOPs) or other uses of stock in qualified retirement plans — can help in a company's efforts to engage the overall workforce, encouraging people to devote their discretionary efforts to the company's best interests.[1]

Good Hedges Make Good Neighbors

Stock-based grants can also work as a financial hedge against pay cost obligations. Making an option grant on 2 percent of the company's shares limits shareholder costs, pre-tax, to 2 percent of shareholder gains until exercise. And it does so under a wide range of business performance and share price gains (though losses are not shared). A stock grant has dilution consequences that are even more predictable across a wide range of performance levels. Compare this to another kind of executive pay geared toward capital accumulation during the participant's career — executive pensions. These cost obligations accumulate largely irrespective of whether management's performance paid off much for shareholders.

Bonus plans don't correlate that well with shareholder gains, either. Companies can rack up big bonus costs while shareholders are racking up losses. Performance plans often have the same problem. There are direct fixes for this problem, ones involving the targets and metrics in such plans.[2] It's also possible to make plans more effective so they reward value creation in a more compelling way. Encouraging better performance — and actually getting it — is the best hedge for incentive pay costs, after all. However, using shares as award currency works as an indirect fix. In a performance unit plan or a bonus plan, cash pay obligations are set directly by achievement of goals, whether those goals and the way they were achieved are proper or not. In a performance share plan, by contrast, award potential is denominated in shares. Good results mean more shares earned, but those shares are not worth as much if those results have not enriched shareholders. A participant might earn 150 percent of the targeted number of shares, but the value of that award is only 75 percent of target if the stock price ends up at one-half of its expected level.

Good Trades vs. Bad Trades

There are perfectly proper uses for company stock in the pay structure, particularly at the senior management level, but the structural role of stock is often larger than it really should be. The key questions in this area can be addressed using the more general design principle of form following function. What will the function of equity be in pay delivery? How much award leverage will stem from stock price movement, as opposed to performance against goals? What forms of equity, subsidiary equity, or equity derivatives will be used within the incentive structure?

Let's start by drawing a few general perspectives. One design goal clearly should be to try to get the most bang for the buck expended on incentive pay. Stock options are complex and risky. This, combined with the fact that most option-holders have little personal control over the stock price, simply encourages executives to discount the value of these grants. What if your company is giving executives grants that cost shareholders 50 cents in cash, dilution, or both, but have a perceived value of 25 cents to the recipient? The recipient would have been as happy with a quarter in cash. The other quarter of cost simply is an economic loss to owners. A grant of options often is a bad trade from the company's viewpoint.

For most companies a shift from stock options to whole shares makes sense since this means executives are less likely to discount what they receive. Discounted stock options are a halfway point between stock options and whole shares, one combining the upside and downside inherent in stock holdings with the higher award leverage of stock options. They're also less likely to be discounted by participants than vanilla stock options, so they enable a more cost-effective trade between the company and its senior management. Companies that are highly focused on cost-effective incentives should regard vanilla stock options as limited-use instruments for special situations.

A Firm Grip, or White Knuckles?

Another sensible tenet is to take account of the individual's risk tolerances. There is some empirical evidence, for example, that CEOs with heavy stock option holdings are more likely to make risky acquisitions. There is a ton of evidence, of course, that most acquisitions fail. On the other hand, companies whose CEOs hold large blocks of stock are significantly less likely to go for big risky deals.[3] Stock exposes its owners to the full spectrum of upside and downside, while stock options, appearing on their face to be about upside only, may well encourage top management to gamble too freely with other people's money. This doesn't mean that companies should ditch stock options as an incentive device for the CEO. But it obviously does invite them to think through the risk implications of the overall incentive system.

Heavy stock ownership requirements also may cause the wrong side of the risk coin to show its face. As we noted in Chapter 5, investors have high levels of liquidity and can diversify easily. Executives do not. This is not something to apologize for. Investors give executives real power over the enterprise and a very substantial stake in its success. In return, executives are properly required to have real accountability for performance and to see their actions through over time. It is perfectly reasonable for companies to require them to hold illiquid business interests they can't diversify to nearly the extent their financial advisers might prefer. However, at some point — somewhere between a million dollars of stock exposure and a few tens of millions for the range of people we are talking about — adding more exposure arguably goes beyond the point of diminishing returns. That is, the personal risk levels involved simply create risk aversion rather than encouraging the balanced risk-taking involved in business success.

Executive Ownership Is Not About the Company Owning the Executive

Typical executive ownership guidelines may encourage premature option exercises since they often define ownership as share holdings and not option holdings. My general view is that companies should include all forms of equity exposure when counting ownership, including giving reasonable weight to stock option holdings.[4] If companies do not regard stock options as "ownership" for the people involved, in the relevant contexts of motivation and alignment, then they should stop granting them.

The level of guidelines should involve material but reasonable amounts of stock exposure. They should not be so demanding that they prevent much personal diversification. We want focus, not neurosis, and having all of one's wealth in illiquid company shares is just a recipe for the latter. It may also render much of the executive incentive system valueless once the executive discounts it for reasonable things like risk, lack of marketability and lack of control.[5]

Investors sometimes want to see some companies attain higher levels of management stock ownership, but those concerns center upon instances in which holdings appear much too low. Shareholder optics are like optical acuity, needing correction only when noticeably wrong. Ownership should be an aggressively set priority only when there is a distinct problem to remedy, like executives exercising options as soon as they have a little vested gain and then dumping all their shares, or reported holdings that are just embarrassingly low. There is some empirical evidence that companies with low levels of ownership (under 5 percent or so) have poorer performance.[6] This is a reason to consider taking steps to increase ownership. Prudent remedies here work slowly:

- Most companies can't demand, as a practical matter, that their executives suddenly put a huge part of their salary and bonus into stock. What they can do is ask for some reasonable portion of bonus pay and allow holdings to climb over time.

- Most should not encourage executives to get out of outstanding options wholesale and into shares. This just reduces exposure to the stock price. Fierce new requirements for holding actual shares would do exactly that.

If executives can't fund a rapid run-up in their holdings, then the company may consider helping them. Many offer a modest bump when executives elect to take pay in the form of stock or options rather than cash. An election to receive the annual bonus in shares most often results in executives' converting an additional 25 percent of their base salary into stock. Companies should not go to much greater lengths. In most instances, large stock matches are simply a windfall. Overall, companies with low ownership cannot expect to remedy the issue quickly unless they want to waste corporate resources or introduce a frightening new feature to their system of rewards.

For the typical company, there should be no shame in being in the middle of the corporate pack in terms of reported ownership. There is not much to be gained by trying to move to the top. That means the overall number of companies that actually should be aggressive in this area is very small.

Most companies state guidelines as a percent of base salary (143 out of 160 companies surveyed by ECR). Of these, CEO ownership guidelines were clustered strongly in the three to five times salary level. The National Association of Stock Plan Professionals found a similar pattern when compiling data on guidelines, noting that multiples of two or three times salary apply to top-tier corporate executives and a multiple of one applies most often to others. (See Table 11-1.)

TABLE 11-1: STOCK OWNERSHIP GUIDELINES

Multiple of Base Salary[1]	CEO		Next Top Four Executives		Other Senior Management		Other Management	
	No. of Companies	Percent[2]	No. of Companies	Percent[2]	No. of Companies	Percent[2]	No. of Companies	Percent[2]
1	2	3.0%	7	10.8%	16	27.1%	14	60.9%
2	3	4.5%	16	24.6%	27	45.8%	6	26.1%
3	9	13.4%	27	41.5%	12	20.3%	2	8.7%
4	14	20.9%	8	12.3%	1	1.7%	0	-
5	26	38.8%	4	6.2%	2	3.4%	1	4.3%
6	5	7.5%	2	3.1%	0	-	0	-
7	3	4.5%	0	-	1	1.7%	0	-
8	2	3.0%	0	-	0	-	0	-
10	2	3.0%	1	1.5%	0	-	0	-
12	1	1.5%	0	-	0	-	0	-
Totals	**67**	**100.0%**	**65**	**100.0%**	**59**	**100.0%**	**23**	**100.0%**

(1) If a company indicated a range for each employee group, we averaged the lowest and highest multiple of the range.

(2) Based on total number of companies that provided the multiple of salary for each employee level.

Source: NASPP 2000 Stock Plan Design and Administration Survey.

Is Time on Your Side?

Many of the voices in the public debate about executive pay insist not only on higher mandated stock holdings, but also on grants that simply do not vest for long periods of time. To me, this approach appears dysfunctional. If the capital-accumulation part of your pay package is unusually illiquid, the best people won't come to work for you in the first place and those with poor alternatives are most likely to stay. An extreme example of the effects would be to offer a nonqualified pension with cliff vesting at retirement only. This would not only be unhelpful at recruiting time but at all other times, since risk aversion would persistently suppress any entrepreneurial impulse. In the end, these restrictive approaches risk using the costly currency of stock to purchase a mediocre, careerist culture. Government bureaucracies often do a better job in this area, creating the same culture at a much lower cost in pay. Retention is a valid goal, surely, but it can be taken too far.

Companies sometimes try to move stock holdings upward through big, long-vesting grants of restricted stock. Unfortunately, these are a good way to make shareholder wealth disappear. They're expensive to shareholders, yet largely valueless to executives. As a general rule, the vesting interval of five to ten years is dangerous water. Incentive grants with vesting periods greater than three to five years are discounted heavily by recipients. To shareholders, on the other hand, these grants are a very likely cost since the actual incidence of turnover and forfeitures is rather low most of the time. And the cost is high. A stock price of $100 is a present value already, and it is most likely to mount, in shareholder cost, over a period of many years. The executive may see it as $100 payable a long time from now and therefore worth much less. It is obviously a bad trade.

The modal three- to five-year vesting schedule is a sensible, market-driven solution. Longer vesting defers liquidity and gains beyond the time horizon of most business decisions and therefore beyond most motivational effects of incentive pay. Longer-vesting grants also beg to be discounted by participants and thereby end up wasting incentive pay resources. Shorter vesting than three years is just unnecessary; the competitive market does not demand it and it does not do anything for shareholders.

Who's Who

Whether stock options and other forms of stock-based pay can motivate, and what they can motivate, depends upon who's holding them. Addressing that issue will involve making sharp distinctions among participants in terms of rank, influence, actual contribution and prospective value. These sensitive distinctions are evaded to a certain extent in the traditional incentive system. The current accounting treatment causes everyone to use the same option-heavy structures, so the long-term incentive media and mix the companies have aren't a result of active design choices. This is going to change as companies become a lot more discriminating about their executive pay plan designs over the next few years.

To see how things will change, let's start with the very top officers. For them, stock clearly has some real incentive power. There are a few people at the company, mostly at the corporate level, who have real impact upon the stock price, and they know this perfectly well. The stock price from one week to the next might be a happy or nasty surprise to them, to be sure. But they believe, probably correctly, that it will eventually reward them for whatever high-quality business moves they're planning now. In their cases, the directional shifts in incentive structure that make sense are twofold:

- Less reliance upon stock options and their upside-only format
- More of a role for long-term operating goals in the incentive plans.

This is going to play out at a lot of companies through fewer stock options and more performance shares. This can be done best if changes also include better targets, ranges and metrics and more focus upon business unit results for those in business unit jobs. Still, long-term incentive pay for top officers will continue to be denominated almost entirely in shares. These people will continue to live and die by the stock price's trajectory over time. For them, stock-based rewards have a leading role.

The balance of senior management has a huge impact, in total, on business results and the stock price. But any impact is small or nonexistent when assessed by team or by individual participant. Still, stock-based pay has real plausibility as a motivational device throughout the senior management group — if it is used properly within the overall structure of rewards. Stock-based grants can reinforce messages not captured as well by operating incentive plans. They align executive gains with shareholder wealth, consistently reminding this important group of decision-makers about whose interests they were hired to serve.

In well-designed plans, though, there is not much difference between the business priorities expressed by operating goals and those that the stock-based incentives are trying to get across. Good incentives, after all, focus directly upon the most controllable, management-driven elements of value creation. That means the operating goals and share price elements of a corporate performance share plan, for example, are largely concerted, mutually reinforcing things.

Stock as a Problem-Solving Device?

Much of senior management is found at the business unit level. A performance share plan based upon business unit results can be a good way to create a compelling long-term stake in the business unit while maintaining strong ties to the company.

These plans are denominated entirely in corporate shares and can serve to emphasize corporate priorities as well as the business unit results that teams at this level can affect most strongly. Again, however, the shares and the business unit goals have mainly consistent messages. The overriding corporate interest in business unit affairs, after all, is that the business unit produces the best possible results and the highest returns on corporate resources used. The best way to encourage this is with properly structured goals set at the business unit level. There aren't many cases in which the business unit and corporate have economic interests that are genuinely at odds. Many of the conflicts companies cite in this area actually stem from incentive plans or from issues linked to the way incentive metrics work (e.g., competition for capital, transfer prices and allocated costs, effects upon enterprise-wide sharing of resources, teamwork generally, perceived unfairness of plan goals). Most such problems are addressed through better design of the operating elements of the plan design. This means charging business units properly and fairly for capital they use and other corporate resources they exploit, having properly-set targets, and having a structure not obsessed with the short term. Denominating awards in corporate shares does not by itself create model corporate citizens, but it surely reinforces the mutuality of interest between corporate, business units and shareholders.

However, if your incentives create any serious conflicts of interest among corporate management, business unit management and shareholders, you should not pretend that paying everyone in stock is going to solve the problem. Companies sometimes believe that stock-based pay creates an over-arching interest in value creation, one strong enough to overcome the mixed performance signals coming out of many bonus plans and to rally business unit management around the corporate flag. As you may by now have gathered, I don't think incentives work that way.

However, other terms of incentives can address problems like conflicts of interest, many biases in areas like teamwork, time horizons and risk, and the general situation of weak stakes and accountabilities. After all, these are problems that incentive plans often have a hand in creating or perpetuating. By fixing the incentives, companies can reverse the harm they do.

The incremental role of stock in the program is to reinforce the specific, positive messages of the plan's design. To be effective, incentives must:

- Interest managers, stapling some real money to items in their in-box

- Convey clear messages about which actions pay and which don't

- Correlate pay with decisions that create value.

Stock-based pay does not meet these criteria entirely. Companies do face performance issues that can be addressed using incentives, but they must address them directly rather than attempting to paper them over with stock and options. That just won't work.

Last Things First

To confront real problems, the incentive designs need to be right for the senior management group. For the top few officers, in contrast, the consequences of design error are not as great. In the pay package for the top few corporate officers:

- The long-term incentive component is very large within the pay mix and will remain so

- Stock-based pay in one form or another will continue to comprise just about all of long-term incentive pay

- The amount of these grants and the way they accumulate over time (possibly encouraged by ownership guidelines) mean that top officers will have an overwhelmingly strong exposure to stock price movements.

These people can affect the stock price over time, and they have huge equity stakes. So the system will ensure they have a direct financial interest in results and that it will work in a directionally correct way. But the system clearly could be more directive for them. Again, the stock price does not come with instructions on which actions create value and which do not.

So, how to make the system more directive? Here, *the best way to ensure you have effective incentives for the very top officers, including the CEO, is simply to ignore their incentives during the bulk of the design process.* Instead, I recommend focusing upon the balance of senior management. Companies should design the system of incentives up to the much higher standards of efficacy and line of sight needed to work well across this more dispersed group. In this regard, the senior managers in the broader group are like canaries in a coal mine. Incentive problems that might carry a whiff of inefficacy for the top officers are deadly to the system for the broader senior management group. By meeting the high design standards needed for senior managers overall, you'll have subsumed most of the design work needed for top officers.

Once you reach this point, you'll probably decide that the top few officers should be paid using the same general set of instruments and premises that applies in the broader senior management group. You may do this for reasons of alignment, but you may also find that by then you'll have the right system for your company and that it obviously should apply at the very top. At that point, top officer pay is a matter that can be extrapolated up a step or two from the balance of senior management. As examples, top officer pay might be distinguished by a higher weighting on stock options (if you still have those in the mix), a complete focus upon corporate operating results rather than those of business units, and generally greater pay at risk based upon stock price movement.

This approach is backward, in relation to the usual process. However, where the usual process falls down is in focusing far too much on the top few officers and particularly upon the CEO. One of the reasons we have such a heavily stock-centered system now is because it *is* sensible to use stock as the core of the pay structure for the very top officers. Extrapolating that prescription much deeper is a mistake, but it is one easily made if you're only paying close attention to the top few officers. And failing to extrapolate our high concerns and standards about management pay beyond the top few is another mistake. Making the system work for the broader senior management group — a group that is, again, pivotally important, yet subject to a highly ineffective incentive system — is the much bigger deal. The role for the top few officers in the executive pay design process is deciding how best to use incentives as a performance device throughout the balance of the senior management group. Chapter 1, addressed to the CEO and concerning pay, was not about how to pay the CEO. It was about how the CEO should use pay as a business governance tool. Overall, what is the role of stock in the incentive structure for the broader senior management group? It is a supporting role, not a lead.

Ownership with a Capital 'O'

Beyond the senior management level, paying in stock is not the same thing as issuing performance incentives. A grant of performance shares may well function as an incentive for someone at the staff manager level in a business unit, for example. The manager may have displayed great performance to get the job that gets the grants, to be sure. Good performance might lead to salary increases and bigger salary-based grants. And the operational goals involved in the performance share plan might well be ones our manager can affect.

There surely are numerous performance sub-plots in this story. We might just stop here and say that, fine, this person's grants are encouraging good performance. But we are not going to do that. We are presenting shareholders with a really big bill, every year, for these incentive plans. So we are going to continue to be really persnickety about the whole question of how well they work, focusing on where the incentive effects originate and where they do not. And they do not originate in stock. This manager has no impact upon the stock price, so the stock part of the pay system is not a performance incentive.

For people like this manager, stock happens to be used as the incentive medium, but it is not in itself an incentive. It surely can enhance the incentive effects the grants are meant to create, though. Here, beyond the senior management level, using stock as an award medium is more about enterprise culture, affiliation, engagement, and message reinforcement than about any specific performance incentive effects.

Magic Tricks?

I have asserted a mainly prosaic view of the concept of ownership, defining it from rather mechanical, behavioral angles like financial stake, information, power and accountability. But there is a more poetic view of stock — a more cultural, humanistic view — that has real validity. Employees' lives often are heavily invested in their careers. Granting a piece of the enterprise — a piece connoting real ownership in the traditional sense — seems to perfect the pay exchange in a way that parallels the commitments made by employees. This is one view of a role stock might play in the overall rewards system. There are lots of others, too, as well as some empirical evidence on broad-based stock ownership and how it can contribute to business performance.[7] One has to acknowledge that there is some magic to using real stock of the company when rewarding its people for their efforts.

Having some stock involved in qualified retirement plans, as one example, seems like a pretty good idea, as long as it does not leave employees unable to diversify properly. In the United States, qualified plans involve one of the few big tax advantages left in the pay arena by providing current deductibility for the corporation and deferred income recognition to the individual. Qualified plans usually involve some vesting, so washouts and bounders don't get much out of them, but the people who make a commitment do. There's nothing wrong with that part of the system. Lastly, whole shares hold obvious value to the employee; unlike options, which are complex derivatives offering only suppositional reward.

In some instances, such as for principals in a consulting firm, stock-based pay may actually have a value in a ceremonial role exceeding its redemption value. On the other hand, all-employee option granting seems to me to be on the wrong side of all the important trades between a company and its workforce. Option gains are unpredictable, heavily deferred and utterly uncontrollable. How much cash would people need to make them as happy? Not much. How much do shareholders save when the company cuts back on option grants? A lot.

The Rulebooks Are Changing

These considerations don't matter much now. Rather, all the big decisions apparently are driven by the accounting treatment of stock options. Companies can issue them without including any cost on their income statements. This has skewed the structure of executive incentives at many companies, encouraging extremely heavy use of options rather than other kinds of incentives.

This situation is coming to an end. The rulemaking authorities are on course to require an expense for options. Although the outcome is not clear as of early 2004, employers should not count on continued favorable accounting treatment of stock options after 2004. Other forces are also spurring change in incentive practices: the uncertain stock market, dicey business conditions and a new wave of criticism of how executive incentives are delivered. Overall, it is a pivotal time for this issue. Companies are likely to change their incentive practices very soon and to a very large degree.

This kind of change does not happen very often. Companies have a lot of competing priorities. It is difficult for them to array their decision-makers and resources, focus them on a given matter, get a high-quality decision outcome and follow through. They can't do this very often, and they can't do it for too many things. Due to these accounting changes and other pressing factors, companies have a great chance right now to re-examine how they use incentives in business governance, overcome a range of deficiencies in the approaches used commonly now and get better returns on the enormous costs involved. This is the best chance in a generation to get it right.

Once the accounting rules change, companies will seek a new equilibrium in their incentive structures, resulting in heavy redesign over the next few years. Accounting treatments will continue to vary at least mildly among types of incentive plans, and they will vary over time as governing boards sort out their new rules and implement them. So concerns about accounting effects still pose a risk of skewing incentive design choices and harming the efficacy of these critical arrangements. We're already seeing incomplete, short-term responses and ideas sprouting up on the landscape. Here are a few of them, just to give a general sense of what may go on in the marketplace and how to respond to it:

- *Some companies will revert to heavy use of restricted stock grants, if restricted stock rules end up being seen as less punitive.* This tactic may help with genuine concerns about share usage, retention and perceived grant value. On the other hand, this approach creates poor incentive leverage and the risk of remarkably inappropriate outcomes in terms of performance and reward. In the United States, it can bring tax problems that can greatly increase after-tax costs of some grants.[8] Using restricted stock purely to get grant date accounting, just to dodge the higher or more variable charges that may accompany some better designs, could be a particularly damaging move.

- *Reducing the term of options probably will be an effective way to reduce the valuation of grants and their expense over time.* Reducing the term of stock grants, however, makes options even less effective as an incentive. Stock gains, as statistical objects, move around for reasons mostly unrelated to performance during the medium term. It takes many years for a reliable linkage between results and value to emerge. So shortening grant terms will make stock options even more of a crapshoot for many holders. Companies might try to increase share exercises in various ways as well, rendering pointless the core concepts of stock option leverage and connection with shareholder wealth.

- *Lengthening the vesting period of grants reduces per-period amortization.* This actually may be a sensible reaction to softness in executive labor markets. It is not a bad thing in itself for shareholders since it effectively restructures executive labor contracts in favor of owners. But, when pursued for accounting effects, it is a classically short-term tactic. Over time, the annual amortization of option grants will be driven by the amounts of those grants, not their amortization term.[9]

- *Companies may cut back too far on stock options if their accounting treatment is seen as being marginally less favorable than alternatives.* As the accounting bias toward options is repealed, companies will grant fewer stock options to fewer people. This makes sense. Stock options can have beneficial features and a valid role in the management pay mix, but they are overused at present. They will need to be recast into a more appropriate role at many companies, balancing their real cost with any incentive effects and with the value and influence perceived by holders. They are obviously going to work best for top officers at the corporate level. They'll also continue to be a good fit in certain settings — high-tech start-ups, for example — in which they capture prospective performance and its valuation effects more accurately than other approaches. There is, however, a clear risk of the pendulum swinging too far against stock options.

- *Companies may add complex or demanding performance conditions to option grants, greatly reducing their present value and book cost.* If not for the accounting treatment, companies would probably have used indexed options to a greater extent in the past. Indexed options can create a "pure play," handicapping performance against a relevant market and focusing on management's differential contribution. But adding tough conditions without increasing grant sizes may simply have the effect of reducing the value of the grants, and along with it any motivational value. Companies may increase grant sizes to make up for such reductions in their per-share present values, but if they do that they will not have reduced the accounting charges.

- *In a play on statistical quirks in some option pricing models, companies may implement limited price appreciation options.* Under this approach, you might get options with an exercise price set at the current $20 stock price that allow gains only up to a $40 share price level. Since the Black-Scholes model attaches most of the value of an option to the comparatively few scenarios with really big gains, such an option would be valued at a level much lower than a regular one and would have lower book costs.

This approach could disintegrate in time. It would be odd and potentially dysfunctional, in an incentive sense, to cap executive stock price gains. To create a more continuous claim on the upside, as companies certainly should, there will have to be more grants involved — ones that entitle the executive to gains on the next $10 or $20 in appreciation and so on. At this point, the strategy stops working. You can make all those additional grants now or promise them unconditionally, in which case you've basically granted a traditional option, in sum, and will bear all the same costs. Or you can make them later on, once the share price gets over $40 and other hurdles, but you'll still end up with big book charges over time.

Many of these ideas, once put into place, may well involve effective pay cuts since they reduce the per-share value of stock-based pay. It is not improper for a company to consider reducing the value of the incentives it provides to executives. In fact, here are some forces that have been in place in recent years — ones reducing market data on executive pay:

- Performance plans of all types simply are paying out less as corporate earnings come in at disappointing levels.

- Formal fixed-share grant guidelines ratcheted down the value of long-term incentives at many companies from 2000 to 2003, and dilution concerns are working similarly in others.

- The decline in the value of many companies amounts to a devaluation of all of management's potential actions and results, a factor that could lead to lower market-clearing prices for executive compensation over time.

- Changes in the accounting for stock options may cause a shift in their supply curve. Concerned about more visible option costs, compensation committees may simply be willing to supply fewer of them.

- Business performance and public criticism may recast the image of the "imperial CEO" and other officers into that of a more replaceable talent. At the same time, forceful board members are stepping in earlier, more often and more actively, reminding the corporate world about the contingent nature of executive authority. If individual executives come to be seen as having a less pivotal role, the demand for their services will be more elastic, and their price will fall.

- When restructuring equity-based incentives, companies may reduce the value of their grants, measured from a corporate perspective, while increasing them or leaving them constant from the viewpoint of individual participants. At many companies, plan participants value whole-share grants more highly in relation to economic cost than they do appreciation rights such as options. The economic cost to shareholders of a restricted share often is about equal to that of two options. Participants' risk tolerances, on the other hand, cause them to place a higher relative value on restricted stock. They may be happy to give up three options they would otherwise receive for one share of restricted stock. A restructured grant policy can create a win-win situation, retaining or improving participants' satisfaction while lessening economic cost and accounting expense under FAS 123.

Executive pay will rise or fall if the market says so. But it should not fall simply because of corporate overreaction to some new accounting rules. Adding tough and complex new terms to existing plans, or just cutting back across the board, is a big pay cut for those concerned. I wouldn't advise that, as a general matter, any more than I would suggest showing up at work tomorrow and cutting everyone's salaries by a fourth. Moving senior management pay to uncompetitively low levels is a bad way to save money. A better approach is to let the level of incentive pay be determined by the competitive market over time and by the values that employees place upon the grants, let its terms be driven by pursuit of efficacy, and let accounting have essentially no role in the design process.

How to Choose

When setting up incentives at the senior management level, I suggest going into the design process with these two things in mind:

- How prominently the operating part of the incentive structure — the part having to do with setting long-term goals and hitting them, as opposed to stock price movement — ought to be in the overall scheme for the various levels within your senior management team

- How prominently stock ought to figure into incentive delivery for the various levels of executive responsibility.

Having nearly 100 percent of long-term incentive pay based upon stock movement is within a reasonable range for the CEO and perhaps a few other people, though in most cases they really ought to have at least 25 percent linked to operating goals, and I often suggest 50 percent or more. In private companies and some business units, basing 100 percent upon operating goals is a very practicable choice for the reasons of line of sight and fiscal control discussed in Chapter 10.

As far as stock-based plan designs are concerned, you don't need 100 choices on the menu to get this done. There are many complicated designs on the market, but much of this profusion stems from accounting concerns and tax issues. Accounting concerns should simply be discarded. For most taxpaying U. S. corporations, the tax issues can be discarded as well. Getting capital gains treatment for the individual typically involves foregoing a valuable tax deduction for the corporation.[10] Stock options offer unusual flexibility in deferring income and controlling its timing. But most executives forego this, exercising before the out years of the grant term are reached. In any event, elective deferral plans can create similar tax benefits, particularly when considering the fungible nature of cash received through stock sales, salaries or cash incentives.

Dilution is not a big issue at most companies, either, when considering changes to equity-based incentive methods. The directional changes in equity plan design are toward use of more whole shares of stock and toward more limited eligibility for option grants, so share usage is likely be less of a tripwire than it was in the past.

We can narrow down the criteria used to make design decisions. Overall, to make these important choices, I recommend structuring incentives to maximize business results as job one. As far as the specific choices are concerned:

- In earlier chapters, we reviewed a sizeable portion of the menu of LTI choices from the perspective of value rules — performance plans, phantom stock and subsidiary equity. Each can be used effectively if designed well.

- Restricted stock grants are simply inappropriate to use as the centerpiece of long-term incentives for management in most settings.

The two most common forms of equity-based incentives — vanilla stock options and vanilla restricted stock — are basically the pick-your-poison section of the menu. Here are the most prominent items remaining on the menu of equity-based incentives that your organization may find palatable:

- Performance shares that are earned based upon operating goals

- Performance shares that are earned based upon relative total shareholder return or other peer-based measures

- Stock options with performance or indexation terms

- Stock options with premium or rising exercise prices

- Discounted stock options.

Performance Shares Earned Based Upon Operating Goals

Performance share grants allow participants to earn shares based upon achievement of pre-set goals. The eventual value of awards depends not only upon the extent to which goals are hit, but also the company's stock price performance during the grant term. Dividends typically are accumulated and paid along with any shares that vest.

The target-setting and measurement apparatus of such plans is an ideal setting in which to apply value rules. The performance and granting apparatus can be set up essentially like the value-based performance plans and phantom stock plans described earlier. In these plans, whole shares of company stock are the award currency, delivering the clearest title of ownership in its most direct form. They are denominated exclusively in shares, so they adhere to owner interests without the upside-only format and potential bias of stock options. They reflect the value of shareholder interests in a way that is fitting for senior management of a public company. As we've noted, this is an excellent way for companies to create compelling business unit incentives while maintaining strong allegiance to the enterprise's overall owners. They're not stock grants, though. They have real performance contingencies — real teeth. They don't allow management to run the company into the ground and still walk off with valuable shares. Nor do they allow decisive performance at the business unit level to go without significant reward.

Within this format, performance shares offer a very specific opportunity to improve the efficacy of long-term incentives:

- Whole shares of stock involve less leverage than stock options. Depending upon how the performance schedules are set up, performance share grants can be made to base most award leverage upon business goals rather than stock price changes. If you look again at Figure 10-2, you can see the whole-share form of equity grant is the least leveraged of the common varieties:[11] This naturally increases the comparative importance of the plan's operating goals, reducing its susceptibility to any stock market movements unrelated to business performance and outside of management's control.

- At the same time, performance shares deliver pay entirely in stock-based form, linking plans in a full and visible way with shareholder outcomes. Operating goals, struck at the corporate level or various others, may be in the driver's seat of this vehicle, but its *marque* clearly is stock.

As noted earlier, these grants are hedged to an important extent. Since they are denominated in stock, their costs rise and fall depending upon how performance and other matters work out for shareholders in the company's share price. And, when their structure of goals is based upon value rules, plan costs are hedged properly against financial results.

Hedging dynamics apply in the accounting arena as well. Under current rules, variable accounting applies to these plans, requiring companies to record estimated plan costs in a variable fashion as they mount over time. This is usually seen as a bad thing, because these expenses obviously are larger than the zero expense levels indicated for stock options under current rules. If the new option accounting rules look like the current FAS 123 methods, option expense in the future will be based upon the value of the options at the time of grant. Like restricted stock, the fixed value of such grants is amortized over the vesting period. Therefore, stock option and restricted stock expenses are fixed by their grant date values. Related expenses are likely to be lower than the eventual gains earned by executives on the grants after a few years of appreciation. Performance share grants may involve expensing that varies based upon performance.

Fixed accounting charges are not entirely advantageous, however, even if your company cares greatly about accounting effects. What matters, it seems to me, are effects of these charges across a range of outcomes rather than just their possible amount at target. Expenses for performance shares are variable under current rules, but in many contexts a variable cost is considered well behaved while a fixed cost is not. If performance and stock price are low, then expenses and dilution are as well. Expenses may actually run negative during a downturn, for example, as previous accruals are reversed.[12] Stock option and restricted stock amortization, in contrast, will march on unreduced. When performance share cost is high, on the other hand, company financial results and stock market value are high as well, hedging their impact on earnings and value. Also, the subtraction of variable plan charges from measured performance — the performance that drives plan gains — acts as a formal hedge as well.[13]

Implementing value rules is a critical element that should be taken into consideration in the design of these plans. Companies should not just shift the pay mix out of stock options and into traditional performance share plans without first improving their metrics, designs, and target-setting methods. We have seen that traditional approaches can cause pay-related bias in company business planning, encourage income manipulation and simply pay out good money for bad business results. Increasing the load on this vehicle without improving its balance simply increases the likelihood that it will end up in the ditch.

Indexed and Peer-Based Grants

Total shareholder return, or TSR, is equal to the company's stock price change plus its dividends paid. It is typically stated as a percentage of the company's beginning share price. Relative total shareholder return is TSR in comparison to a group of peer companies or a stock index. Relative TSR comparisons are depicted in public company proxy statements in the United States. They appear in such filings as an overall indication of business performance for shareholders, inviting judgments of management pay against relative TSR performance.

Performance share plans of this type allow participants to earn shares based upon relative TSR. This approach to executive long-term incentives is the darling of many commentators on executive pay design:

- These plans offer many of the general benefits of performance share plans. They offer a whole-share deal rather than the upside-only structure of an option while providing a general connection with shareholder wealth.

- They're specifically admired for their relative TSR measurement approach. This involves comparing company TSR with peer companies. It naturally handicaps the individual company's performance against the general business conditions and expectations affecting a group of business peers. In this regard, it delivers rewards based upon a "pure play" measure of management performance. If assessed against the general market rather than a peer group, relative TSR still does the valuable service of stating company TSR on a basis net of general market movement.

As peer metrics go, TSR goals are the easiest to set. Expected TSR is equal to a company's cost of equity. Expected TSR performance against peers is equal to the 50th percentile, assuming company business risk and capital structure are similar to those of peers. Reasonable goals for growth in operating income or sales, in contrast, or in terms of margins or return on investment capital (ROIC), could be equal to any percentile of the peer group for a given company.

Relative TSR plans comply pretty well with the financial dimensions of value rules, even though they don't involve explicit operating goals for income, capital and the cost of capital. Relative TSR is an admirably resilient and complete way of looking at a business's performance for its owners and zeroing in on management's contribution.

Performance share plans using relative TSR do not do well in terms of clarity and line of sight, however. For management simply to know how it is doing under such a plan, they need a handle not only on what their stock price performance has been, but also what it has been for peer companies. To understand that picture, they need a sense of what has been driving stock performance in the industry and what role each company's management has played in it. Only then can they gain a sense of the management performance contest at the center of the plan. For the plan to be at all informative, they need to know what they can do to improve the stock price. TSR against peers, just like the company's own stock price, is silent on that critical matter. And, lastly, for the plan to be effective in a prospective sense, participating executives need to have an impact upon its outcomes. For people aside from the top few officers in the company, relative TSR plans do not meet this criterion. After all, relative TSR plans involve no actual business goals.

Ultimately, these plans commit the same sins as stock options. They do not come with instructions on how to create value, and they do not connect with actions of almost anyone in senior management. Relative TSR performance share plans can be a productive part of the incentive structure for the CEO and a few others. The relative TSR performance framework can offer better line of sight for these key folks at the very top than stock options do. Beyond this group, these grants are no more effective than stock options. They may align gains more closely with a company's specific performance, but this advantage seems offset by their higher level of complexity and, in particular, their "moving target" aspect. Use of relative TSR plans for the broader senior management group should not be based upon specific hoped-for incentive effects. Rather, it should be based upon more general choices about the proper weight of company stock price movement and stock market movement in the incentive structure.

Relative TSR plans also carry the risk of paying out big awards when actual stock price performance has been poor, but not as bad as that of peer companies. This by itself should not be seen as a non-starter, though. Companies should unlink pay from the stock market in search of greater incentive efficacy. As a result, they will see incentive payments based less on stock market results and more on business results management can affect. This is true in relative TSR plans just as it is in plans based upon operating results measured at the corporate and business unit levels. Nonetheless, many boards will balk at the prospect of paying for negative results simply because they are relatively less negative.

There are a couple of mechanical issues with TSR measurement warranting note:

- Just as in measuring the performance of investment managers, relative TSR results are very sensitive to the performance period chosen and, in particular, to the beginning stock price at that date. The solution is to use a structure of overlapping grants with uniform terms and measurement dates.

- To the extent percentile measures or rankings are used, results can be affected by discontinuities in the range of peer results, making the award scale lumpy and jumpy. A TSR gain of 1 percent in one interval of the award schedule might have the same award impact as a 5 percent gain in an adjacent interval. This can be addressed by standardizing the range of peer data and making inferences about relative performance against a smoothed distribution rather than against the unadjusted range of peer data points. This method takes into account the dimensions of peer performance that are important when establishing a ranking — central tendency and dispersion — in a more effective way. This technique is applicable in most peer-based measurement situations, not just those involving TSR.

- Whether percentile rankings are used or not, there are target-setting issues that concern the spread in TSR results of the company and its peers. A plan that pays out maximum awards for attaining TSR of a certain number of points above the peer median, for example, might work out to be inappropriately easy to reach. In such a case, it might also create extremely high leverage and incremental dilution within a small range of company stock price changes. That could create a moral hazard, just as a similar situation could within a bonus plan schedule. Award schedules in such plans need to be set up carefully, just as they need to be in bonus plans and performance share and unit plans. In the particular case of relative TSR plans, this means closely examining the statistical behavior of the company's stock price and those of peers.

Performance share plans also can be based upon operating measures that are compared to those of peer companies — measures like earnings per share growth. The motives created by these plans resemble those associated with TSR plans, but they are likely to remain less prevalent due to greater measurement issues.

Indexed stock options have strike prices that rise or fall in tandem with peer company stock prices or the value of a stock market index. These plans have a lot of the same relative performance dynamics as performance shares based upon relative TSR. They enlarge gains when a company's stock price does well against an index or peers, and vice versa.

Stock Options with Premium, Discounted or Rising Exercise Prices

Premium options involve a strike price fixed at a level above market value at the time of grant, while the exercise price on a discounted option is set below market. Other grants have exercise prices rising at some annual rate. One Mexican company, for example, uses a 7 percent exercise price growth rate corresponding to the cost of the arrangements it uses to hedge option-related dilution. Premium and rising-price options have lower values than grants made at current market, so companies need to make more of them in order to meet a given competitive guideline. These larger grants, coupled with the higher performance demands they contain, create a more leveraged payoff curve than traditional grants. Discounted grants do the opposite.

Discounted stock options are an interesting device. As mentioned earlier, discounted stock option grants create a kind of happy medium between the upside-only structure of traditional options and the low-leverage nature of restricted stock grants. These grants may offer some accounting advantages, when new rules emerge, for the many companies that remain highly concerned about such matters. If the exercise price on an option grant is discounted by $50,000, this is likely to increase its valuation and book cost by far less than $50,000. A $50,000 separate grant of restricted stock, on the other hand, would result in the amortization of a full $50,000. Premium grants are on the wrong side of this dynamic. Large increases in the exercise price do not decrease value and accounting expense by much. Discounted grants have some tax advantages as well, since executives are not taxed on the discount, as a general matter, until exercise. Restricted stock, again used in contrast, causes taxation upon vesting dates that often come much sooner. Adding performance features to option exercise prices essentially turns them into premium or discounted options based upon performance. Currently, shareholder activists see discounted options negatively.

Summary

Vanilla, fixed price stock options are losing their current position as the centerpiece of the incentive structure for company management. These complex instruments, offering almost no cause-and-effect incentive to the people who receive them, became extremely popular due to their fictitious "no cost" portrayal in company profit and loss statements. With that treatment on course for revocation, companies will abandon their heavy option usage as well as the bulk of the business rationales that supported it.

Stock-based pay generally, on the other hand, is here to stay, particularly for top officers of public companies. When choosing which stock-based vehicles to use, however, companies will be much more discerning about who gets what types of stock-based grants and what those grants will accomplish, precisely, within the context of total rewards for each participant group. Companies will no longer slather the management workforce, or the entire workforce, with stock options every year, without rigorous thinking about what this approach costs and how it might contribute to business results.

The tipping point for this trend was reached in mid-2003. Microsoft is the biggest stock option issuer in history as well as the biggest name in the option-addicted technology sector. In June of 2003, it announced that it would discontinue stock option grants and begin using whole shares of stock as long-term incentive currency.[14] In the broader workforce, Microsoft announced that it would make future grants in the form of restricted stock. Among the top 600 officers, in contrast, share grants will be earned based upon goals in areas like customer growth and satisfaction.

This type of shift — away from options and toward whole shares and performance goals — is predictable for many companies. What I recommend is that companies take the design process a few steps further. They should not only be more deliberate in the matter of which stock-based vehicles go to whom, but also should link incentive pay with business goals that participants can affect within an overall structure tied directly to value creation.

Endnotes

1   See National Center for Employee Ownership and the ESOP Association web sites for a range of research citations regarding broad-based employee share ownership and company performance.

2   Also, some of the disconnect between bonus pay and stock price movement is a timing difference. Bonuses are based upon actual performance, while stock prices reflect anticipated performance. This time gap is addressed in Chapter 4.

3   An example is Sanders, W.G., "Behavioral Responses of CEOs to Stock Ownership and Stock Option Pay," *Academy of Management Journal* 44: 477-492, 2001, in which CEO stock option grants are positively correlated with (risky and often economically unsuccessful) acquisition activity, and block share ownership by CEOs and outsiders is negatively correlated with it. A large number of studies document poor corporate performance in the area of mergers and acquisitions. The book, *The Synergy Trap*, by Mark Sirower, sets forth his research and summarizes much work by others.

4   For example, by counting the number of shares that could be purchased using the in-the-money option gain amount.

5   Data on discounts for lack of marketability and control appear in the book, *Valuation: the Analysis and Appraisal of Closely-Held Businesses* by Shannon Pratt and Robert Schweis.

6   See Morck, R., Shleifer, A. & Vishny, R.W. "Management Ownership and Market Valuation: An Empirical Analysis." *Journal of Financial Economics* 20: 293-315. 1988.

7   See organizations cited in Footnote 1.

8   Generally, those made to proxy-named executives with pay over $1 million.

9   A grant of $100,000 per year worth of options with a two-year amortization schedule would require $50,000 per year in straight-line expense. Since two such grants would be outstanding any time, the stable "run rate" of expense would be $100,000, equal to the annual grant amount. The same would be true with four-year vesting; $25,000 per year would be amortized on each of four outstanding grants. Note that vesting term may affect the value of the option itself.

10 Foregoing a corporate tax deduction, for a U.S. company, normally means increasing the after-tax cost by 50 percent or more. Most companies would be better off simply increasing grant sizes by that amount or less. In any event, U.S. competitive norms do not demand that companies provide grants that allow favorable capital gains treatment to individuals. Instead, almost all incentive gains are subject to taxation at ordinary income rates, once received. Rates and norms vary greatly between countries, of course.

11 This chart was used in Chapter 10 to describe phantom stock leverage, but it applies equally to grants based upon real equity.

12 Note that FAS 123 does not allow previous accruals to be reversed in the case of grants that fail to vest due to stock price performance.

13 As noted in Chapter 10, spikes in plan cost reduce income, performance and, circularly, plan costs. This has the effect of smoothing out costs over time and making them even more strongly contingent upon sustained financial performance.

14 Microsoft also announced that it would expense stock options beginning in 2004, and it experienced no apparent share price penalty.

12

The Medium
Is the Message

One of the platitudes of incentive design is that proper communication of incentive plans is pivotal to their success. What's said less often, though, is that the plans themselves are important communication media. When we talk about communication of incentive plans for senior management, the most important thing to recognize is that the medium is the message.

Formal communication initiatives will not work if the plan design itself is ineffective. If an incentive plan does not pay out based on things people can affect, then no number of seminars or brochures will make that plan an active contributor to business results. You cannot talk, write, or gesticulate your way around goals that are infeasible or upside claims that are weak and diffuse. If you do not shut down the linkages between bad business decisions and incentive rewards — either through the terms of the plans themselves or through other governance tools — then you bear a risk of value destruction irrespective of how often your training programs warn against it. Multimedia rollouts do not help when none of the media convey credible messages.

Money, on other hand, talks. Senior management knows that better than anyone. Well-designed incentive plans speak for themselves. If your company wants to communicate about performance, you should take business goals and incentive plan terms that are clear, use them to create compelling financial stakes in long-term business success, and grant them to people who are in a position to do something about business results. *That* is saying something.

One communication platitude I *can* get behind is, "You can't not communicate." If you don't convey a clear set of messages, people will supply their own based upon the evidence they hold. In the executive rewards arena, there is no such thing as a news hole. Nature abhors a vacuum, and executives' natures do, too. They each have a standing set of presumptions about what is and is not rewarded in businesses generally and, normally, a fairly precise sense of the ground rules in their current setting. They're not novices, after all. These are people who attained and now hold senior management jobs. The traditional incentive structure creates a vacuum. It does not draw a compelling linkage from high quality business decisions to rewards. When silent, vague or implausible on this important matter, incentives invite executives to fill in their own messages, maybe cynical ones, and risk creating a mediocre, careerist view of how the company really works.

Here's another valid principle of corporate communication: Leadership's actions are more important than formal communication media. Newsletters, brochures and seminars often carry little of the real persuasive power around major new initiatives. What really matters is when leadership gets behind a new initiative and clearly communicates that support to employees. Here again, the medium is the message. The most important communications within a company are handled directly by the CEO and a few other top leaders and are expressed most compellingly with actions rather than words. In the context of a senior management incentive plan, the most important factor is that the CEO demonstrably supports the "deal" that the incentive plan creates. And why should he or she? Because effective incentive pay plans for the broader senior management group can improve company performance and stock value. No matter what form future incentives take, the CEO will have lots of money at stake based upon the company's stock price. That is why I wrote Chapter 1 directly to the CEO, pointing out how implementing value rules can improve business performance, shareholder wealth and the working life and rewards of the CEO.

Value Rules from Finance's Perspective

Many of the big changes demanded by value rules — metrics, target setting, business unit valuation and other explicitly financial features of incentive design — lie directly within the skill set of the finance function and are within its authority. Since incentives are about encouraging good business decision-making by rewarding actions that create value, there is a lot of overlap between this mission and the work of the CFO. In practice, incentives really ought to make the CFO's job easier, and there are many ways in which value rules can support key responsibilities of the finance function. Unfortunately, it doesn't always work this way.

Budgeting. The typical, negotiated incentive structure hurts decision-making. It creates short-term bias, it may instill risk aversion, and it sets up adverse interests within senior management. Better methods for incentive design and target setting can encourage a longer-term focus and a balanced view of risk, at the same time uniting the financial interests of the parties. Examples include setting targets based upon shareholder expectations, using various financial algorithms to set targets consistently each year, and applying value-based methods to performance measurement and plan calibration. These methods use consistent external standards for target setting rather than letting pay-related goals create a set of one-off disputes between corporate and each business unit. And these plans create shared upside since each party is rewarded for the same stream of economically profitable results.

Long-range planning. This process can suffer from many of the same problems as the annual budget, enlarging the risks of biased resource allocation. In a target-setting process framed by shareholder expectations or other value-based criteria, a business unit manager who maintains, "Things are very uncertain in our sector, I can't promise much income growth, and I need a lot of investment," is really saying something else to corporate leaders and to peers: "My business isn't worth much."

Various kinds of phantom stock and performance plans can be very helpful, since they connect pay with achievement of long-run goals, making it difficult for operating management to continually defer promised performance gains into the out years of "hockey stick" plans. These plans also can help put companies with differing performance on a fair and comparable footing for judging success and delivering rewards. Under the total business return (TBR) approach that was explained earlier in the book, the rewards in a company with high growth and big capital requirements might be similar to those in a company posting more modest growth but highly distributable income, provided each has growth and yield levels adding up to the same level of TBR. This approach can result in truer, better-informed business planning. It causes business unit management to fully expose their insider views of business prospects as they position the unit for growth or cash yield (each of which is lucrative to a participant in an incentive plan based upon TBR). This technique has another virtue. It sidesteps much of the target-setting process since it does not require the company to set hard and fast goals (e.g., separate goals for growth and return on invested capital [ROIC] in a bonus plan) for each business unit.

Investment evaluation. Incentives can provide a full, clear accountability for the use of capital, for business risk, and for long-run returns on investments in the company. Then, managers know they are spending their own money when they propose big capital outlays, initiatives or acquisitions. They have no incentive to inflate forecasts at the time of deal approval or to continually defer accountability to the out years of business plans. This behavior can be reinforced by using value-based designs that clearly account for capital when setting incentive targets under any of several methods and that lengthen the effective time frame of the company's incentive structure.

Financial education. Well-designed incentive plans can help educate the management workforce about the basic connections between business results and value creation. These linkages — which we boiled down to the interplay between long-run operating results, the use of capital and its cost — are ones that finance executives would like to see the broader management group applying in many things they do. Value-based incentives reinforce financial training because they reflect the basic value drivers clearly, and they make the training message compelling in money terms.

Cost control. Incentives can create a clear entrepreneurial interest in business success. This encourages management to spend money as if it were its own. Outlays are seen from a "best bang for the buck" viewpoint, and costs offering no return are cut out quickly. Companies can use consistent target-setting methods each year. They can use incentive plan designs that create a stake in business results that is clear, continuous, concrete and long-term. Under either method — or when using both — participants understand their financial interests are like those of an entrepreneur and should act accordingly.

Financial performance evaluation. The inconsistent, incomplete nature of many traditional financial metrics confounds the basic performance assessments they are supposed to enable. These metrics often fail to disentangle the effects of financial leverage, historical and future capital usage, risk, and other factors. One example of how value rules address this issue is the suite of TBR solutions we applied to measurement, valuation and target setting. They recognize both the growth in a business's income and the amount of free cash flow it generates. TBR redresses an unusual number of the issues that can crop up in incentive plans. It is unaffected by financial leverage, taking into account only changes in capital and reflecting business risk directly. It enables more meaningful benchmarking of a company's financial results and their effects upon enterprise returns.

Financing decisions. Incentive plans ought to encourage the broad management group to focus upon operating performance — upon the things they can affect most strongly. Instead, plans tend to make the entire management workforce a stakeholder in financing decisions as well. That is because the pay media and methods used are often ones affected strongly when the finance function makes decisions about things like debt levels, dividend policy, share repurchases, leasing, joint venture structuring and initial public offerings (IPOs). In a certain number of cases, such pay concerns can put undesirable pressure on finance. In almost all cases, the plans interpose financial policy between the company's operating results and its pay outcomes, reducing line of sight and efficacy. Many incentive plan formats — generally, those setting targets and measuring performance from a total capital perspective, tracking enterprise returns in one way or another — can remove the effect of capital structure from pay and link it more strongly with the operating results that most of management can drive.

Value rules have some impact upon company risks as well. They can encourage senior management to take a balanced view of risk, one that creates the most value for shareholders. In this regard, their impact upon risk is like that in many other areas. They encourage the broader senior management team to take the perspective of the finance function, which in this case means taking account of business risk as investors would.

Incentive plans are an invisible hand guiding many, many decisions in all areas of the business. Financial management cannot participate in every business decision, but it would like to see the principles of finance and value creation reflected consistently in actions of the broad management group. The company's incentive structure may be the CFO's best opportunity to do this.

Overall, value rules should change the finance function's focus within the enterprise. Its current role is far too much about policing and control at a tactical level — deflating some forecasts and removing sandbags from others, unwinding bias and gamesmanship, directing attention to the basic financial rules of business success. Finance is too often a bulwark against the negative impulses of the enterprise and the people in it. Incentive plans based on value rules can help position this critical function to guide economic behavior positively, and through it the broader affairs of the enterprise.

Value Rules from HR's Perspective

We could repeat that last paragraph when talking about the view from human resources. But we don't need to add a long discussion about it. This whole book has been about how the compensation arrangements typically run by HR can be used to get better business results throughout the enterprise. This is a strategic opportunity for HR to initiate change and collaborate with the CEO and CFO to make much better use of the stock and cash consumed each year by executive incentive plans. The gains are low-hanging fruit, as performance initiatives go. And HR can do this, proactively, in an area that is bound for change anyway. But both finance and HR will have to deal with some complex challenges to get it done properly. A lot of hard work being done right now by the stock market — business target-setting, performance evaluation and pay delivery — will have to be taken back within the company in order to make the system more effective.

Complexity itself can be called a business trend, and more companies are taking on complex initiatives in order to pursue competitive advantage. Consider some examples of the kinds of things that companies have done to squeeze a bit more money out of their operations in recent years. They've been out reengineering all business processes, rightsizing their workforces, implementing six-sigma (meaning, roughly "one defect per zillion") and implementing new IT systems and web-based commerce.

However, while we may deal with a lot of complexity during the design process, when it comes time to roll out the incentive plan, we have to simplify the plan's description to the greatest extent possible. Typically, this means conveying to participants that they have a big claim on company value that they can influence in some simple and direct ways.

Well-designed incentives ought to make HR's job easier, too, even if setting up the plans is harder than tallying up a year's option grants. HR is very concerned about company systems for performance management and rewards and their effects upon attracting, retaining and motivating key people. Consider the following two offers, and ask yourself which one today's top candidates would prefer:

- You don't have to spend your whole career here. Just work with us for 15 or 20 years. You'll get advancement in accordance with your contribution to a big, experienced team. You'll be subject to lots of oversight and a well-developed structure of approvals and safeguards, but you'll receive lots of support. The main way you get paid is with option and stock grants. Over time, you'll get bigger and bigger grants of stock and options based upon your salary and rank. And, over time, these grants are quite likely to pay off because our stock reflects our good performance over the long run. You'll also share in the company's profits through a cash bonus each year (based upon actual profits against budgets) and you'll receive a competitive pension accrual, a car allowance, executive dining room privileges and, one day perhaps, an office featuring 240 lineal feet of hardwood molding and some maritime prints.

- We need you to devote the next (three/five/seven) years to help our team (start up/grow/turn around/ lead/ generate returns on/raise to the next level) our business unit X. You'll have an unlimited financial stake in the success of the business, consisting of your interests in the annual and long-term incentive plans. These plans are based upon operating performance, and you get a cut of whatever cash the business generates. So, when you invest in this business, you're effectively investing in your future wealth. If you think you can get good rates of return on investment, then invest heavily. If not, then milk the business for cash. By the way, you also get a competitive benefits package. We're talking about the long run here, with incentive grants that mature over a three- to five-year period made each year.

The first pay package is about stewardship. It appears to have been designed for William Whyte's "Organization Man." The second is for the more mobile and entrepreneurial candidate. Focusing just upon two dimensions of the traditional design — time horizon and line of sight — is enough to warrant a major restructuring of the incentive plan to engage higher performing candidates. It is reasonable to focus on business unit heads for this purpose, by the way. For every corporate CEO and management team, there are at least a dozen teams in groups, divisions, profit centers or other largely stand-alone ventures.

Being able to recruit the more confident, performance-oriented types not only makes HR more successful, it improves performance of the whole business. It serves everyone in senior management and places HR squarely in its "strategic partner" role.

Design Process

An unflinching incentive design process also is important to success in the area of senior management incentives. The design process needs to provide thorough, decision-quality information to top management and the board, including the pros and cons of the incentive changes being considered. Value rules might lead to more challenging relations with the broader senior management team. They also can point back at senior management, exposing decision-making flaws and business errors that often go right to the top. This is a good thing for the business and its owners. Value rules are about getting business gains by correcting flaws in business decision-making. The design process should go looking for trouble, because that's where the gains are to be found.

The CEO and board need to be well informed about the pros and cons of value rules to understand how they are likely to play out in their company's particular situation. If they hold an incorrect or incomplete picture, disappointment is a real risk, and so is failure. Executives in the plan need to consider whether these rules are likely to offer gains in their particular business situation, taking into account the possibility that gains may come from sources they don't know. If they're quite certain that these methods don't offer gains in their particular setting, they should pass on them altogether.

Many incentive plans have been hampered by problems associated with the process used to design and roll them out in the first place. Many suffer from lack of imagination in their basic design, poor commitment among participants and little continuing support once they are in place. A high-quality design process, on the other hand, engages stakeholders with basic steps like these:

- State the precise role that incentives will play within the overall system of governance and rewards.
- Pursue input from a wide group of people.
- Involve senior leadership and the board at proper junctures.
- Infuse the design project with high-quality information.
- Develop real, actionable alternatives to design.
- Evaluate alternatives in terms of how well they meet objectives.

- Apply formal simulation and testing tools to the design of the overall incentive structure and its components.

- Bring expertise, experience, integrity and independence to the process.

- Commit to an implementation plan and execute it.

- Communicate the plan fully to all participants on an ongoing basis.

A successful rollout certainly does not require full unanimity nor full trust. Unanimity is an unsuitable goal. An incentive structure that pleases everyone will be ineffective, too expensive or both. And trust is built over time. Situations of low trust typically mean that past incentive plans have been changed a lot or otherwise discredited. That is good news because it simply increases the potential business gain from doing things right.

I do not suggest doing a lot of navel-gazing as part of the design process. Value rules are meant to distill the real choices involved in effective incentive design and to streamline the process by ignoring extraneous criteria and approaches. If you are going down this path, you don't need to grapple with the general question of how incentives should work in the senior management group or the basic characteristics of measurement and pay delivery. Value rules stipulate all that up front. The role of management is to maximize value creation, and incentives should support such efforts in clear and compelling terms. Under value rules, incentive design is about how to bring these propositions to bear in a particular company's setting.

Flexibility, Stability and Plausibility

The design process should try to achieve stability, even permanence within the incentive structure. The basic drivers of the incentive structure are more or less permanent, after all. Indeed, one of the distinctive features of value rules is that they are never repealed:

- Senior managers are in the decision business. The essence of their role is not defined by a particular market, like the one for electric utility services or Beanie Babies, nor by a particular set of business conditions. Their specific, unique and enduring charge is to make business decisions on the part of shareholders.

- Senior management's product, in the end, is business results that create value for owners; not cars, dishwashers or rent-to-own marketing of saxophones. That is true for a single-line business just as it is for a conglomerate or even a private equity fund that continually enters and exits businesses.

- Investors always have had measurable standards for performance and return, ones continuously reflected in markets that compete for their capital and ones permanently applicable to judge success of management teams that run the affairs of business on their behalf. This was true in corporations 400 years ago and is still true today.

Warren Buffet is among the richest people in the world. When asked about his investing methods, Mr. Buffet continues to cite a 1940s Benjamin Graham textbook on fundamental security analysis, one containing many of the basic assertions of this book. Jackie O. never seemed to change her hairdo, either, you might have noticed. The classics never go out of style.

Business conditions change all the time, though, and so do the structures and fortunes of companies. Management teams turn over from time to time while shareholders can come and go on an hourly basis. Strategies change, and so do business buzzwords. But the underlying connections between management and owners are not transient things. The incentives that formalize these ties need not be either:

- The basic moving parts of value creation — long-run operating income, capital usage and risk — apply in all business conditions. Incentive plans that flow from these basic drivers never need fundamental change.

- Metrics themselves can be set up to endure, flexibly, through a range of business conditions. The metric TBR, for example, automatically captures the benefits of business investment and growth when favored by market opportunity, and cash yield when not.

- The mechanics of value-based incentives are flexible, as well. With each new grant under a long-term performance plan, the company can re-sync goals based upon changes in performance expectations or the cost of capital.

- Basic adjustments can handle the effects of big acquisitions, divestitures, or volatility in operating results without disrupting the incentive system or interrupting management's financial interest in long-term business success.

- Unpredictability, volatility, and cyclicality can be addressed in the target-setting, range-setting and measurement aspects of plan design.

However, company incentive plans get changed all the time, diluting their credibility and contributing to a short-term focus. This, combined with other design flaws, has created a norm in which senior management does not have a plausible financial claim upon their own results over time. Value rules are flexible over time and across a range of business conditions. This enables companies to have more permanence in their pay structures, making them more credible and effective.

Rollout, Communication and Training

The formal communication process for management incentive plans poses its own sizeable set of issues, but this is an area in which improvements in the typical company's practices are easily envisioned and made.

Participants in many operating incentive plans don't have a strong sense of how various decisions may pay off under their incentive plans. Companies should run seminars at least yearly regarding goals and how to reach them. A spreadsheet model can be devised for just about any plan, one that tells exactly what will be earned at various performance levels and the impact of specific business decisions and scenarios on those performance levels. Armed with such information, participants can easily figure out what they'll be paid for various results they might pursue. There is nothing wrong with this because well-designed plans are meant to affect business decision-making. They're probably doing this anyway, so the company may as well make it easy.

Business decisions are supposed to create value for shareholders, and the results of most companies can be converted rather simply into a valuation estimate. Linkages between business decisions, business results and value creation should be made clear in plan communication. This ought to be a compulsory step for any company making use of stock-based incentives, but it is particularly useful for those using operating incentive plans that were designed based upon value rules.

Incentives are valuable at the executive level — and so is total pay. The value of each pay element, as well as the basis for earning awards under incentive plans, needs to be made clear through effective communication.

John Cronin guided roll-outs of new value-based plans twice, as part of leadership roles in the Grand Met organization and its successor, Diageo. His advice is that, if performance measures are new to the business, don't first introduce them to managers through the incentive plan. First, begin to use them in day-to-day management, so managers are familiar with them, before tying their pay to them. He also recommends integrating the communication and operation of the plan with business strategy and processes so the plan is not seen as HR policy but as an integral part of managing the business.

There are great opportunities to dovetail with other corporate messages and strategies. There also is all the opportunity in the world to be creative, have fun and come up with particularly memorable ways of getting the key messages across. I've done a lot of financial training, for example, and have used methods ranging from lectures and team case studies to a competitive quiz show format complete with cheap yet "fabulous" prizes.

Again, keep in mind that many of the communication problems with executive pay — the issues causing real dissonance — do not relate to communication, but to design. Executives are smart. When they are unhappy about pay, they often have real, design-related reasons for being unhappy; in those cases, propaganda does not help. True communication problems, as opposed to flaws in design, tend to stem from basic failures to communicate the value of what executives have, how it might pay off and what they can do about it. First, fix the design problems. Then, tell them what incentive opportunity they're getting, what it's worth and how they can earn it.

Bottom Lines

A tiny portion of the world's population largely directs the affairs of commerce. A typical Fortune 500 U.S. company has a few hundred of these people. Little companies have from one to a few. They are senior management — this means they, either alone or working within a team, have material impact upon the value of a business enterprise — a private one, public one, or a business unit of either.

Their roles endow them with great impact on the business. But, in the case of most bigger companies, they don't own the businesses they run. Instead, they manage these enterprises at the pleasure and behest of shareholders and their board representatives. They draw their remuneration in various ways and are responsive to the terms of their pay programs. Such plans are important subject matter because business enterprises — their efficiency, innovation and success — create the material benefits we have in society. They provide household income and the goods and services it buys. They also fund, directly or indirectly, the goods and services provided by government and the non-profit sector.

Ultimately, the material wealth of a nation relies upon a few intangibles. These are things like the industriousness of its people, the liquidity and information held in its markets, the degree of freedom individuals have in commerce and the general trust and confidence they hold in markets and laws. Among these key intangibles is a properly functioning system of rewards for top management, one that uses the self-interest of executives as a way to get the best performance for owners. Actions of those at the top of enterprise have societal impact, strongly affecting resource allocation, economic efficiency and competitiveness. A business environment that rewards success, particularly for those in key decision-making roles in the economy, contributes importantly to national welfare. The design of senior management incentives is an essential component of this system. It is worth doing well.

Glossary

accumulated depreciation (AD)
> A balance sheet account that records the cumulative amount of depreciation for an asset since its acquisition.

agency theory
> The branch of economics concerned with management of shareholder-owned companies in which shareholders are obliged to hire professional managers to run the company on their behalf (as their agents).

capital asset pricing model (CAPM)
> A model that describes the connection between the risk of a security and the return investors expect from it. The model was developed by economists Jack Treynor, William Sharpe and John Lintner.

cash value added (CVA)
> A cash-based version of the metric economic profit (EP). (Chapter 8).

CFROGI
> Cash flow return on gross investment (Chapter 8).

CFROI
> Cash flow return on investment (Chapter 8).

discounted cash flow (DCF)
> A method for estimating the value of a business by making a projection of future cash flows from the business's operations and discounting them to present value (Chapter 4).

earnings per share (EPS)
> Net income available to common shareholders (after subtracting preferred dividends) divided by the number of outstanding shares (Chapter 7).

EBIT
> Earnings before interest and taxes (Chapter 7).

EBITDA
> Earnings before interest, taxes, depreciation and amortization. Under U.S. generally accepted accounting principles (GAAP), since companies no longer amortize intangible assets, the "A" part of EBITDA is vestigial (Chapter 7).

economic profit (EP)
> Also known as residual income or economic value added (Chapter 8).

employee stock ownership plan (ESOP)
> A type of retirement plan in the U.S. in which company shares are held as retirement assets for employees.

Financial Accounting Standards Board (FASB)
   The independent organization that promulgates accounting and related reporting rules for U.S. companies.

forecast-term income
   Income projected to be earned during the explicit "forecast period" or "forecast term" in a discounted cash flow (DCF) analysis, normally a period of five to 10 years.

free cash flow (FCF)
   Cash flow that can be distributed from a company's operations and used to satisfy the claims of investors by paying dividends, repurchasing shares, paying interest costs, or paying down debt (Chapter 4).

hockey stick plan
   A forecast of poor near-term business results that are rationalized by expectations of large improvements in performance three to five years in the future.

incentive
   A monetary inducement for employees to take actions desired by the company and its shareholders.

incentive stock option (ISO)
   A tax-qualified stock option under U.S. law.

initial public offering (IPO)
   The act of a company selling its shares to a large number of investors and listing them on a stock exchange for the first time.

leveraged buy-out (LBO)
   The purchase of a business, typically by an investor group including company management, financed mainly by debt.

long-term incentive (LTI)
   An incentive plan that measures performance and pays out rewards over time cycles exceeding one year.

net income
   Revenue minus all expenses including taxes (Chapter 7).

nonqualified plan

A retirement plan that does not qualify for favorable tax treatment under U.S. tax law and is not subject to the statutory reporting and funding requirements. Participation in such plans typically is limited to a select group of highly compensated employees.

optics

A vernacular term for the general appearance of executive incentives from an external perspective like that of a shareholder or regulator.

performance unit plan

A plan that pays out awards based upon measured performance against goals over a period of more than one year (Chapter 10).

phantom stock plan

A long-term incentive plan that does not involve the use of actual company shares, but is based one way or another one share price performance (Chapter 10).

premium option

A stock option whose exercise price is higher than the market value of the shares at the time of grant (Chapter 11).

real value added (RVA)

A residual income measure — like economic profit — that has been adjusted to take account of inflation that has occurred since company assets were placed in service (Chapter 8).

return on capital employed (ROCE)

Operating income after tax divided by capital employed (debt plus equity). Generally equivalent to return on invested capital (ROIC) or return on net assets (RONA) (Chapter 7).

return on equity (ROE)

Net income divided by stockholders' equity (Chapter 7).

return on invested capital (ROIC)

See ROCE.

return on net assets (RONA)

See ROCE.

shareholder value added (SVA)

An estimate of how current financial performance contributes to the overall value of a company (Chapter 8).

total business return (TBR)
> A two-part performance measure that tracks how much a business has increased in value and how much income or cash flow it has generated for its owners (Chapter 8).

total investor return (TIR)
> Like TBR, but stated more precisely in market-value terms. The amount of the increase in the value of an enterprise plus the free cash flows it generates (Chapter 4).

total shareholder return (TSR)
> Capital gains plus dividends earned on a stock investment.

value-based management (VBM)
> Using principles of corporate finance and valuation in a prominent and explicit way in business processes, usually encouraged by value-based incentive plans.

variable accounting
> An accounting treatment for many cash-based incentive plans — one in which variable charges are accrued against income depending upon estimates of what the plan eventually will pay out to participants.

weighted average cost of capital (WACC)
> The overall rate of return that a company needs to earn on its investments in order to compensate its debt and equity investors for the risks they bear (Chapters 4 and 5).

Index